# Musings

## of a 20-something Mom

### and the perils of being a
### Mommy Blogger

Jenny Schoberl

First Edition

Cover design by Jeremy Johnson

ISBN 978-1-4679-0444-5

# Dedication

For my Mom, who made me the sarcastic stubborn and strong-willed person that I am today; I wouldn't have it any other way,
And for the two boys who drive me absolutely insane but give my life meaning: Holden and Parker. I hope that one day I can inspire you like you have inspired me.

# Acknowledgments

Thomas, for putting up with months of late nights and
frustration during this intense process.
Jeremy J., even though you put me in a serious bind, I think it
made the book better. You gave me a ton of completely selfless
help and encouragement, and I appreciate every little bit.
Jennifer L- who has been the greatest support, and always
made time to brainstorm with me and listen to me bitch until I
was blue in the face; you deserve Saint status.
And every other friend who I wrangled into reading through
rough draft after draft, whined to you, or asked you to help-
Thank you all! I couldn't have done this without you.

# Contents

# Foreword

When I started my blog, Holdin' Holden, 3 years ago, never did I imagine the wild ride it would take me on; culminating in me standing in my kitchen in the middle of the day (yes, standing, because what Mom has time to sit down?), writing the foreword to my first book.

It has been one hell of a rollercoaster, and if you're reading this now- I want to thank you for making it this far.

This has most certainly been a labor of love for me- and some of the names and locations have been changed for the protection of not only my own ass, but the innocent.

I hope you enjoy the book as much as I enjoyed writing it- and when you're done- come and find me in my little corner of the internet.

# Disclaimer:

This book is a firsthand account and telling of events as experienced by the author. Other individuals who shared some of these experiences have differing opinions on how those experiences transpired.

# Prologue

Mommy Blogging- what's so hard about that? All you have to do is write about your boring ass day wiping butts and picking crusty boogers off of your little crotch blossom's face. Big deal! It seems so simple, so menial, so granola with a side of apples snooze fest; no stress involved. Certainly not exciting or challenging!

Well, that's what I thought too, and I was DEAD wrong. Blogging about parenting and children is like stepping into a veritable minefield. You never know what is going to blow up on you, or what limbs you may lose along the way.

If you had asked me 5 years ago if I imagined my life today as being a stay at home mom, popping out 2 kids before I turned 27, I definitely would have laughed in your face.

The life I have now is most certainly not the one I planned. Not even close! It is so far from where I thought I would be today that it's crazy to even think about the differences, but to get to the end we need to start at the beginning, so let's begin the right way.

My name is Jenny; I am 27 years old, and the mother of two crazy little boys. I've been married for 4 years to a guy named Thomas- the last person on earth I ever thought I'd end up with. Oh, and if you couldn't tell by now- I'm a blogger. Next to my family, writing about them is my life. I love it, I hate it, and I live for it.

In my own household I'm the queen bee. The only vagina in a sea of penis. The Head Bitch in Charge.

If you ask around? People might tell you I'm a cool chick, but in the grand scheme of things- I'm pretty friggin' normal. I have no delusions about being more special or interesting than anyone else, just a mom with a strange sense of humor who started a blog about my life that returned a lot of strange lessons and more than a few consequences.

Five years ago I wasn't even contemplating the thought of children, or even getting married. To the contrary really, I thought I'd be single forever and most of my friends would have agreed I'd be the *last* to settle down. I was a somewhat professional musician, had quit my job and was touring the east coast playing shows. A goal I had worked so hard for, for 7 very long years, in hopes of getting a record deal and skyrocketing to 'stardom', whatever that is. Or at least more than playing half empty bars and pandering my CDs and T-shirts to people who had never heard of me but might believe someday I would "make it," as they say, and they "knew me when."

My mother passed away when I was just 19 from complications after a kidney transplant. We had a very tumultuous relationship to say the least, and though she was incredibly sick for the last few years of her life I never once expected her to die. I always thought she'd get better. That was always the goal, to get her back on the track to a normal life. That's all she ever wanted: To live happily and healthy in her new condo next to the beach.

That didn't happen. And when it didn't, my life changed drastically. I can't say at that point I immediately wanted children... it was the opposite. I didn't want my possible future children to lose me at such a young age without ever really knowing me or being old enough to ask REAL questions. What that event in my life did to me was to make me more focused on my music; I lost myself in it. *Really* lost myself.

Thomas and I met our senior year of high school. I can't say we ever meant to be friends, because I don't really believe that was either of our intentions from the beginning, but something

xii

always kept us apart. His douche bag tendencies, or the fact that I was currently in a relationship with one, something always managed to get in the way.

There was one time in particular when Thomas had invited me to his house, 30 minutes away, and I thought maybe we'd *actually* get to be together that time after talking about it for so long. Shady business already since I had a boyfriend- but it was Thomas I really wanted to be with. After I showed up though, so did another girl… who promptly kissed him on the lips. He introduced her as his 'girlfriend.' I tried to play it cool, but inside I was screaming at the top of my lungs. I'd been double crossed when I was double crossing! That was just one of many lies he told me that played a hand in keeping us apart.

About a year after that, I moved to California to pursue my music, or that's what I like to tell people. If you want to succeed as a musician, Hollywood is the place to be! The move was honestly more of an escape from my life in order to not have to deal with the fact that I'd lost my mother, and my current boyfriend was my escape car… my incredibly abusive psychotic escape car.

The night before we left, in front of a few of our closest friends, he screamed obscenities at me for reasons I can't exactly remember, and chucked a full can of soda straight into my stomach. Mild compared to what he usually did to express his frustration with me.

Anyone in their right mind would have ended it right there- and all that were witness to what had taken place begged me not to leave- but I was so desperate to run away from reality that I went anyway. I don't think anything could have stopped me.

My stay in sunny California only lasted 7 months, but in that short time, while I grew to love music more, I also got to know

myself better and realized more about who I was.
Unfortunately there was a road block named Thomas in the
way. I never fully got over him. We never stopped talking, and
had become 'best friends' even though we both knew being
friends was never really possible because of our underlying
feelings. Friendship quickly (and finally) turned into love.
Against all reason we decided that he should come and visit
me, a visit that was approved by the crazy boyfriend- but little
did he know that we had such strong feelings for one another
and we planned to finally, at last, be together.

By that time the abuse from my boyfriend had hit a boiling
point. It was an everyday event and if I had ever been in love
with him, I certainly wasn't anymore. Yet another situation I
desperately wanted to escape but couldn't because I felt
completely trapped.

When Thomas arrived it was March of 2004. Instantly I was in
heaven, happier than I'd been in a VERY long time. Totally
smitten, head over heels in love and oblivious to the reality of
the situation. I was living with my abusive boyfriend and had a
boy I was in love with staying on my couch, and 3,000 miles
away from home with nowhere to go if things happened to get
ugly.

During the visit, the boyfriend got increasingly agitated, until
one night when Thomas and I were up late watching a movie
and I gave him a peck goodnight. Boyfriend, whom we thought
had gone to bed hours ago, had actually been watching us
through a crack in the bedroom door and instantly up and lost
his damn mind.

He smashed through the door screaming and threatening us
both, generally being terrifying. Thomas and I grabbed his
things and left, sped off in my car and eventually checked into
a local hotel. Not even a few hours had passed when we got a
call on the room phone. My not-so boyfriend had scoured
every hotel in town looking for us until he spotted my car. It

was a very scary and surreal moment. I had known he wasn't quite right in the head, but never imagined he'd stalk me. More threats were made, he said he'd cut off my phone, turn off the electricity, get rid of my cats, etc. etc... and then he left. I was shaken and panicked, and from the distant demeanor of Thomas, I'm sure he was as well.

A few days passed that were relatively calm, and then it was time to drop Thomas off at the airport so that he could go home to Virginia. I cried, and he promptly told me *"there's no crying in baseball,"* A line I wouldn't soon forget.

Since I had nowhere to go after that, I decided to suck it up and go home, back to my apartment with the boyfriend. He was there waiting... and as soon as I walked in the door we got into a fight that led to him physically picking me up and throwing me outside, locking the door so that I couldn't get back in. After 10 minutes of me crying hysterically and pounding on the door, the neighbors called the police. When they showed up, I denied physical abuse, but the boyfriend claimed *I* had punched *him* in the face, and I was told if I didn't leave the property immediately I would be arrested. I could not believe it. After everything I'd been through, the punches to the face, the hair pulling, being choked and having my head slammed into hard surfaces, now suddenly *I* was the abuser? Had I stepped into some parallel universe? What could I do other than leave? I certainly didn't want to be arrested in a state where I had no friends or family to bail me out.

I got in my car and drove away, quickly realizing that I had absolutely nowhere to go. I can remember pulling into the Von's grocery store parking lot and bawling my eyes out. I ended up calling the only person's phone number I had in the entire state of California - a coworker. He had been made aware through conversation of what had been happening with the boyfriend behind closed doors and immediately told me to come over. He then graciously gave me his couch to stay on for as long as I needed.

During that time I called my Dad and told him what was going on. I told him about the physical abuse and that I'd been thrown out on the streets and just wanted to come home. He didn't believe me. I'd kept it a secret for so long; I'd waited so long to admit it out loud that now not even my Dad believed me. I hadn't even told the boyfriend's parents when they asked me to my face if he was hitting me because they knew he had issues. It took a lot of convincing to get my Dad to help me get the hell out of California.

The decision to come home seemed like an easy one. I had nothing in California left for me. Yes, I was playing my music, but what good was that if I was miserable there? What good was it if I had nowhere to live and very few friends to support me? If I moved back home, I'd finally get to be with Thomas with nothing getting in our way- for real this time. I bought my plane ticket, a serious red-eye for the next week, and then attempted to call Thomas to tell him. I thought for sure he would be happy, since we were so happy together over the past week. He didn't answer any of my calls, and the now ex-boyfriend had cut off my cell phone so if Thomas had tried to call me, he wouldn't have been able to get through.

My last night in California ended up being the first blog I ever wrote. I started it for the sole purpose of writing about what I was going through, attempting to reach out to Thomas. Why won't you answer my calls? What is going on? Aren't you excited I'm coming back?

Once I got home and was *finally* able to talk to Thomas, via instant messenger, he hit me in the gut with a ton of bricks. He didn't want to talk to me anymore. He wanted absolutely nothing to do with me. He thought *I* was crazy. Everything he'd witnessed in California he blamed on me. From my driving, my ex, the whole situation was just too much for him and it was over. Period.

I tried to convince him that we were meant to be; we could be together now. The boyfriend was no longer my boyfriend; he was completely out of the picture. Thomas was the one! I knew he knew that!

He couldn't. Wouldn't. That was it. It was the last time I spoke to him for 2 years, other than his "anonymous" comments on the blog I'd started back in California attempting to defend his position. I later found out that once again he'd had a girlfriend the entire time he was with me, and had once again kept it from me. Old habits die hard I guess.

I realize by writing all of this, I make Thomas sound like the biggest self-centered asshole on earth- but honestly, what 18 year old male isn't?

So I, refusing to be deterred once again, began playing music as much as I could. I was incredibly hurt, crushed even, but if nothing else it gave me a lot of fuel to write great songs.

I played shows in all kinds of places and states, with big bands and small bands, big venues and tiny venues- it didn't matter. All the while just scraping by with crappy jobs that made me miserable, but paid the bills. At one point I even quit my full time job to tour the east coast. While all of this was great for me because it got me out of the rut of a stifling full time desk job that wasn't me *at all*, it still wasn't totally fulfilling. I found myself sad, lonely, and unhappy throughout the entire process. Something always felt like it was missing.

I still didn't get the record deal I so longed for... and at the end of the tour, found myself once again homeless and for the first time, hopeless. This was not what I signed up for. This was not what I'd dreamed of. This was not what I'd expected after *all* I'd gone through and all the work I had put in to get to that point.

As always, I found a way to make it work. I got a townhouse and a roommate and had *finally* gotten away from being a serial monogamist, only dating whack-jobs and assholes, and was happy just to be single for once; able to really focus on what was important to me, but somehow I still wasn't happy or complete. How could that be?

The musician's life wasn't an easy life at all, but it was the one I had chosen and the one I so desperately wanted... and I have been bound and determined to make it happen. After 7 long and hard years of trying to break my way into the business, it was about time I finally achieved my dream.

That was... until Thomas came back into my life in 2006. I had written MANY angry songs about him over the past two years and performed them to the masses, and even though I seriously never thought I'd speak to him again after that huge falling out, I was still slightly hung up on. What can I say, I don't give up easily.

One night in the townhouse I shared with a "friend" of mine, I got bored and began lurking the internet. I don't know why or how I came across Thomas' profile on MySpace, but I did, and found that he had not only graduated college, but he'd broken up with the girl he had been hiding from me back during our tryst in California. So against my better judgment, I e-mailed him.

Things that are meant to be will just be, and that October, he came tumbling back into my life and it was a whirlwind from that point on. Turns out, time had done us both some good. He grew up, as did I. Neither of us were looking to be together like we had once dreamed of, but as I had told him before- it was meant to be; an undeniable force of nature.

We went from *finally* dating, albeit on and off because not only was he still dating someone else (and once again hiding it from me), but I was still dating other people as well, and not so willing to give up my newfound freedom- to a pregnancy scare that led to a 'serious' drunken conversation about getting married at the court house- to soberly considering marriage and a baby.

 Less than a month later we were *actually* planning to get pregnant and married- and then very surprisingly- it happened. Who'da thunk?

We got pregnant, engaged, and married all in the course of a few months. When you look at the big picture, it was about damn time.

 For some people it takes a very long time to get pregnant, which is what we had both expected- but things never go the way they are supposed to for us. First lesson learned in a long line of surprises. Maybe I should have taken that as a sign of things to come.

In my life I never do things slowly or traditionally though. There's no doubt that no one in my inner-circle or Thomas' saw any of this coming, and we were met with a hell of a lot of negative reactions. People just didn't know how to handle our lives changing so drastically, so quickly, when they were all still at the age of going out and having a good time with little to no responsibility, and partying until all hours of the night. Very suddenly, my life went from being a "wild child" to buckling down and getting myself under control for the sake of the baby growing in my belly. The baby I never really expected, but had somewhat planned and wanted so badly. That came as a shock to not only others, but myself as well.

You see, I never really liked children. Scratch that, I HATED children. The whining! The diapers! The poop!  I never babysat, not one single time, never wanted to- even if the money was good. Taking care of a whiny brat was the absolute *last* thing on earth I wanted to do growing up. I would have rather lived off of my measly allowance than deal with someone else's spawn.

I wasn't sure I'd EVER have children, and had no problem imagining my life without them. Even swore to myself and to others that kids were not in the cards for me.


Perhaps once things are "right" in your life, your viewpoint on those things that you were *so* certain about before change. Things you couldn't imagine become possible realities. Not only possibilities, but things you long for. Things you never knew you wanted become the things you dream of.

Once Thomas and I finally grew the hell up, he put on his big boy underwear, and were able to be together with no loose ends dangling in the background, everything seemed to just fall into place.

# 1 The Conception

While some women would be offended by their friends being not-so-enthusiastic about the idea of a baby growing in their womb, and rightfully so, I however was not surprised in the slightest.

You see, the music industry is made up of 98% boys who are essentially living on a prayer (and I use the word boys for a reason)... all with a Peter-Pan complex. *"I don't wanna grow up!"*

When it comes to talking about futures, children, marriage and the like- you're more likely to get a huge laugh and a roll of the eyes than a serious conversation, or to ever be taken seriously.

The somewhat negative reaction was expected, and I suppose it didn't help that my strong dislike of small children wasn't any big secret. Why the hell would I want one of my own? That's something that even I can't even answer.

Age? Biological clock? Desperation? Love?

I was not only one of very few females in my circle of musician friends, but one of the oldest in the crowd as well. Even though I knew I would lose a lot of those friends once I started taking leaps and bounds toward a mainstream life that they were all so repelled by, I was still beat up about it for a long time. I did take part of them with me though- and that part became embedded in my personality.

Being surrounded by smelly immature dudes around the clock does something to a woman, and I don't mean something of the

warm and tingly kind. What I mean is that I learned *very* quickly not to let myself get pushed around,
If you give them an inch, they take a mile. You're a small fish with a vagina in a big stinky pond full of testosterone fueled penis. Being a woman in the music industry is *not* an easy thing to be.
So I went from being somewhat shy and quiet, to being loud, outspoken, blunt, and incredibly crass.
I'd always been that way in the music I wrote, but never when it came to handling actual people face to face. I also learned that I needed to be quick-witted in order to survive, and in order to not crumple into a ball of girly lipstick stained mess on the floor from being harassed and teased by a bunch of gnarly males. If you don't grow a thick skin, and fast, you won't last a day on tour, or in the music business for that matter.

Going from having a rather large network of single friends, to being married, pregnant, and rather lonely is somewhat of a stunning experience. There I was, wishing for someone to talk to, to discuss all the strange and slightly disgusting things going on with my body- and while I had some friends left, not a single one of them was pregnant, had ever been pregnant, and were probably not considering having children in the near future, if ever- so I didn't exactly feel like I could turn to them for sympathy or understanding.

I imagine at that point I did what a lot of women would do in my situation: I turned to the internet.
It didn't take long before I found internet forums full of pregnant females. Some with slightly similar interests, or those that lived in the south-east as I do, but the one that stuck was a forum of women due in the same month as I was on a website we will refer to as MomSpace. They were all going through the same horrifying things as I was at the same exact time. How often do you find all of that in one place?

I'd love to say I immediately felt at home, but it became clear very shortly after I joined that my brass, no-sugar coating sense

2

of humor was not shared by fellow preggos. I found more women that were happy to think that their precious bundles of joy would be shitting rainbows and butterflies instead of oozing (and sometimes shooting) putrid liquid from their nether regions. The *only* thing we had in common was that we would be pushing a kid out of our snatches at the same time. That doesn't leave a lot of room for making friends.

Even me *referencing* baby bowel movements as "shit" made some ladies pack up and leave. Why would I reference something so nasty with a cutesy word like "doodoo" or "poopy"? Baby shit is not *poopy*. It is worthy of a much stronger word, and I have no issue using such words in reference to children. That leaves a bad taste in some peoples' mouths.

Being that I didn't really see any other options to make Mommy friends, I stuck it out on the MomSpace message boards. Hell, I even *created* a few side boards just for variety. That was my only connection to other Moms throughout my entire pregnancy with Holden, and just about the first year of his life before feeling too stifled for that to be my only place to go to discuss projectile vomit, screaming babies, and nightmarish crap that defied gravity.

I'm not a big fan of rules and regulations; I'd never make it in the military. With a message board FULL of women? More specifically *pregnant* women? I *completely* understand the need for a serious amount of rules, but that doesn't mean I liked them.
You put that much estrogen in one place and you're bound to have drama, mudslinging and catfights. You also run into the problem of Moms who think everything THEY do is right, and therefore, by default, everything YOU do is wrong.

Conventional is not a word i'd *ever* use to describe myself, my style, or my parenting views. I'm not what most people would consider the "Typical Mom." I hate cooking and cleaning, I can't ever picture myself as a member of the PTA, I don't do crafts, I don't wear mom jeans or tube socks, and I'm covered in tattoos and piercings. Combine that with my foul mouth and I found myself on the receiving end of TSK TSK's and criticism quite frequently.

A lot more frequently than I really wanted to deal with when I had a kid who came out of the womb screaming in reflux pain and rarely ever stopped until he was 6 months old.

Once the screaming stopped, the attitude started, and the screaming turned to whining (which is quite possibly the most annoying sound on the face of the earth).

That being said, I still didn't like not being able to fully speak my mind or curse, or make slightly dirty jokes without getting slapped with an infraction or starting an internet flame-war on the MomSpace boards. Context and sarcasm are lost on the internet.

I found myself feeling suffocated by all of the rules and regulations, so I took the chance- I pulled no punches and had no problem expressing my frustration and utter annoyance at the sound of whining constantly offending my ears; it was the MomSpace moms that had issues with how I felt. I thought I was being honest... and maybe a little bit funny, but you'd have thought I'd recently taken a trip to club baby seals and then came back parading their fuzzy little head around as a hat with the reactions I got.

Man the harpoons!

I swear, you tell a mom that you don't think your crotch fruit is a precious little angel sent from heaven who can do no wrong, and you'd damn well better be prepared to have your head torn off.

To me, anyone who doesn't think their kid is an evil ball of brat at *least* twice a day is either completely delusional or a big fat liar. Or even worse- a Mommy bragger. You know the type. Don't pretend you don't!

The mom who says her 4 month old can recite the alphabet backwards... *in Latin*. The mom who claims her baby is a TOTAL genius because he or she can speak full sentences, crawl, walk, babble, speak, crap anywhere other than their diaper, or drool all before the estimated dates suggested by their pediatricians.

All those things combined, and I *definitely* wasn't happy... and I highly doubt a lot of the other members were pleased with my crude and honest view on motherhood and the things that excrete from children either.

Once I realized that I was making more enemies than friends, I knew I needed another outlet for my thoughts and feelings on pregnancy, childbirth, and children in general; One where I wouldn't be censored or having to constantly worry about offending someone. The MomSpace board was still important to have as a resource for advice in areas of parenting where I found myself utterly lost and confused, which I'll admit happened a lot, but it was not the place to go to, to express myself (unless myself was someone else.) I needed my own domain, my own space... And that is what birthed the blog for which this book gets its name.

In the art of full disclosure though, I do have to admit that having a place to express myself was not the only reason I started blogging.

While taking care of Holden full time was better than *any* job I've ever had- let's be honest- it certainly was not helping to pay the bills.

I had a strong desire to be able to contribute, and also a need to actually be able to afford getting my hair done and buy new clothes so I could get OUT of the maternity wear I'd been stuck in since I was still too 'fluffy' to fit into most of my pre-

pregnancy clothes. I'd been independent since I turned 18; sitting on my ass was never my style, so I did what anyone else would do: I Googled.

I did a lot of searches online to see if there was anything I could do from home to help bring in some extra cash. The options were slim to nil, y'all. Unless I wanted to sell makeup or do cold calls (or hook on the corner), it was beginning to look like I was shit out of luck on the money front.

Just as I was getting discouraged, I came across a website with a post on making money by "Mommy Blogging".

I was no stranger to blogging- I'd had blogs in the past... granted, most of them were full of teenage angst (like the one I mentioned that was directed at Thomas) but, it was something I had experience in keeping up with; writing had *always* been something I loved to do.

As a child I wrote short stories, as a tween it was fan-fiction (yes, I said fan-fiction), and I'd written songs since I was first able to write coherent sentences.
The thought of being able to make money from writing a blog about being a Mom? That sounded like a perfect fit, especially since I was already looking for a new outlet in which to purge my 'abnormal' parenting opinions.

# 2 Holdin' Holden: The Infancy

It would be an understatement of mega proportions to say that my blog got off to a rocky start. I wasn't quite sure how to go about writing a good blog about parenting, being that I'd never done it or even considered it before, and I'd had so much pent up frustration that I couldn't vent elsewhere, that for a while the majority of my first blogs came out as just blatant bitching about Holden. That was *definitely* not my intention. I didn't even realize that was what I was doing until the backlash began. There were comments and whisperings made both behind my back and to my face of complete and total disapproval of what I'd written.

*"What if Holden reads this when he gets older? Won't you feel bad?"*

My answer was of course: **No!**

I didn't see anything wrong with having a place to vent about all the stresses and frustrations of being a stay at home mom. Better to get it out in a blog than to take it out on your kid, right? Or that was my thoughts on it anyways. Besides, I thought by the time he got old enough to actually seek out and read my blog (if he ever felt so inclined), he'd be old enough/smart enough to understand that raising a kid is HARD.

Too bad for me, not many other people saw it that way. I was off to a very rocky start to say the least. The place I'd hoped to have to go to be 100% honest without repercussions was turning out to be the same old drama, just in a different venue.

My unquenchable thirst for always wanting to be the center of attention didn't help either. That has *always* been a part of my personality, and most likely started when I ventured into the music world as a profession and not just a hobby.
You generally don't play music just for yourself, as you can't support yourself on no money, and my main and ultimate goal was always to get more and *more* people to hear my music; to know who I was; always aiming for that one end goal: a record deal.

A blog that could have been private without *any* consequences for any of my 'taboo' thoughts had I let it just be... I didn't really *WANT* to just be that way. It's not in my nature to stay under the radar. That's not to mention that the more readers my blog acquired, the more money I would make; and, *any* money was good money for someone who made nothing to begin with.

My primary thought process was: *"I want EVERYONE to read my blog! I want it to be the most popular mommy blog on the internet!"* And so off I went - promoting it however and wherever I could.
Friends, family, Facebook, MySpace, blog sites, the MomSpace boards I was a member of... If you knew me, or even if you didn't, I wanted *you* to go to my blog and read it.

Maybe I just didn't fully understand how OUT THERE my blog was for everyone to see by promoting it so heavily, or maybe I was just naive in thinking that everyone who visited my blog would be the type to love it, understand me and my sense of humor.
Or *maybe,* I'd just attract those who had a similar viewpoint on kids and the need to vent.

What I failed to *really* realize before diving head first into the Mommy blogging world was that although it was MY blog, there were no moderators and no rules. By posting my thoughts and feelings online- it's called the World Wide Web for a reason- I was giving anyone and *everyone* access to my personal inner-most thoughts. That included people who didn't know me at all and people who have nothing better to do than to crap all over someone else's writing by tearing every little word, phrase and thought apart. People could say and think whatever they wanted about me based on what I had written, and unlike the MomSpace boards, there was no one to stop them.

This would eventually change my life in more ways than I ever could have expected. It would shape me as a person, a parent, and a writer; I just didn't know it yet.

## 10/10/08
# Another one of 'those' days

Today was another day where I questioned how good of a mother I actually am. I do not claim to have the patience of a saint... hell; my patience has been ridiculously thin for a LONG time now.

Having a child who screams all day long, whether playing or eating, is wearing it even thinner. I don't know what's wrong with Holden, but I know it needs to stop. NOW.
I feel bad for him because it's so obvious that he's completely miserable, he doesn't have the spark in his eye that he normally does, he isn't laughing or smiling nearly as much;
and I feel bad for my head because it's pounding from him screaming in my ear all day long. Today was another day where I felt VERY close to snapping. I just wanted to get up, and walk out the door and clear my head- but I know I can't do that because Holden deserves better... and I know he isn't screaming just to be a brat- but because he's feeling like total crap.
Still, in the heat of the moment, I find myself white-knuckling. I try to stay calm, but I'm not perfect. I'm human... and what

human wouldn't get irritated with someone screaming and yelling for hours on end?

I admit that blog was not one of my finer moments, but being new to the mommy blogging world, and being pent up for so long and so incredibly frustrated- it felt natural and normal to let it all hang out. I'm naturally pretty open about my life, why should my writing be any different?
Without thinking twice I wore my heart on my sleeve, and to be honest I've written worse;  but I was completely open and sincere in that blog entry, and in reality I'd written a lot worse; regardless, I caught a *lot* of heat for it (that and other blogs like it).
Behind my back, via anonymous comment through my blog, or just through other friends who had been confronted with uncomfortable questions about their "friend's blog that was just so offensive", the disapproval began flooding in.

 Not that now in retrospect I don't understand the flak I got for it, but at the time I was totally clueless. I hadn't found my voice, had *no* idea just how far I would end up taking the blog, or what direction I even wanted to go in. My main goals were to vent, feel better, and maybe make some cash in the meantime.

After a little while of blogging about the same old shit day in and day out, all while attempting to be funny, I was doing a lot of whining and getting a ration of crap for it. That didn't feel so great anymore.
I soon came to realize... I'm a bitch! A Negative Nancy. A pessimistic whiny turd- and probably coming off as someone who absolutely hates my life.
Why would ANYONE want to read about my monotonous days full of an ornery child? What is fun about reading those things? No one likes having days like that, so why would they want to read about someone *else's* days like that?

10

Of course anyone would hate to have a craptacular day, only to come to my blog and get dragged down too. A few jokes don't make up for two pages worth of *"poor poor me"*s.

I stopped wanting to blog about the same things over and over again, and I *did* start feeling bad that the only things I ever seemed to have to say appeared to be negative, when my life with Holden was not that at all. That's not me, that's not the person I am... and it's definitely not how I wanted to come off to other people.

I thought to myself:
*I love my son. He is the greatest person I have ever met, and has completely changed my life for the better!*

Still, I have my same sarcastic, brutally honest sense of humor and way of looking at life. That's never going to change, and it's actually one of the things I like most about myself. I don't take parenting too seriously, and I fully believe that without having a sense of humor about all the crazy, irritating, loud and obnoxious things children do... that you will absolutely go insane. *Especially* when you're with them 24 hours a day, 7 days a week, 365 days a year.

So how do I get that across without it coming out as bitching? How do I get my point of view across when not EVERY day is a good day? I can't lie; I can't make things up or make my life more interesting. I wanted to be honest. I may be MANY things, but a liar is not one of them.

That moment of realization was when instead of writing about daily life for every single blog, I started telling stories from my past. I had a LOT of stories, that at the time were absolutely horrifying to me, stories from pregnancy and Holden's infancy that now I could look back on and laugh... and maybe make others laugh too. Maybe I could WARN moms & mothers to be in advance about these weird happenings and strange bodily functions. All things I missed getting to write about since I started the blog well after Holden was born, that now I could

11

reflect on with a sense of humor instead of a negative undertone due to currently being in the thick of it. That point was when blogging really hit home for me. It's when I really started to LOVE writing again. THAT was when I really came into my own and the backlash died down for the time being

# 3 The Post-Pregnancy Blogs

From stretch marks to leaky boobs, you name it, I blogged it; but I'm not one to stay inside the box. I like to put it *all* out there, usually at my own expense, in vivid, horrid detail. What good is life if you can't make fun of yourself as much as humanly possible? Self-deprecation is an art form, one I like to believe that I have mastered.

My pregnancy with Holden wasn't what I'd consider a typical first pregnancy. He was planned (which I still to this day have a hard time convincing people of), and I was incredibly happy to be pregnant, but my body just didn't seem to agree. Instead, it decided to give me a run for my money.

Morning sickness? Screw that! I had ALL day nausea but could never puke. It felt like a permanent hang over. I had intense Braxton-Hicks contractions from about 20 weeks on, and went into what was considered "pre-term labor" at 26 weeks, had to quit my job since they still wanted me to perform manual labor, and was then stuck on modified bed rest for the remainder of my pregnancy. I was told not to get out of bed, or even roll from my left side unless I had to shower or shit.

Next came the high blood pressure and constant trips to Labor & Delivery to be monitored for fear of preeclampsia, and then *finally* being induced at 39 weeks. Yes, Holden was stubborn before he ever took a breath of anything other than amniotic fluid.

All of that aside, I got a huge kick, and countless hours of amusement out of horrifying pregnant mommies-to-be, and making those who had been through the pregnancy, birthing,

13

and postpartum process a good chuckle. Once I started writing pregnancy blogs, I got on a *serious* roll, I was unstoppable! It was like opening the hormonal floodgates. Things I'd repressed, blacked out, and had burned their way into my mind became blogs.

Here are some of the best... or maybe I should call them the best of the worst.

## 10/11/08
# "It's like throwing a hot dog down a hallway"

You've all heard the rumors, and those of you who haven't had children probably believe them. Giving birth will stretch you out like an old rubber band, or so the urban legend would like you to believe. Now, I can't speak for women who have had 10+ children, but I can speak for myself and friends I've spoken to about this subject and it just isn't true!

Most of us are not lucky enough not to tear, or not to have the unfortunate experience of an episiotomy (getting snipped to make it easier for the baby to come out... in my case, twice) and while it's a VERY painful recovery process to have either of those things happen- in my opinion it might be for the best. Unless your OB absolutely hates you, they'll stitch you up tighter than a virgin (seriously). That with the fact that any sane person will wait at least 6 weeks to have sex after giving birth due to pain- and it gives your nether-region a LONG time to heal and essentially, for lack of a better term, 'snap back.'

The way I see it, a vagina is like a piercing hole. If you put an earring in, and leave it in, of course it will stretch to allow the post to comfortably stay there. Take the earring out for a prolonged period of time? It will go back to the way it was before ever having it pierced; closed.

Obviously, a baby doesn't stay in your birth canal long enough to get your snatch used to the feeling of being stretched to its outer limits, so saying that you'll be loose after having a child doesn't really make a lot of sense when you think about it logically. If you make sticking/expelling large objects in/from your hoo-ha a hobby it might be a totally different story...but a child or two? Maybe even three? Not going to give you a gaping hole where your vagina used to be.

So tell your significant other/friends to shut up- the rumors aren't true!

Now, the rumor about post-baby sex hurting worse than losing your virginity? That I can confirm.

10/16/08
## Pumping, A.K.A, Milking your boobs

Holden was a formula fed baby, but for the first 7 weeks of his life I pumped. Five times or so a day for 30 minutes at a time; I pumped my boobs until I could pump no more. It was hell. Time consuming, uncomfortable, and basically fruitless. I'm not saying that pumping is bad, maybe my boobs are just broken. No matter how much I pumped, the most I ever got was 3 ounces at a time, and by the time Holden was a month or so old he was eating that much or more at every bottle. The more I pumped the less I got, so I ended up having to give him half a bottle of formula, and half a bottle of boob milk (and only once a day, ALL that work for 3 oz. a day if I was lucky by the end). Twice the hassle, twice the mess.

Add the reflux to the equation, and you had a screaming child while I was sitting there helpless with my boob being sucked into a pump, only causing me to become highly frustrated with the whole situation (and I was told crying babies helped the milk flow... not true).

Let me clarify, I used a MANUAL pump, which basically means I was trying to suck the milk out of my boobs by hand. Even if you get the good brand (which I had, a Medela), they just aren't as effective as the electric pumps, and they are incredibly messy.

The entire time I was pumping I would try to situate my boob to get the best flow and the best suction, causing my hard-earned milk to splatter and drip everywhere while make farting sounds. Super embarrassing when your husband is sitting right next to you wondering what the deal is, and why the hell it sounds like your boob is queefing.

To me, electric pumps are terrifying. They reminded me way too much of cow-milkers, especially the double-suction pumps-not to mention the lofty price- but I suppose if you're really looking to give your baby breast milk (because we ALL hear that 'breast is best'), but don't want a kid nibbling at your nip-it's the only way to go. You can be hands free while extracting the good stuff (and MUCH more of it compared to a hand-pump), what more can you ask for?
Of course there is a downside: the misshapen mess your tits end up looking like by the end of a pumping session; Frankenboob syndrome.

If you don't want to BUY an electric pump you can always rent a used one from the hospital if they offer it, and if you don't mind using a pump that's sucked the milk from Lord-knows how many other women's ta-tas.
But hey, they're sterilized!

The moral of the story is: extracting boobie-juice with a hand pump is like masturbating with a vibrator sans batteries: Your hand gets tired before you make any progress, leaving everyone tired, frustrated, and unfulfilled. Literally.

16

10/23/08
# Pregnancy Perks

Yes, growing a miniature human-being in your rapidly expanding uterus is obviously pretty damn cool… but let's get real- i'm not good with the sugary sentimental crap, so we're going to move right along to the less obvious perks of pregnancy

**Porno-Titties**
The boob-fairy never came for me. I was never blessed with big-uns, and although it took nearly the course of my entire time spent on earth, I learned to love my small boobs (huge floppy tits never really were very appealing to me).
I didn't even get the small boobs that I now have until late in my teenage years. Just like I was a late-bloomer in life, I was a late-bloomer in pregnancy.
When I FINALLY got pregnancy boobs, it was like Christmas morning. I went from a size B, to a C/D seemingly overnight. Not just big boobs, but big, full, perky boobs… without the hurt on my pocket implants would cause.
They were every boob-challenged girls dream. I felt confident, and hell, even sexy. They of course were trumped by the huge belly that sat underneath of them, but beggars can't be choosers.
Sadly, I lost the huge porno-titties a few weeks after giving birth and am even smaller than I was before getting pregnant (double damn!) but they were fun while they lasted.
Now I know why women love having implants, big perky boobs are great!

**Condomless Sex, yay!**
Condoms are obviously a good thing, they protect against unwanted pregnancy and STDs…but if we're being honest here- they feel like sandpaper rubbing your vagina raw, and lube does NOT work the way the commercials would like you to believe.

If you're already pregnant, the damage is done. You obviously can't get pregnant AGAIN (and if you're with a steady partner), why not let loose and go bareback? We all know it feels about a million times better.

Go ahead and give your hoo-ha a break- assuming your significant other isn't totally freaked out by preggo-sex. Then, I'm afraid, you're screwed- and this time I don't mean literally.

**Goodbye Tampons**
Or pads, if you choose to use the bloody-diaper (eww). One of the things I was most excited about during pregnancy was that I would NOT have a period for 9 long months. No more period cramps (pregnancy cramps are another story), no more sticking cotton up my snatch to stop the week-long bleeding, no more hideous bloating (bloating is exciting during pregnancy because you actually think you're showing when you're not). Trust me, it's fantastic not to have your period. I certainly don't enjoy having it back.

**Playing the 'Pregnancy Card'**
As bitchy as it might seem, I definitely used being pregnant to my full advantage. Don't want to get up and get a drink or snack? Play the pregnant card. If your husband isn't a total twat- he'll get up and get it for you. People will give you their seat if all seats are taken. Strangers go out of their way to make you comfortable or to get things for you, it's pretty awesome. You feel like a queen. A fat, swollen, tired queen, but a queen nevertheless.

**Solid excuse to be fat**
Eating like a cow during pregnancy will come back to bite you in the ass after giving birth, but I won't lie and say it isn't fun to stuff your face while you're pregnant and not have anyone bat an eyelash (well, except your OBGYN). Most people have heard the saying "eating for two" and take it at face value, so when you're shoveling down your second serving of cheesecake- people smile and write it off to the fact that you're pregnant and need the calories.

Gives a whole new meaning to being fat and happy.

**Never-ending shopping**
What woman doesn't love to shop? During pregnancy, the shopping-spree never ends. Whether it's shopping for clothes to fit your fat ass (and the ones you buy at the beginning of pregnancy probably won't fit towards the end, meaning MORE shopping), or shopping for baby.. there never seems to be a lack of the need to shop and spend ridiculous amounts of money.

**No more birth control**
It's a no-brainer that you stop birth control when you're knocked up. If you were taking it before and a sperm accidentally got through, well- that sucks- but you won't need it anymore for obvious reasons.
No more remembering to take a pill, or sticking a new ring up into your cooch. No need for an implant under the skin on your arm (um, OUCH!), or to get a *"tiny plastic insert"* shoved up into your cervix, or even to stick a patch on your arm.
You *will* have to remember to take pre-natal vitamins, which might just make you horribly nauseous, but... well... I'll just keep this as a pro for now.

**Being a bitch is a-ok**
Some people might argue that it's never ok to be a bitch... but c'mon, with all those extra hormones floating around your bloodstream during pregnancy, it's hard NOT to want to snap at least twice a day and tear someone a new asshole. All you have to say? *"Sorry, hormones!"* and all is well in the world again.

Ain't being pregnant grand?

Of course, there are many awful, uncomfortable, and disgusting things that come along with being pregnant, but I'll save that for tomorrow's post. Let's all bask in the positive glory that is pregnancy right now.

10/24/08
# And now for the bad news

Yesterday I wrote about the perks of pregnancy... but there is a dark side to the magical joy of growing your very own spawn. I'm never one to gloss over the bad stuff, so let's get right to it. Put your reading glasses on, because this is going to take a while.

**"Battle Scars"**
I'll readily admit I got lucky when it comes to stretch marks. My stomach is basically in the free and clear (minus one ugly one on my bellybutton from a piercing-scar gone wrong). I've seen pictures that would make expecting-mothers scream in horror.
Almost no one is safe from getting them. You might think you're doing well during your 6th month of pregnancy when one morning you wake up, look down, and your tummy looks like an over-stretched balloon. Ugly purple and red marks going in all directions.
Regardless of what the commercials say, that famous name-brand cocoa butter the commercials SWEAR will keep your skin from streaking like a college frat boy? DOES NOT WORK. It just doesn't. It doesn't stop that horrendous itching you'll experience either.
I went to a store called "The Body Shoppe" and bought the most expensive cocoa butter I could find. In lotion form, in body wash form... in every form you can think of to ward off looking like a zebra, and then proceeded to oil myself up like a Thanksgiving turkey.
Unfortunately, I missed my ass. I don't know how. I guess I was just so focused on the part of me that was obviously expanding the fastest that I didn't even think twice on my poor rear end.
It now looks like a roadmap. Lucky me, mine are white and not pink or purple. It just kind of looks like I laid in a tanning bed

the wrong way, wrinkled up my skin and missed some (read: a lot) of spots. Whoops.

Also, for a few months after pumping, my boobs looked like starbursts. Ugly white stretchies all around the nips. Sexy Lady!

Try telling the women who end up with terrible stretchies that they are just "battle scars", then duck- because you'll most likely get a well-deserved smack to the back of the head.

**Braxton Hicks**

Or as I like to call them: *"just kidding, you're not really in labor!"*

Some women describe these 'fake contractions' as just uncomfortable- but for me- from 6 months on they were pure hell. I had them just like regular contractions, constantly. I was put on medication to stop them that made my heart race, body shake, and caused migraines... I was in and out of L&D, had Non-Stress Tests to make sure Holden was still ok, etc. etc. All thanks to the wonderful Mr. Braxton Hicks.

In short, they suck. There's no two ways about that.

Braxton Hicks also made for quite a few false alarms towards the end of my pregnancy (that, and accidentally peeing a little which I assumed was my water breaking).

I was never told what I was having were in fact BH, so when I went into REAL active labor, I was blindsided by the intense pain. BH are NOTHING in comparison to active labor. I just wish i'd known that prior to being induced; it would have saved me a total freak out in the delivery room.

**Touched by a stranger**

Get used to having your vagina stared at by strangers, ladies. I cannot honestly count the number of hands that have poked and prodded my cervix during pregnancy. I consider myself pretty shy when it comes to being naked (I hate it, to be exact), so growing even somewhat used to the nurses and doctors at my OBGYN was a huge feat for me.

It's a totally different story when it comes to all of my trips to L&D for monitoring.

Big fingers and tiny little short ones are by FAR the least fun of them all. Having a petite woman shoving her hand as hard as she can into your snatch to try and check the progression of your cervix? Nightmare.

I actually had a complete meltdown when my doctors thought I may have been in actual active labor at 26 weeks, and a random male on-call doctor at the hospital wanted to shove a strip in my cooch to see if I was leaking amniotic fluid. WASN'T HAPPENING. It's one thing to have 100 different women sticking their fingers in there, some random (and extremely young) looking male doctor? No way in hell.

Once you're *IN* labor? The rumors are true: you stop caring who sees your vagina and what's coming out of it. You just want the baby OUT and don't care who has to see every bit of you in order to make that happen.

## Waddling
There's no escaping the preggo-waddle. Your body just isn't sure how to handle all the weight protruding from the front, so it makes you waddle like an emperor penguin… or like you have a gigantic poop in your pants.

It's the worst in the last trimester. People see the waddle and immediately tell you *"Man you're about ready to pop, you look so uncomfortable!"*

DUH! And thank you for reminding me. The HUGE stomach didn't give that away?

## Preggo-Brain
You'll feel like a crazy old woman with Alzheimer's.

Suddenly, you can't remember what you did yesterday, what you were supposed to be doing now, your age, maybe even your name. Pregnancy is like having a perpetual brain-fart, and I have bad news for you: I'm over a year post-partum and my brain *still* hasn't fully recovered.

22

**Fat Assness**

Get used to the idea of getting fat. It's a given during pregnancy. You're going to gain weight whether you like it or not (unless you are already over-weight, then you may get lucky and might not gain any at ALL other than what's growing and floating around inside of you due to baby). No matter how little or healthy you eat, the weight is coming, and there's no stopping it. Your ass WILL get fat, your thighs WILL get big, and cellulite will start popping up in places you never dreamed of having it. Hell, even your face gets fat.

It's easier said than done to just accept your new found fatty-status. I know I was completely horrified when I stepped on the scale at my OBGYN and was told i'd gained 10 pounds in 1 month (even more horrified when I was told to *"stop eating so much"*) but your body is going to gain what it thinks it needs to in order to grow a healthy baby, so there's not much you can do other than just embrace yourself as festively-plump and move on. Really, you should be more concerned with having to push something the size of a watermelon out of your vagina instead of whether that fourth ho-ho you're cramming down your throat is going to put an extra pound on your ass this week.

**Preggo-Clothes**

Sure, they look cute. You can't wait to wear the flowy pretty clothes you see in all the ads at stores like Motherhood... but they're much prettier on paper than in practice.

I had a hard time finding ANYTHING that fit, and what I did manage to find was astronomically expensive.

Finding pants was the biggest thorn in my side. Those pants with the huge stretchy tummy panels meant to cover the entirety of a baby bump were straight out of my nightmares. U-G-L-Y, and sweaty. As if a pregnant woman isn't uncomfortable enough, let's just put unbreathable spandex over her stomach!

Size 1 preggo-jeans? Too big. It's like they expect your legs to be built like a lumberjack. I was never even a size 1 BEFORE getting pregnant; the sizing just makes no sense at all.

They also expect you to have size G boobs, so everything hung

off of me in the boob area, and I wasn't about to expose myself to random strangers (though i'm SO SURE they would have liked to see lactating tits staring them in the eye). I ended up going to regular stores, and buying a larger size. Luckily, empire waisted shirts are the stylish thing to wear right now.
The preggo look is *so* in.

**Morning Sickness**
Is a crock of shit.
The first trimester is an all-day hangover after an all-night bender.

**Pissing like a racehorse**
Not only will you be peeing upwards of 25 times a day (and getting up 5 times during the night), but you'll find your bladder weakening as your pregnancy progresses; to the point where if you sneeze, you pee. If you cough, you pee. If you laugh, you pee.
Basically you're peeing ALL.THE.TIME.
The worst is that you'll feel like you have to pee SO BAD, rush to the bathroom, sit down... and only get a *tiny* little drop out.
Talk about unsatisfying.

**Just call me Granny**
Being pregnant is like being old. Really, *really* old. Your joints hurt, your muscles ache, and you're tired and irritable all the time. I even started developing carpal tunnel in my third trimester (it's gone now, thank God).
Consider yourself a night-owl? Kiss that goodbye. I found myself dozing off at 8pm every night without fail.
Try and stop yourself from calling people whipper-snappers though, then you may be too far gone.


After giving birth it doesn't get much better. Your body is going to take a long time to recover.
You can look forward to:

**National Geographic Boobs**
Remember how I said you'd get porno-tits DURING pregnancy?
Mmmhmm, well, after you give birth (assuming you aren't breastfeeding. If you are, this will happen later) kiss those bad-boys goodbye.
My boobs went from being perky and fabulous pre-pregnancy, to weird looking and lacking fullness post-pregnancy.
I honestly can't imagine the train wreck my chest would be if I had big boobs beforehand.
Wait...I can. Long, saggy, and thin like two strips of bacon. Yum!

**Birthing Hips**
Your hips have to expand during pregnancy to widen your birth canal. While they do get a tiny bit smaller after giving birth, they NEVER go back to normal. Prepare to hear beeping sounds if you ever have to walks backwards. It's a wide load comin' through.
I am having to face the reality of throwing my 'skinny' jeans away and accepting the fact that my hips will just never be small again.


Things I could list but left out:
Bad skin, pissing in a cup, urine-labs, getting massive amounts of blood drawn, no more drinking or smoking (unless you're a total moron), bad skin, and frizzy unmanageable hair.

I feel like this blog is getting incredibly lengthy and may scare women out of EVER getting pregnant, or freaking out those already knocked up so I'll cut it short and say this:
Even after all that my body/brain has gone through, after all is said and done, i'd do it again no questions asked.
Not any time soon mind you, but someday. Maybe...
The saggy tits, the water-bed stomach, the fat ass, all just become a moot point because of the wonderful, whiny bundle

of joy that comes out of you in a big bloody goopy mess.
It's worth it, I promise

# 4 It's a... Boy?

Before even the idea of getting myself knocked up crossed my mind as a reality, there was one thing I always knew- IF I ever had kids (and that was a *big* if up until it actually happened), I wanted a girl. Just one girl and my life would be complete.
I can't really fully explain, even to this day, why I was so obsessed with the idea of having a little girl. Maybe to have a better relationship than my mother and I had for so many years. Maybe to be able to name her after my mother to feel closer to the person I missed so damn much.
Or perhaps it was the never-ending repeats of Gilmore Girls I watched on a daily basis and wanting that super close relationship with a daughter that a woman just doesn't get by having a boy.

For the first few months of my pregnancy I had myself completely convinced that I was indeed growing a girl in my belly. No one could tell me otherwise and anyone who did was met with a serious stink eye. Thomas and I had *only* girl names picked out, and he'd taken it a step farther than me by buying a pink onesie.

During the gender determination ultrasound, I was SO positive the heavens would smile on me and give me a little princess. Even the ultrasound tech took one look at my belly and said *"looks like a girl!"* I was feeling pretty secure about the contents of my womb. When I heard *"it's a boy!"*- a punch to the gut could not even come close to accurately describing how I felt.

*A boy? What in the hell am I going to do with a boy?*

27

*I don't know anything about boys other than that they have
penises, and they eat a lot, and they smell.*

*I don't play sports, I don't watch sports, I don't even LIKE
sports! And Thomas is the same exact way. I'm not particularly
fond of dirt, and I'm not even a big fan of being outside. What
good would we be for a boy?*

None of that was even a reality once Holden was born. Sports
and other things of the stereotypical male nature didn't play a
role in our lives; babies can't exactly kick balls around- though
they can grunt. I felt ridiculous for even thinking about all of
those things instead of *really* preparing myself for all the
physical elements that come along with having a boy.

I don't have boy parts, and contrary to popular belief- I did not
spend a hell of a lot of time before mommyhood staring at
penises and familiarizing myself with them in the medical
sense; or any sense really. Penises are ugly- who wants to study
them?

From the outside it may seem simple enough. What could be so
complicated about a penis? It's nothing more than another
appendage, at least it isn't an *inside* part like a female. People
will tell you *"boys are easy!"* but I found myself baffled by all
the strange things that came along with Holden just because of
that one extra body part.

From the circumcision care, to peeing straight in the air, to
attempting to potty train a little boy when I have never in my
life held a penis and aimed, and had no idea just how haywire
those things can go. Not even at the most drunken rager I
attended did I EVER offer to hold a male friend's dangle so he
didn't piss all over himself. Maybe I should have. It would
have left me better prepared for what was to come.

11/17/08

# Peeps

If you've been reading this blog, you should know by now that by "Peep" I don't mean that brightly colored disgusting ball of marshmallow goop that rears its sugary head right around Easter time.

That's right, by "Peep" I mean PENIS. More specifically, baby penis. Something I never in my life thought I would have to deal with, and was not prepared with all that comes along with it.

Once I found out Holden was a boy, I immediately became totally creeped out. Why? The thought of his little baby peep rubbing all over my insides. Trust me, I know it's a weird thing to think about, but when you're pregnant, you're crazy, and you think about crazy things. That is my only explanation.

The decision on circumcision was a no-brainer for Thomas and I (a lot of people relent over it). I have never seen an uncircumcised penis in person, nor do I ever want to; and I certainly didn't want to be pulling back foreskin to clean the head all the time, or having to teach Holden to do so once he got old enough. I'll pass on the pig-in-a-blanket speech, thank you!
Did I feel bad about 1 day old Holden getting his peep skin cut off? Sure- no one wants their child to be hurt- but it's better to do it (if you're going to at all) before they can remember it.

Since I was on bed rest in the hospital, I never saw Holden's uncircumcised penis. I never even got the chance to change a diaper until I got home. Needless to say, I was very squeamish about seeing his pained little peepee in all its glory. The only thing the doctors really tell you is to put petroleum jelly on the head to help in healing, make sure their PENIS DOESN'T STICK TO THEIR DIAPER (SHUDDER), and so the feeling of cold air on something that's been so warm all the time doesn't hurt them.

His 'wound' from the circumcision wasn't as nasty as his creepy black umbilical cord stump, so I got used to dealing with his peep, and it healed pretty quickly.

What I was not prepared for then? Two main things:

Baby boys get erections. Obviously not for the same reasons as adult males, but they get them- and they're beyond creepy. And you'd better watch out when the peep starts perking up at full attention, because you're about to get pissed on. I didn't think i'd have to deal with Holden getting any kind of boner until I inevitably walked in on him masturbating into a sock during puberty.

It gets worse.

I started noticing that Holden's peep was looking… well… *funny*. There was no definition of a head anymore, just a lot of skin and a tip. My brother, who has a son 6 months younger than Holden, was visiting one day and during a diaper change I happened to ask him if he thought Holden's peep looked weird (i'm sure this story would completely embarrass Holden), and he replied that it did in fact look funny to him as well. That's when I realized that something definitely *was* wrong with Holden's peep.

Immediately I asked a girl on the MomSpace board I post on who is a nurse what was going on, and she told me something that has most likely scarred me for life:
Holden's circumcision had reattached.
I had no idea it was even POSSIBLE for that to happen. Turns out, it's actually very common. When doctors do circumcisions, they don't want to cut too MUCH skin, so they leave a little excess for baby to essentially 'grow into.' It makes sense I

guess.

Apparently I was not being firm enough at diaper changes with this excess skin and it proceeded to... *adhere* to itself. Are you cringing yet? I am.

Even more disturbing was the action I had to take in order to fix this situation. I had to take Holden's poor little peep between two fingers on one hand, hold it still, and *tear the skin down* with the other. The thought alone made my stomach turn- but the last thing I wanted for Holden was to have a disfigured penis because I was too much of a pussy to fix something that I myself had let happen in the first place.

So I did it. And I could *feel* the skin pulling apart; it was like pulling two pieces of tape apart. Holden didn't flinch one bit- but the job wasn't done. I had to do it again to fully get the skin un-attached. He wasn't so pleased this next time, it even bled a little. Broke my heart, but I was so happy his penis looked normal once again.

Happy until it re-attached again... and then again one more time after that.

Being *extra* firm was not firm enough. You have to be MEAN with the excess skin. As much as you want to be gentle, or maybe you're just a little too bashful to really take hold, you just can't be.

Do I regret having a circumcision done on Holden? Hell no. I'm just glad he didn't have to have ANOTHER one done due to me not being mean enough to his peep.

Am I still creeped out by his weird baby penis? Sure am.

Penises are weird enough to look at in adult form; Mini-penis with excess skin is doubly weird.

Like a mutant pinky finger. That pees.

31

## 1/19/09
# Peep Funk

Never did I imagine that in Holden's first two years of life he would develop a funk in his nether-region so strong it would make a grown man grimace. With perfect, soft baby skin, baby wipes, and cold weather- it doesn't seem like there are the right components for his taint to smell like a grown man's after working out in the summer heat, but somehow, to put it lightly-he stinks.

I blame it partially on potty training, and partially on myself. Without potty training, he'd get wiped down at every diaper change, which would alleviate any kind of funk from forming. Now that I sit him on the potty, and the wipes are in the other room, unless he actually USES the potty he doesn't normally get wiped down. TSK on me. I really need to move the wipes container to the bathroom and scrub that funky smellin' region down every time he gets off the potty.

Then again, think about it this way: MEN don't wipe when they go pee. They shake, put it away, zip up, and go. I can't imagine that EVERY man has peep-funk just because they don't wipe down their balls with a baby wipe after using the bathroom, so why Holden?
Now that i'm actually putting thought into it, it's most likely because he's running around in a damp diaper for the majority of the day, and urine SMELLS. Rubbing urine around on your lower parts for a while, which are usually pretty warm anyways, is conducive to making that area stink, *badly*.

Really all of this could just be solved if the kid would START USING THE POTTY AGAIN! Give mommy a break! It seems that Holden is starting to think that 'potty time' is 'book time', because that's ALL he wants to do. I read him one, he picks up another and shoves it in my face saying *"THIS! THIS! THIS!"* until I read it to him.

Kid needs to learn to multitask. He can listen to me read him a book WHILE expelling urine and releasing his bowels. Don't most men read while taking a shit anyways? You'd think this would be second nature.

# Early potty training for Dummies like me

If I had a nickel for every time I got a nasty, strange, disapproving and confused look when I said I was going to begin potty training Holden as soon as he started walking full time… Well, I wouldn't be rich- but my piggy bank would be pretty damn heavy.

Once children go from infants to toddlers and their crap starts looking and smelling like adult feces instead of wet cement-diapers, for me at least, cannot be handled or tolerated. It's just not right! Pulling open a diaper and seeing something staring back at you that looks like you yourself could have put it there? That is an experience I wanted to avoid by any means necessary.

The bigger the kid, the bigger the crap... and Holden was above the 100th percentile in weight and height. Let your imagination run wild there. I can tell you one thing: it's a poop you do *not* want to have to clean up.

It would appear that the older children get, the more curious they become about what's going in and coming out of them. Have you ever tried to clean poop out from under fingernails? It's not an easy or a pleasant task.

Early potty training just seemed like it would be a win-win situation for all of us. We'd be spending less money on diapers, and wouldn't have massive toddler crap blow outs all over the house. Who likes changing diapers anyways? I was incredibly tired of it after the first two months alone, and with everyone telling me how hard boys are to potty train, starting early would hopefully put us ahead of the curve.

Like other areas of parenting though- since I had zero experience with potty training and really didn't have a single clue what I was doing- it was an obstacle course of surprises and stinky messes.

I tried going the normal parent route by asking for advice and buying expensive books. The kind that promise to have your kid out of diapers in an extremely short amount of time (none of which I actually took the time to read), but really I just winged it.
Forged my way through the accidents, setbacks, triumphs, and a potty that constantly leaked piss all over not only the floor, but anyone within range of the distance Holden's dangle could manage.

The following blogs are just a few of my early dabblings into the potty training world, because little did I know just how LONG it would take and how much my life would change in the course of just a handful of months.

## 11/21/08
# Late Poop Bloomer

I remember when Holden was younger, reading posts made by other moms with babies the same age about their children constantly grabbing at their poopy diapers as soon as they came off.
Holden never did that, and I sort of giggled at the posts and considered it a bullet dodged.

Chalk it up to one more thing I was wrong about.

Holden apparently has jumped on the *"I wanna play with my poo-filled diaper"* late. About 8 months late.

He's never really had an interest at all with his diapers. Clean ones, sometimes- he likes to grab them and carry them around the house like they're buried treasure, but when he's on the changing table he's more interested in yelling at me for cleaning his butt with a cold wipe than grabbing at the diaper I've just taken off of him.

This week is a totally different story. As soon as his (shockingly bad smelling) poop diaper comes off- his hand goes directly to his diaper. I, of course, start freaking out because I don't want him putting his hand in crap and then trying to eat it like a delicacy like he does with lint or old wrinkly peas that I miss during dinner cleanup- so he crinkles his face and then tries to touch his poo-covered butt. Not just once, but over and over.
It's not a fun situation, i'm trying to clean him and get him to stop from covering himself in gag-inducing baby crap at the same time, and he's getting mad because I won't let him.

I started pondering why he's just started doing this now as opposed to when he was under 6 months old like other babies, and I think it could be because his crap has changed consistencies from runny 'baby poop', to sticky gross corn kernel filled 'toddler poop.'
I'm sure it can't be comfortable to have a huge nug of nastiness stuck between your cheeks- but why try to touch it?? Just let mommy do the dirty work and dig it out of your crack, simple as that! Maybe I could just hand him a wipe and let him go to town- but I think the results would be horrifying at best.

Or, y'know... He *could* poop in the potty when I sit him there during his regular poop time, and we could alleviate this problem altogethcr! Knowing Holden, he'd turn around, reach his hand into the potty and scoop the poop right out to play with. Ew.

## 12/4/08
# Toddlers cannot be trusted

Toddlers are evil diabolical geniuses; planning and plotting your downfall. Have you seen 'Family Guy'? Small children are just like Stewie, with a dash of Cartman from 'South Park' thrown in for good measure. Rubbing their chubby little hands together and giggling as you run around after them and pick up toys they've flung across the room (probably at your face).

Today Holden got me all excited, jumping up and down and giving him a cookie because he took a pee in the potty. Then he wowed me again later by peeing and pooping in the potty minutes after I sat him down (his normal routine is to make me wait about 15 minutes before doing anything, if he decides to do anything at all). This was all part of his plan. Once he pushes his nuggety turds out, he says to me *"Done!"* (Which sounds more like 'duh,' but *I* know what he means). So I ask him, "are you done pooping?" and he replies *"Done! Done! Done!"*

I pick him up off the potty, make a huge deal about his poop and pee (while trying not to gag), clean out the potty, wipe down his butt, and give him a potato chip for being such a good boy, and then proceed put a diaper on him.

Not five minutes later, he's running around downstairs and this putrid smell comes wafting across the room and offends my nose. I look over at Holden, who is grinning like a madman, and I just KNEW what he had done: pooped in a fresh diaper right after pooping on the potty. Lifts me up and then slams me to the ground! I cursed the sky and changed him again; *Evil* little child.

Toddlers simply cannot be trusted! They lie, steal, and cause an enormous ruckus, mostly just to get attention or maybe to just make you look stupid. You never know what's going on in that round little head of theirs.

And then he spilled my tea all over the floor, for the second day in a row, which he thought was totally awesome until I locked him in his playpen with no toys. Take THAT!
I'm fighting poop with fire.

Sometimes I think maybe babies are not human at all. Maybe they are evil little aliens implanted in your uterus, hell-bent on making your life totally insane. They have hidden cameras and video tape your every ridiculous move, making short movies of the stupid faces you make at them to hear them laugh, and then airing it on a show on their evil baby planet called *"Stupid Human Tricks."*


12/6/08
# Poo Fright


Have you ever been in a public restroom alone, sat down to pee, had someone else walk in, and suddenly just not be able to tinkle? You concentrate and try to push that pee out, but nothing happens because your bladder suddenly gets shy due to the fact that someone else might be able to hear your stream hit the water?
It's happened to me too many times to count. Not like I really care about peeing when someone else is in the room but can't see me. When you gotta go you gotta GO, and i'm not one of those girls that slips a squeaky fart out as soon as I start peeing, so there's really nothing too embarrassing about it. My bladder disagrees, it seems to have stage fright.

39

Holden seems to have a case of 'Poo Fright.' This week is the first week where he's actually pooped in his mini-potty (YAY!), but there are conditions that come along with his bowel movements. You can be in the room, you can be sitting two feet from him, but the one thing you can NOT be doing is looking at him while he's trying to push a turd out.

I'm still in the honeymoon phase of Holden pooping and/or peeing on the potty, so of course when I hear him start to grunt I get super excited and immediately look over at him. In return I get the look of death

*'Don't you dare look at me while i'm POOPING!!!'*

And he stops all bowel movement. As soon as I stop looking at him, he resumes happily pushing.

I can totally understand not wanting someone staring you down while you're trying to rid your colon of crap- although Holden definitely does *not* understand the concept of embarrassment yet (obviously, he loves running around naked from the waist down with his peep dangling for anyone and everyone to see).

I guess I should just thank my lucky stars that potty training is moving along swimmingly (almost literally), and that Holden finally seems to actually *enjoy* potty time, and understands that i'm not just sitting him on a plastic torture device for my own personal enjoyment.

To go a tad off topic, this weekend is the first time Thomas has actually been home to witness Holden go #2 on the potty. I don't think he quite believed the absolute disgustingness that is cleaning baby turds out of a mini-potty. He thought I was exaggerating.

So being the awesome wife that I am, when Holden dropped a deuce and Thomas was around- I announced that HE would be the one to clean it up while I went to get Holden a potato chip as reward.

And what did I hear coming from the bathroom?

*"OH MY GOD! EWWWW, THE SMELL!!!! THIS IS DISGUSTING!"*

Ahhh, the sweet sound of satisfaction.

I think having to clean out the mini-potty is the ONLY downside to potty-training I've encountered so far. That and the potent smell of baby shit wafting through the air downstairs. Two words: It lingers.

2/26/09
# Hit with the Fire hose, Round 2

The one thing some people may enjoy about their little boy getting older is that they tend not to piss straight up into the air so much when you change them.
Holden didn't do this as much as other babies i'd heard about (parental horror stories and many cautionary tales, I think people were just trying to scare us), but he did it often enough to arm myself with a cloth to shove over his peep area if I ever saw it coming to full attention (which I still keep around for emergencies, and for if the wipe gets his ass too wet, we do NOT want diaper rash).

Now that we've been potty training for a good while, I haven't had to deal with getting sprayed in mid-air at all. I can't remember the last time he did it to be honest, but that's mostly because he RARELY gets put on the changing table. He's even grown to completely loathe the changing table and will scream when he knows he's about to get laid on it, so these days we do standing diaper changes.

Potty training and standing changes lead to other messy situations when it comes to having a boy with an out of control penis.

Holden has this habit when he's sitting on the potty of playing with his peep. Not constantly, but whenever I ASK him if he's going to pee-pee, he'll touch it. And he ALWAYS touches it when he IS peeing.

And not just touches as to say *"hey i'm peeing"*, but he pulls his peep OUT of the potty and sprays the floor. I don't sit close enough to get hit, but it's still a whole lot of piss to try and clean up- all while trying to celebrate that he peed 'in' the potty (even if technically the piss didn't make it IN the potty, it still counts).

This has happened more times than he EVER pissed straight up into the air on the changing table. He's really gotta learn to POINT DOWN.

Then comes the standing diaper change...

If he doesn't piss in the potty, you run the risk of him pissing right there on the floor while trying to get a diaper on him, and he never holds still so it takes a good minute or two to get one securely fastened.

That isn't as common as him running naked from the waist down out of the bathroom and pissing on the living room floor.

He even used one of our couches as a urinal before.

That stain never came out.

All joking aside, the random peeing never ends. He's like a wild animal.

I realize little kids don't understand WHEN they're peeing, or don't understand the feeling that they have to go when they have to go, but Holden needs to learn before he's marked the entire house as his territory. That is NOT the scent I want people to be hit in the face with when they come in to my house.

# Roaches, Rats and Mold, Oh my!

Around the time Holden was 15 months old, the three of us had finally become what one would consider a 'tight family unit.' We had our routine down pat and the days were floating by smoothly.

Reflux had finally subsided (which meant no more screaming for hours on end), he was walking and talking *just* enough that I actually understood what the hell he wanted… but one thing was strikingly clear-
The longer we lived in our small two bedroom townhouse (with three people and two cats) the worse it had become, and through no fault of our own (honestly!)

Since before Thomas and I got married and up until that point (for SHAME! Living together before marriage!) we'd lived in an older brick rental complex comprised of flats and townhomes. And it wasn't just old in age; it was old in looks, structural integrity, and maintenance as well.

Our bathroom, for instance, was blue. Perhaps that doesn't sound so bad to you- but EVERYTHING was blue. The bath tub, the toilet, the sink, literally everything. We figured that was a lucky break considering the only other option was mauve. Straight out of the 50's, that place was.
Our stove and fridge looked about as dated as the bathroom, but was sadly less functioning.
It left a lot to be desired, and that's being kind.

For a "first place" it was decent (if you have low standards, which we did)… but it got old, FAST. The problems started early, but we just didn't take it seriously enough at the time.

We figured that every old place had its kinks and that we could learn to live with them.

For the price we were paying monthly, the townhouse was a decent size and in a quiet neighborhood. We couldn't afford to be any pickier, so why complain about a few seemingly harmless issues?

Harmless becomes nuisance after months on end of the same crap over and over again.

Imagine (if you can) being 7 months pregnant. You've already been in the hospital multiple times for "pre-term labor" and you are supposed to be *'taking it easy.'* No stress allowed, and definitely no big movements. If it were up to my doctor I would have only been out of my bed to pee and shower. Otherwise I was to be on my left side at all times; it was that serious.

Suddenly, you find your nose assaulted by the smell of rotting flesh seeping through the walls in your home.

Zombie apocalypse? House built over an old grave yard? It all seems plausible when the smell is THAT strong.

Thomas and I, unfortunately, could never seem to locate the source of the stench. It just got worse and worse until it honestly didn't seem like it could smell any stronger, and then just as suddenly as it came, it disappeared completely.

We may have forgotten about it altogether had the invasion of the mutant flies not begun shortly thereafter.

7 months pregnant and jumping in the air in order to kill the BIGGEST flies you've ever seen in your entire life? That is *definitely* not a good idea, especially for a woman who is supposed to be on modified bed rest. It was an absolute nightmare. From what we could deduce, it would seem that whatever was rotting in the walls had now decomposed to the point of maggots turning into flies.

And unfortunately it didn't stop there. That was only the beginning of a disgusting downward spiral in that townhouse.

From mutant flies, the problem moved on to bigger and better: rats. I never saw one, but man oh man did I find the droppings. If it were back in a dark corner of one of our closets I may have let it slide, but the droppings were always only found in our kitchen. Coupled with loud scratching sounds in the walls, it was just a nasty situation. And the cats we had at the time were not hunters; they did us no good in catching those plague carrying vermin.

I'm not scared of rodents- I actually find them sort of cute and harmless (other than their history of spreading the Bubonic Plague), so while finding rat crap in our kitchen was a little gross, it wasn't anything I couldn't handle. It was an old townhouse; we'd just call maintenance and have it taken care of.
What we learned though, is that maintenance never came and *really* fixed anything. Band-Aid on a gunshot wound is how I would describe their handy work.

The battle line was drawn once I started noticing spiders the size of my palm come lurching threateningly out from under our couches in the living room- making beelines for Holden who was too young, and therefore, too dense to realize that spiders *are* in fact something to run from. He would just stand there with a puzzled look on his face, watching the spiders inch closer and closer to him.

I have no problem admitting that I am absolutely **terrified** of spiders. I'd even dare to call it severe arachnophobia. So bad that I have recurring dreams about being locked in a closet and HUGE spiders come down from the ceiling to eat me. So bad that I can't even see a spider on TV without having to look away. I can't see a drawing of one without cringing, and even the tiniest of spiders makes me scream like I'm auditioning for a horror movie.
 I blame my Mom for that level of sheer terror. She never should have let me watch the movie Arachnophobia at such a

young age! What has seen cannot be unseen; I've never been the same!

Thomas and I called the rental office multiple times about the spiders coming after our small child. It just wasn't something I could comfortably live with. I needed the issue taken care of. *Immediately.* In my teenage years, after a very drunken night, I passed out on some stairs and got bit by a spider on the back of my neck and broke out in hives all over my body. I may not remember the night, but I remember the bite. I can only imagine what a spider bite would do to my toddler.

What did property management do to rectify this problem? They sent out an 'exterminator' (I use that term lightly) who walked in and sprayed two little squirts in our living room next to the back door and left. That was it! Two squirts! How in the hell was that going to get rid of gigantic blood thirsty spiders living under my couch??

At that point I'd honestly had just about enough. All things combined, it was too much to handle. We'd already considered moving, but I guess we just needed that *one* last push over the edge to really reach our final breaking point.

That push happened once we'd learned that the complex we were living in had been given away. We may have had issues with the management before, but at least they acted like they cared about the welfare of their occupants- even if they did only send out morons who half-assed repair jobs.

The new owner (aka, the old owner's asshole son) cared about nothing but money. They didn't care about complaints or the families living in the complex who considered it home. Instead, they decided to go ahead and terminate everyone's leases, forcing you to either re-sign at a higher monthly rate (and with far more and ridiculous stipulations), of course, or get the hell out.

As you can probably guess- that didn't fly with us. No *way* were we going to pay more for a place with problems that never got fixed, and a management staff that treated us more like prisoners than paying tenants.

If all of that wasn't enough to make a normal person run for the hills already, then came the mold; Just one more thing to really kick us into gear to pack up and move out. We had in our tub what looked, not only to us but to everyone else who saw it, like black mold- that the morons in the rental office insisted was *'just mildew'*, and perhaps we should *'try cleaning the tub instead of calling them and complaining.'* Yeah, because I hadn't tried that already!

Did I mention that the tub had then sprung a leak that bled through our kitchen ceiling that no one bothered to come and fix no matter how many times we called? They just sent someone out to cut a hole in our ceiling who never bothered to come back to patch it. A hole, by the way, that HUGE roaches (management called them 'water bugs') constantly crawled out of. Yep, we had a roach infestation as well.

1/17/09
# Water Bugs

In previous posts, I've talked about how I live in a total crap hole at the moment. The longer I live here, the more I hate it.

We have roaches. We've always had roaches. Sometimes they go into hiding, but they are always here…waiting for the perfect moment to pop out and strike.
Ever since maintenance came and carved a hole in our ceiling because the toilet upstairs was leaking shit water into our kitchen, and NEVER CAME TO REPAIR IT, the roaches have been in full attack mode.

Bigger (we're talking about 2 inches long) and angrier, and these bitches can JUMP.

It's not just us getting hit by them either; it's our friends right next door as well. Since we're connected through a wall, they just go back and forth between us, never really going away. We both called the office to complain, and both got a visit from the exterminator on the same day (even *he* thought the hole in our ceiling not getting fixed is ridiculous). He calls the roaches 'waterbugs' too. I do not believe that for one second. They sure as shit look like ginormous roaches to me. If it walks like a duck and talks like a duck, right?

So the guy sprays the kitchen, and then sprays the neighbor and leaves. Soon after I put Holden down for his nap, the neighbor starts frantically calling me. I can't answer the phone because Holden, the perpetual light sleeper, will not allow me to have phone calls during sleepy time- so I text Thomas and tell him to call the neighbor to see what's going on.
A few minutes later he texts me back.
*"Heather says roaches are pouring out of her utility closet and wonders if the same thing is happening to us."*

Instantly I get the heebie-jeebies. I glance out the bedroom door (which is upstairs), just waiting for a swarm of roaches to come crawling towards Holden and I, ready to feast on our flesh (can you tell i'm scared of roaches?) I've lived in houses before where i'd be sleeping and would suddenly get pegged in the head by a roach falling off of the ceiling, so I think I have the right to be a little paranoid.

Once Holden's nap is over, we go down to inspect the damage. I only find about 4 roaches. One alive and kicking, 2 dead, and one being torn apart by my wonderful cat. We didn't get it as bad as the neighbors, who killed over 20, and when you kill them, they STINK.
Still, 4 is enough considering their size. And since then we've found a few more trying to make a quick escape. Ew. Shit ain't

right!

The funniest (or maybe most frustrating) part of it is that later that night we were outside talking to the neighbor about the roach infestation, and the property manager walks up and tries to start a confrontation. She went as far as to try and claim that the only reason WE have roaches is because we have a hole in our ceiling. A hole THEY have left in our ceiling for over 2 weeks.
A) She's dead wrong; we've had roaches since day 1.
b) You can't justify a problem with a problem YOU created in the first place, dumbass.

*Ohhhhh*, I really hate this place. I can't freaking wait to move out!!

On a lighter note, I received a check in the mail from my oral surgeon for $94.00 for overpayment. Woohoo! Maybe Karma has decided to finally give me a break.

---

Thomas and I had been scouring the internet for weeks looking for just the right place to move into. After all we'd been through in our current residence we did NOT want to rent again. I couldn't handle any more roaches, rats, or spiders that I had no control over getting rid of. I didn't want to have to answer to someone else, or rely on them to solve our housing problems… only to *never* have them resolved.

We wanted to BUY a house; that seemed to be the only acceptable solution to our issues. A frantic search for a place to live began. Availability? Immediately. We wanted out of that townhouse *yesterday*.
Among the stinky, creepy, straight out of a scary movie houses we sifted through, we actually found one we liked being 'sold'

by a rent-to-own company. It had enough space, it was in the right area... it just seemed to be the perfect place for us.

The problem? Money. And that spawned yet another unexpected issue.

# 7 I'm just not that into you

1/5/09

## Tomorrow is D-Day, again.

No, i'm not getting more teeth pulled from my head...although; since I got my wisdom teeth pulled my mouth has been hurting a lot. Could be that 'decaying tooth' in the back of my mouth, who knows.

ANYWAYS, Tomorrow is D-Day in the fact that tomorrow we should find out whether or not we get the house we want.

A lot of factors go into the decision. The normal things like other people who are interested in the house, and our credit. The main thing that could swing it either way is our down payment. I have 2k in my savings to put down right away (although I would rather not), but the other 8k i'm planning on putting down is tied up right now in my trust fund.

Yes, I said trust fund. Yes, I have one. It's not anything to gawk at, but it's enough to put down around 10% on this house.

The problem lies in the fact that my trust fund is totally screwed up. When my mother passed away, my grandmother was made executor of the estate. Meaning she was in charge of tying up all the loose ends my mom left behind. She couldn't handle the load, so she signed up my aunt as co-executor; I'm not really clear on what happened. Then my grandmother passed, so my aunt was left being the executor of the estate. When she took back over, things were already messy. Taxes hadn't been filed for two years and things just weren't being done by the estate lawyer who'd already been paid in full.

This leads to problems now, because if the taxes aren't filed, and things aren't closed out- no money can be distributed. I don't think so anyways.

The company we're working through is fine with not getting the extra 8k right away, as long as they get it before we buy the house (in a year). I worry that they're going to call the estate lawyer to confirm that the money actually exists, and the lawyer (who is basically a shady douchebag) is going to mess things up for us. I don't know what he's going to say. That the money isn't available? That there is NO money (heads will roll if he says that because that would mean a substantial lump of money disappeared in the past 3 years)? I'm really not sure what's going to happen.
Best case scenario would be that he says the money is there, and once the estate is finalized it's free for the taking (of course it's a tad more complicated than that, but i'm simplifying so I don't have to go into length. Boring length).

Obviously, i'm worried. If things had just been done correctly in the first place this wouldn't be an issue, but the fact that they're so screwed up is troubling.

I even went as far today as to call the county clerk to see WHAT exactly is holding this whole process up so I can light a fire under SOMEONE'S ass and get this done. There technically should already be a huge fire lit considering it's against the law to leave an estate like this, to not file taxes and all the other things that are supposed to be happening that aren't.
She couldn't tell me much other than what I already knew. Nothing's been turned in since '05. I asked whose fault it was. She said the executor, who would be my aunt. Which is different from what my aunt is saying- she's blaming the lawyer, and I agree that the lawyer is at fault. In order for my aunt to FILE the paperwork, she has to GET it from somewhere.
I got re-directed to another lady who was supposed to be able

to give me more info, but of course she did not answer, and did not return my message. Guess who's getting another call tomorrow?

Can nothing in life ever go smoothly? I mean, really, come on. ONE little break here or there would be nice.
I'm back to crossing my fingers that IF the company can even get a hold of shady douchebag lawyer tomorrow (that's another problem altogether), he keeps the process moving and doesn't screw us out of a house, because other than making phone calls, I have NO power whatsoever to do anything but sit here and hope that it all works out. Shitty.

My nails do not appreciate all the biting going on, that's for sure. Wish me luck. It could not be a better time to get out of this townhouse. Still no one has come back to patch the hole carved in my ceiling from the leaky toilet that they claimed to re-seal and did not, it still wiggles. UGH!
Get me outta here!!

1/6/09
## The Saga Continues

You're probably wondering if we got the house or not.

The answer is yes and no. The house is ours if we want it. We go in tomorrow to talk about the house and everything that goes into it; repairs, rent/mortgage, and all that fun stuff. If we decide we want it, we put our 2k down then and the house is officially ours.

There are really only two concerns left after that.

The first being the concern that once we go to get financing in a year to officially purchase the house, that our mortgage will skyrocket to the point that we really can't afford it. Taxes in our city are the highest in the area. Why? I honestly do not know. Most people don't want to live here if at all possible. It isn't as bad as people say, but some areas are not nice. I'd more expect the taxes in the city over to be sky high since everyone and their mother wants to live there. It's safe to assume that what we're going to be paying in rent is far less than what the REAL mortgage will be- and that's worrisome. We can afford a little more, but not a LOT. So we're going to have to have an in depth conversation about that tomorrow.

The second concern, of course, is the trust fund. It figures no one would be able to get a hold of the shady douchebag estate lawyer to verify that the money exists and that it's mine (and my brother's).
While I knew the situation was messy, I had no idea just how fucked up everything is. Be prepared for your head to hurt, I know mine does.

I finally got in contact with the people at the commissioner's office in charge of my mother's estate today. They are not happy. Not only has nothing been filed since '05 (which I knew), they have no paperwork that says my brother and I are the beneficiaries of the estate, nothing. The trust fund, as far as I know, has not even been set up. The money is still floating around the estate waiting for the trust to be set up. Problem? Obviously, the paperwork that they need, but there is also NO trustee. No one to oversee the trust fund. Apparently that job was my grandmother's, and when she passed it disappeared. The estate lawyer has it, but since he has been completely noncompliant- no one else does. I got asked all kinds of questions about why my brother and I were paid half of the trust fund in '06 because they don't have the freaking Will and have no idea that we are officially entitled to it, or that that's how it was originally set to pay out. If they don't get that paperwork, we could be in trouble, and it isn't even our fault. Obviously, no other money can be doled out until that crap is set up, and since there's no trustee and no paperwork, it's all up in the air.

The Hail Mary might be my Dad, who never trusted the estate lawyer in the first place and has the original copy of the Will in his files (so he thinks). Thank God for my Dad, right?? Without proof that I am one of the beneficiaries entitled to my Mom's money, the down payment I was planning on putting down for the house is nonexistent to anyone but me. This would mean our mortgage payments would be well over 1k, which we were not planning on.

The court is so upset, in fact, that tomorrow they are issuing a summons to my aunt (the current executor of the estate). If she doesn't get everything done in 30 days, she'll have to go to court and explain why to a judge, and most likely get in an assload of trouble (which is not fair to her because it isn't her fault that the lawyer won't give her the paperwork needed to finish this crap). This is all because my grandmother laid a lot of the work on douchebag lawyer, who's been sitting with his thumb up his ass for years and never returning any calls. If it were me in charge, i'd have gone to his office and fired his fat ass, and then taken the paperwork to someone who would finish it in a TIMELY MANNER. No one was to know when he was hired that he wouldn't do the job he was PAID to do, it just seems totally unethical. How is this guy still in business?

I'm not trying to be a conspiracy theorist here, but the court also hasn't received receipts of any of the checks written from the estate; money that is essentially coming out of my brother and I's pockets. They have no proof that the checks that have been written are valid or that they actually went to who they claimed they went to. How ridiculous is that? Could douchebag lawyer be skimming off the top? I wouldn't put it past him.

I just don't understand HOW this got so messed up, and i'm pissed that right now it might fuck me over.

Bunch of ridiculous bullshittery if you ask me.

Today has just been a weird day all over. We couldn't get into the house to show my dad, the combination to the lock box didn't work. That sucked. My dad is much pickier and notices more than Thomas or I so it would have been nice for him to be able to scour the house before our meeting tomorrow.
Then, Holden choked until he was blue in the face. I have never been so scared in my life. We kept trying to pull food out of his mouth only to find there was more in there and he just KEPT choking. I don't even want to think about it. I never want that to happen again, and I think I'll most likely have nightmares for the rest of my life about it. He's fine, thank God. He's probably forgotten it by now, but I don't think Thomas or I ever will.
If you're pregnant or thinking about getting pregnant, take a parenting/childcare class. Even though most of it is common sense, I cannot stress how important it is to know how to get food out of a child's throat, or how to perform the Heimlich maneuver.

UGH.

Anyways, we should know by noon tomorrow if the house is ours. Then my obsession with watching house flipping shows will finally be put to good use. Or bad use.
LET'S DEMO THAT WALL! WOOOOOO!
I may have to physically restrain myself.

---

Those two blogs spawned a reaction that almost permanently severed my ties with the majority of maternal family I had left. A reaction I not only didn't expect, but never intended. All of the going on and on about money and trust funds may make me sound like a spoiled, petulant little brat, and maybe I deserved a light verbal lashing for depending so much on money that didn't really belong to me, but I think that assumption leaves a lot out of the actual circumstances behind the whole complicated situation.

My Grandmother, back when my Mother's money was first put into an account, had always told me that if I ever needed money, *really* needed it, to call and it would be no problem to get. I rarely ever took her up on that offer besides some medical bills when I was very ill and help with my broke ass car. I'm not a big fan of asking for help- but a home for my family seemed like good enough reason, and something that I am positive my mom would have helped us with had she still been alive.

The thoughts that run through my mind aren't always what come out through my fingers and into the blog, and may not always be the way others see the same situation; my family being those "others" when referring to the above blogs.

One thing I have had to learn the hard way in blogging is actually *thinking* before I type.
It wasn't an easy process in the slightest. I generally like to regurgitate all of my thoughts in one sitting. I don't even read what I've written before hitting the "post" button. Ever.
I just press it.

Call it diarrhea of the fingers, it's a sick compulsion. I fear that if I start the editing process- I'll get so wrapped up in changing and perfecting things that nothing will ever make it out in one piece. It's the reason why writing this book always seemed like a pipe dream instead of a reality- because I thought I'd get stuck going back, re-reading, and changing things until I was blue in the face and years had gone by. I'd end up never actually getting anything finished and it would in turn become a fruitless task.

So I don't edit myself… or didn't at the time anyways.

Some of my family reacted more than a little negatively to those blog posts, assuming I was attacking *them* instead of the idiot lawyer in charge of the mess that had become of my Mom's estate. They responded by writing pretty nasty comments and e-mails, not only correcting what I'd written, but also attacking me and the lack of what *I'd* done to help get it resolved.

Never had I intended for any blog post to implicate *them* as the ones to blame for the hold up in my mother's estate. That's not even something that had ever even crossed my mind. Some of my words were charged, yes, but laying any kind of blame on my family for anything that had happened wasn't what I meant. How I intended the blogs to read was the exact opposite, but that's the way it usually goes with blogging.

Without realizing it, you can hurt someone's feelings- even if the blog you've written has nothing to do with them. People have an incredible gift of making every single thing about them.

I had to learn very quickly to try to avoid writing personal blogs about others unless I knew for a *fact* that they either didn't read my blog, didn't have internet access, didn't know anyone with access to the internet that could print it off and pass it along... *Or* someone who had a phone and could receive calls from those who had access to my blog. You'd be hard pressed to find someone like that- so it's better safe than sorry.

Of course, if you're a heartless asshole, hurt feelings may not be an issue for you. I know plenty of folks who relish the fact that their blogs could get someone else all worked up, and occasionally do it on purpose for that simple fact alone. Perhaps hurting feelings is your goal- and while I can understand how that may be fun depending on the target- it was not mine, not this time anyways.

Still, even if you'd like to hurt someone's feelings with what you've written- are you *really* prepared for the can of worms writing that blog would inevitably open?

If your answer is yes, your balls are at least ten times bigger than mine.

I've said it a million times at least and am not ashamed to admit that I do not handle confrontation well. I'd prefer to avoid it altogether to be honest, but after the influx of e-mails and comments I received after those 'trust fund' blogs, I felt like I had to clarify what I'd written so that my point was absolutely crystal clear to everyone- even those that had convinced themselves beyond a reasonable doubt that my blogs were specifically about them, for the sole purpose of passive aggressively attacking them.

It wasn't the first or the last time I'd waste a blog on explaining myself or the way that I write in terms that everyone would hopefully understand.
Let me tell you something right now- no matter how many times you re-write your words, someone who wants to pick a fight will still find a way to do it.

A blogger who doesn't want to hurt anyone's feelings but still aims to be honest and open just has to accept that stepping on some toes occasionally comes with the territory- but not without consequence. When writing a blog you have to be prepared for the unexpected. You just never know what you're gonna get in return.


1/7/09
## Context

Reading things in the correct context on the internet is an incredibly hard thing to do. Sometimes it's hard to tell if someone is being sarcastic, joking or serious, or even talking about you at all.
I'd like to think that i'm a pretty good judge of context, but i'm

not totally innocent in this matter. There have been many times while reading something online where I've thought to myself *"Wait... is he/she being serious? Is that about me? What the fuck? What did I do??"* I end up completely overreacting to the situation and then finding out I was all wrong. This leads to feeling like a total moron forever assuming instead of just asking, or just being smart enough to know they *weren't* being serious in the first place. You still can't help but to be a little mad, even if they flat out told you what they really meant. Sometimes you still can't help but think that whatever was said was intended for you- or maybe that's just me. I tend to harp on things a little too much, worry too much, overanalyze, over worry. It seems to just be my nature.

More often than me reading context wrong, people seem to take my words out of it. The river runs both ways. I'm not sure why or how it happens so often. I like to think that i'm pretty straightforward with my thoughts, but people seem to take me seriously when i'm joking, or seem to think i'm talking about them when i'm not.
I'm always flabbergasted when this happens. First is the confusion stage where I wonder if I did in fact say something, but upon realizing that I didn't, I get a little upset at the notion. And then, for some odd reason I cannot figure out comes anger. Getting angry at someone for being angry at you has to be the most pointless thing in the entire world. It serves no purpose, and definitely doesn't help to rectify the situation, but it sucks when someone misunderstands your words and thinks you're just being a total cunt when you aren't. This always results in a long overwhelming explanation of what I actually meant that shouldn't have been needed in the first place, but I give anyways, because the last thing I want is people twisting my words and getting upset, angry, or hurt over something I never said or didn't mean.

There will never be a world without drama. As much as we

hate it, it keeps things... *interesting*. I'd call it annoying- but if you want to look at the bright side- at least we aren't constantly bored, drooling in a dark corner with nothing to do but play with ourselves. Without drama, there would be no reality TV, and as trashy as it is, it's the guilty pleasure of millions (if not billions) of people... including myself. Who doesn't love a little trash now and then?

We should all save ourselves the pain, hassle, and fighting, and stop assuming altogether. Aside from the jokes that could be made, it would do the lot of us some good.
Easier said than done though; jumping the gun seems to be the favorite pastime of just about everyone I know, and I am guilty of the same offense.

So what can you do? Just gotta deal with it as it comes I suppose. If you ever find yourself in question of something i'm saying... you're probably taking it the wrong way. I'm nothing if not blunt and honest. I pride myself on that fact. It might make me a bitch, but it shouldn't ever leave you wondering about what I meant in the end, and doesn't that seem like a better option?

---

Unfortunately for me, the constant context war didn't teach me enough of a lesson to stop the personal blogs altogether. I can't control myself. It *is* a personal blog after all!
I did learn to leave my family out of blogs almost completely- at least things that had any potential to offend. However, that did not stop them from interpreting the most random things as being passive aggressive attacks on them; being sensitive appears to run in the family.
 You just can't control everything, or how anyone thinks for that matter.

My best example of that is a later blog I wrote that still sticks with me today, because I wrote it with the absolute best intentions. For once, I wrote completely and wholly from my heart, and I do not normally do that... ever! Sentimentality isn't one of my strong points.

It's one of the only blogs I've ever written about my mother, and the only one to this day that was about her and her alone. For the first time I wrote about our relationship, her sickness, and subsequent passing. Something I had never done before because the subject was and still is so sensitive to me.

Instead of it just being a testament to how I felt about her and that I was still thinking of her, it instead got taken as a thinly veiled dig at certain family members. It took, to me- something that was very close and very private- and tore it down to nothing but petty personal drama. To take something that I felt so strongly about (in a good way) and turn it into something mean and hateful is a concept I still have trouble grasping. Vulnerability is not a trait I feel comfortable showing, so usually I don't. I'm not claiming to be some tough ass chick, I've just been hurt so many times in the past that when it comes to lovey-dovey sappy crap? I take a hall pass; that's just how I was raised.

Growing up I had parents that were polar opposites on the emotional scale. My Mom was the highly volatile, sensitive, and short tempered type, but fiercely caring while my Dad was the solid, stoic rock. He was the one you knew you could go to if you needed help. I can't remember ever seeing him cry or show huge amounts of any kind of emotion. His anniversary cards were always signed with just his name and a short statement explaining that he was *"not good with the emotional stuff."*

They met in the 70's, both working at NASA. My Dad an aerospace engineer and my mom a receptionist, as different as two people could be in every single aspect. Eleven years in age difference, my Dad on the straight and narrow and my mom a complete and total flower child (even if years past it being popular). I'm not sure what attracted them to each other; the allure of something so different from what they were themselves? Whatever it was, they ended up together, and for a long time complimented each other. What one didn't show, the other would make up for by the boat load.

My mom, being true to her hippie, outwardly emotional roots, always wanted me to be lovey, mushy & cuddly. Wanted me to say 'I love you' whenever we hung up the phone… but I guess I took after my Dad in how shmoopy I'm really willing to get, because the overtly emotional crap just wasn't going to happen. I never felt comfortable with it.
 When I write, I can express *so* many more things than I could ever dream of being able to say out loud. Even I can't figure out the exact reasons why, but when it comes to actually speaking my mind through my mouth- it doesn't happen often.

From my Mom I got the sensitive part for sure, and once Holden came into the picture, the fiercely caring traits showed up… but he was the only one who really got to see that side of me.

When I do let any semblance of vulnerability show- I let it *all* hang out; this time more than any other. So when the words I'd written got taken as anything other than total (and unusually) heart on my sleeve honesty in their intent- I was crushed.

The following blog should be a lesson to anyone that even the most innocent things can be turned and twisted by those who want to turn and twist them. While incredibly upsetting to me, I suppose in the world of blogging I shouldn't have been surprised. Without editing myself, and the amount of bitterness I was still harboring over my Mother's death, I can understand how anything I wrote may have been mistaken for animosity. I didn't realize it in the heat of the moment just how strong my words would be.

3/30/09
# My Mom

My mom gets mentioned a lot around this blog, but other than the genetic factor I don't think I ever go into much detail about the relationship we had.
I'm very protective over my memories with her. She passed away when I was 19, and for 18 years of that we didn't really get along at all. We butted heads constantly, she was on a lot of medication that made her (for lack of a better word) crazy (and even she admitted that towards the end), but despite all of that we were thick as thieves.

I get upset, and so hurt when people question that relationship. It's no one's' place to do that, because no one really knows what our relationship was like except her and I.

When my mom first went on dialysis, I was in high school. I remember it not being so bad at first, just once or twice a day, but as years went by with no transplant, that got upped to four times a day. She had to quit the job she loved (as a teacher) and go on disability. Dialysis basically kept her in the house at all times, because she always had to be doing it to keep her kidneys functioning.
I even dropped classes to come home and help her, because she couldn't carry the heavy boxes of fluid she used for the dialysis from the garage to her room. Most of the time she didn't want to go grocery shopping or clean, so I did that, too. I took care of her by myself. When she had surgery, my Grandma came to take care of her because I couldn't be there all the time, but other than that I don't recall many visitors, if any at all. As an unruly teen, of course I didn't enjoy doing all the housework, I didn't like how she treated me, always yelling, *always* fighting. We took each other for granted because we thought we'd always be there for one another.

In the middle of my senior year my mom decided to up and

move to the beach, and wanted me to make the move with her. I couldn't leave my school and start over in a NEW school in the middle of my senior year. My mom knew that wasn't fair to me and I don't think she ever expected me to go with her, though she tried to convince me to, but she was intent on going, and so she did. I moved in with my Dad and continued going to the same school in order to stay at my alma-matter, to have my picture in my own yearbook, and to graduate with my friends.

Once we didn't live together anymore, my Mother and I, we got along a thousand times better. We weren't there to grate each other's nerves. I think I went to visit her just about every weekend. I tried to get her to come and see me, but most of the time she made an excuse and bailed out at the last second. One time it left me sitting in a Chili's parking lot for an hour before she called and said she'd been pulled over for speeding and was just going to go home.

Then came *the* call while I was at work. She got a kidney. The transplant surgery would be that day. She begged me to come but my work wouldn't let me leave. I realize now that I should have just gone, but I couldn't afford to lose my job and have no way to pay my rent and bills. I promised to go and see her in a few days, and I did.

A lot is fuzzy after that. I think she got released and re-admitted to the hospital a few times. Months after the surgery, she wasn't getting better, only worse. The kidney was rejecting. The thing that was supposed to make her live a LONGER and better life was only hurting her.

She spent a stretch of something like 5 months in the hospital, even through Christmas.
Still working 6-7 days a week, I couldn't see her as much as I wanted to, or as much as she wanted me to, but there wasn't anything I could do. I couldn't drop everything, not pay my bills, and live on the street, and the hospital was a good 45

minutes away. This caused some of my family to judge me harshly. They thought I should be there more. If I could have been, I would have been. I knew my mom understood, we had full conversations about it. We talked on the phone constantly. I took her presents, I made surprise visits. During a few of the visits, that hospital had OVERDOSED HER ON MORPHINE and had her so fucked up that the next time I went to see her, she was convinced I hadn't come for a month, when I had JUST been there the week before. She also insisted she was on court TV and there was an imaginary fly in the room, it was that bad.

The prognosis did not improve, and they finally decided to remove the transplanted kidney. I blame the hospital for this. They weren't taking proper care of her. They weren't making sure she ate all of her food and were messing up her medications... it made me so angry.
We all thought she'd be fine if they could just get that piece of shit kidney out of her, but she still couldn't go home. She was too weak. She got placed into a nursing home. I remember talking to her and her telling me that she hated it because there were cats roaming the hallways. It's not that she didn't like cats, but she had become OCD about having a sterile environment for dialysis.

I remember it being around Mother's Day, only a day or two after being admitted to the nursing home. I was waiting to get my hair done, and decided to call her. I didn't have a reason, just wanted to tell her I loved her. She said, *"where did that come from?"*
I wasn't sure. We were NEVER the type of family to say "I love you", we didn't really hug, we didn't show emotion other than sadness and anger, but that day I just felt like saying it.
I told her I had Monday off, and said I could come and see her at the nursing home then. She told me no, not to come on Monday, which was weird to me. She had no reason to tell me no. She *said "Come Tuesday, call me Tuesday morning for directions."*

I agreed, and hung up. That was the last time I ever spoke to her.

I called Tuesday morning, I was ready to leave and come and see her. A weird voice answered her cell phone number. I thought I had the wrong number so I hung up.
Her cell phone calls me back. I answer and it's my Grandma. She asks if i'm alone.
*"Yes, i'm alone"*
*"Call me back when you're not alone"*
I don't know why I didn't think anything of it. I just hung up and went about my day. In the back of my mind I knew something was wrong, something just didn't feel right, but I shook that feeling off.
I called back later when people were at my apartment. My Grandma answered my Mom's cell phone again.

*"Your Mother passed away last night. I'm sorry"*

*"You're joking right????"*

*"No honey, i'm not"*

I dropped the phone to the floor; I couldn't believe it. This wasn't supposed to happen. She was supposed to get better. She wasn't supposed to die.

To this day I still feel like i'm in denial. I'd still like to pick up the phone and call her. I wish she was here. I wish I could talk to her, ask for her advice, go shopping with her. I wish she'd been at my wedding, seen the birth of my child, her Grandson. I'll never get any of that.

I feel her here though. Ever since I got pregnant with Holden, she's been here, her presence. She's been in my dreams... I can just FEEL her around Holden. He talks to thin air and smiles. I get in the car and hear her favorite song ALL THE TIME lately, and it is an old and not often played song). She's still here. I know she wouldn't be able to miss watching her grandchild grow up, even if she'd hate to be called Grandma.

So yes, I get upset when people question my relationship with her. I get very hurt when people think I wasn't there for her. Maybe over the years, because I just don't talk about it that often, people got the impression that I just didn't care.

If I didn't care, would I have wanted her wedding dress?
If I didn't care, would her picture be sitting above my desk?
If I didn't care, would I have her initials tattooed on one of my wrists, with "Hope" on the other, because I know that's what she would want me to have?
If I didn't care, would I think about her all the time?
If I didn't care, would I be naming my daughter (assuming I ever have one) after her?

Want to know how I knew Thomas was 'the one'?
The last time I saw my mom alive, he was with me. She met him and instantly liked him. She asked me *"Why are you still with 'crazy ex-boyfriend'? He's cute."*

I promised myself I would NEVER marry someone who had never met my mother, even if only for a brief moment. Her judgment meant everything to me- even if while I was young I resented it. She was a good judge of character as far as other people went. For herself? Not so much. She deserved better than the crap she dated after my Dad.

My mom meant more to me, and means more to me than some people will ever understand. And I shouldn't let that get to me, because my mom knew, and that should be all that matters.

If I didn't care, would I have written this blog?

# An unexpected bump in the road

Family drama aside, things weren't all bad. By January of 2009, we had signed a rent-to-own lease for the house we had set our sights on and were scheduled to move in on the first of February.

It wasn't going to be easy though. To say that the house was an absolute dump would be the understatement of the century.

The people who had occupied the house before us had moved in, and according to neighborhood rumors (and all the holes punched through doors) had some extreme marital issues, never paid their rent a single time, and were promptly evicted- or at least were attempted to be- not promptly enough!

In their wake, they left clothes, blankets, dog shit, a leaky kitchen sink, crayon doodles all over the walls... and an unopened box of Tupperware containers (SCORE!)

What we saw in the house, because I'm making it seem so terrible, was potential. A rent-to-own program gave us an opportunity to get a house at a good price with low rent and fix our credit before actually purchasing it, which would make for a lower interest rate later.

While it may have appeared to be a complete shit hole upon first glance, we looked at it as a blank canvas. With a hell of a lot of paint and elbow grease, it could be perfect for our little family.

Did I mention the walls were painted in an array of disgusting shades from Pepto-Bismol pink, peach, and deep purple, and let us not forget the hideous 70's style wood paneling? Classy! The people who decorated that house were either color blind... or certifiably insane.

And maybe *I* was insane for really wanting to take the project on. I'd lived in apartment complexes for so long that I was dying to be able to decorate my own place with whatever colors I wanted. I'd been staring at nothing but white walls for far too long.

My Dad was nice enough to buy us all of the paint we needed for my birthday, so after the painstaking process of picking out the colors for every single room (because every single room looked like the walls had been sprayed with unicorn shit), it was time to get to work.

From the time we signed the contract in early January up until the wee hours of the morning on move-in day; either Thomas or I was at the house working on it. Though I do have to tell you, it was mostly me. I suppose I felt like since it was my genius idea to do such a complete overhaul that I should be the one to bear the brunt of the workload.

I'd never been away from Holden before except for ONE time. He was about 3 months old when I left him with a friend who decided it would be a good idea to wake him up in the middle of the night to play with him; never again. So having to leave him around dinner time to go work on the house was not easy for me at all. It had to be done though, and there was so much to do I couldn't be my usual procrastinating self or we would be moving into a total shithole just like the townhouse we were trying to escape from.

In the beginning I thought painting was fun. What a cool project! I've watched tons of house flipping shows, it can't be that hard!

Painting is like that one person out of your circle of friends who is hilarious for about 5 minutes, and then starts to annoy the piss out of you to the point where you have to physically restrain yourself from reaching out and strangling the life out of them- Only fun in small doses.

Give me a single room to paint, an accent wall, a piece of ugly furniture! Anything but a 4 bedroom 1 bathroom house with separate laundry and dining rooms where every single wall, window frame, and baseboard needs new paint, the tub needs refinishing, walls need sanded, and doors need replaced.

After my first 5 hour shift at the house, I began to realize just what I'd signed myself up for.

Can you guess one thing that would make re-painting an entire house practically single handedly even more miserable?
I can!

The heat went out just a few days into the process. Keep in mind this was the middle of January- Virginia's coldest month of the year. As if painting alone, at night, in an empty house wasn't bad enough (and pretty damn creepy) - let's add freezing temperatures and frost bite to the list!

Regardless of the lack of heat, Thomas or I still spent every single night, and all day every weekend in the house shivering and hauling serious ass to get everything done by move-in day. Most nights I would work for so long that it was 2am when I finally crawled into bed (sometimes even later), and since Thomas had to work in the morning- he was already sound asleep and snoring. *Loudly.*

If it's not obvious by now- we didn't see much of each other that month. I even spent my birthday painting. My Dad brought me dinner and lent a hand for a little while- but the rest of the night I spent alone and very cold. Not that I saw inching yet another year closer to 30 as something to celebrate anyways.

When we *finally* moved in (house partially unfinished unfortunately) I was absolutely exhausted.

Exhausted but also happy to finally be out of that rat, spider, and mold infested townhouse and into a place that I had *literally* put blood sweat and tears into.

As much as I just wanted to collapse and sleep for a week straight, moving didn't mean I could put life on hold… anymore anyways. As soon as we'd unpacked enough to be able to live somewhat comfortably (I am the worst unpacker ever. I hate it even more than packing, and will generally attempt to avoid doing it altogether), it was back to potty training, fleeting attempts at getting back into an exercise routine, and blogging.

On Thursday February 12th I got a call from a familiar number; It was my OBGYN reminding me of my yearly appointment the next day. With all the 'excitement', and how for once in recent history I'd actually been busy- it had totally slipped my mind.

Figures that just as I'd managed to block out most of the memories of having random hands and gadgets stuck up my hoo-ha during my pregnancy, now it was time to go and dredge all of that back up. Yay!

Here's a little secret- I didn't have my first gynecologist appointment until I was a good 6 weeks pregnant with Holden. At 22 years old. *That* is how much I dislike the idea of having people who are practically strangers root around in my nether-region.

One would assume that with how ridiculously superstitious I am that I would have not only realized my appointment was landing on Friday the 13th- a notoriously unlucky day- but that it was most likely an omen of sorts.
Oh naiveté! How you dissuade me from assuming the worst!

As a woman, you do what you gotta do to take care of your lady bits- so when it comes to pap smears it's just a necessary evil. I was actually looking forward to seeing my doctor and all the nurses since they hadn't seen Holden in over a year.

We get there and begin going through the motions- sign in, pee in a cup, watch Holden flirt shamelessly with every nurse in the place. It's all going as it should; swimmingly one might even say- and then the question that *always* gets asked- no matter what kind of doctor you're seeing- comes up once again:
*"Any chance you could be pregnant?"*
I laugh. It may have actually been a scoff now that I think back on it. What a ridiculous question! Ridiculous because I couldn't honestly even recall the last time Thomas and I had made the whoopee. With the remodeling and moving and unpacking- by the time either of us even thought about it- IF we even had time to do that- the other was asleep.
*"You have to **have** sex to get pregnant!"*
She looks at me like she's either feeling very sorry for me, or like she thinks I'm taking crazy pills.

Although the question mostly gave us a good laugh, it did bring up questions I'd had about my cycles. My entire experience with a monthly period has been abnormal at best. While most women consider theirs to be "like clockwork"- I am the exact opposite. My cycle can be anywhere from 1-2 months apart. It's so sporadic, in fact, that I usually just lose track of the damn thing.

After years of always getting surprised by the warm gush of blood- I was damn tired of it! Since I was already there at the OBGYN, why not ask?

My doctor did what all doctors do- ran some tests. She thought it could potentially be some kind of thyroid issue, so I was sent to the lab (which was in the same office, directly across the hall from the room I was in) to have some blood work drawn.

There I sat, Holden in lap, waiting to get my arm stabbed by the tech. I see my doctor come in and start fiddling around with the pee samples across the room when I hear her go

*"Huh."*

She turns to me, and very matter-of-factly says:

*"Well, I know why your cycle has been so long. Your pregnancy test is coming up positive."*

I laugh, because it just sounds so absurd, but my entire body begins to go numb. She's joking, right? That's impossible! No freaking way on earth could MY pregnancy test be coming up positive. That's crazy talk!
So I challenge her. I don't just take things lying down, even though she was suggesting I had done just that.
I told her to test it again; she *must* have the wrong pee. I'm certain of it. That's all it is, a pee mix-up. They all look the same; it's an easy mistake to have made.
This time I watched very carefully as she dipped the strip into the cup with my name written on it- by me.

Positive.

Fuck.

Right there and then, I began to cry. I remember feeling horrified, terrified, confused, angry... and then humiliated as other nurses walked in and wondered why I was crying, only for my doctor to inform them
*"She just found out she's pregnant again."*
Thanks a lot. Make it sound like randomly getting pregnant is something I've made a hobby out of.

In 5 seconds flat the bottom of my world had dropped out.

74

Another baby? We aren't the type of family who gets happy about an unexpected pregnancy. We don't have the money to be that careless. We just took on a new house with a higher monthly rent that we know has already made things much tighter for us.

We don't have money trees growing in the back yard, and winning the lottery doesn't seem like a valid thing to be counting on.

We had no money for a new expense- and that's what a baby is; A very expensive addition.

Not only that- we didn't *want* another baby. Definitely not so soon... maybe not ever! Another baby wasn't even something we'd really discussed, because we knew if it was going to happen, it wouldn't be for a very long time; so much for that plan.

With all of those thoughts running through my head, I left with an appointment that coming Monday to find out just how far along I was and if all was well with... *the baby*. I couldn't even think it. If I thought it, it made it real, and I didn't want it to be real. I prayed that the entire day was an incredibly vivid nightmare, and I'd wake up in a cold sweat and have my life back.

I decided to try and *not* believe the pregnancy was real until I had ultrasound confirmation.

You may be wondering by this point why this chapter, unlike all the previous ones, has no blog entries in it.

The answer is simple: there are none.

I so desperately wanted to get on my blog and spill my guts. Try to get my head together and my thoughts collected. The blog had always helped me do that in the past. This time, I knew that wasn't going to be possible.

At that point and time, I had no idea if I was going to keep the baby or not, and as open as I pride myself on being in my blog, I just couldn't be open enough to discuss abortion. Breastfeeding and circumcisions I can handle, but I knew the level of backlash I'd be facing if I openly admitted to considering terminating the pregnancy would be insurmountable.

I had to draw the line between my personal life and the blog right there; this was just *too* personal. Maybe it would have helped someone else going through the same thing, who knows... but I couldn't knowingly sacrifice myself to the Pro-Life Gods.

Not to mention that if I blogged it, ALL of my family and friends would know, along with all the judgmental strangers in cyber-space. I was *definitely* not ready to face the firing squad. The last thing I wanted was for everyone to find out I was pregnant, only to then find out I'd had an abortion if that was what it came down to.

So at that very moment, I made the conscious decision to tell no one other than Thomas and my best friend until I knew exactly what I was going to do. If I was going to terminate the pregnancy- it would be something never written about on my blog.

I would love to be able to tell you that Thomas and I sat down and had a serious conversation about what we should do, but it just didn't happen that way. Outside of my blubbering and the extreme fear and anger I felt for somehow getting into this situation, coupled with what I think was a state of shock we were both in... we didn't say much to each other at all.

I've been trying to figure out how to word this without making Thomas seem like the bad guy, but I can't figure it out other than to say that Thomas was leaning toward terminating. I can't say that I blame him or that I didn't understand, or even that I didn't agree, but he also saw it differently than me in many ways. While I agreed with how incredibly difficult affording another child would be, and also agreed with that we didn't even want another kid so soon... he's not a woman. He can't understand what it's like to have to consider abortion.

Let me make it clear that I am 100% Pro-Choice. I think a woman has a right to choose what to do with her body (though I don't agree with those who use it as a form of birth control instead of just wrapping it up), but I had never been put in the position to have to consider one for myself. I'm 100% Pro-Choice, but I wasn't sure if that choice was right for me. I didn't know if I could physically go through with it and live with myself afterward.

I was incredibly torn, and Thomas wasn't much help because regardless of what he wanted- he told me that it came down to what *I* wanted to do, and whatever that was we would find a way to make it work.

Unfortunately for me, that didn't make the decision any easier. I still had a lot of doubts running through my head.
It really all came down to a few factors.

Did we really have enough money to care for two children, or would having another baby completely bankrupt us?

Could I really take care of TWO kids? Could I spread myself that thin? Could I love a child I didn't plan and wasn't sure I could ever be happy about? Would this ruin Holden's life, having to have a baby take so much time away from him when he was still so young? He didn't choose this. This wasn't his fault, why should *he* have to suffer?

Still, all the begging, pleading, crossed fingers and salt thrown over my shoulders did absolutely nothing to help my cause because Monday came and there it was; in all its' peanutty shaped glory- a baby with a tiny pulsing heartbeat. And it wasn't exactly little. It turns out I was over 7 weeks pregnant, a

HUGE shock to me. I had had absolutely no pregnancy symptoms whatsoever. A younger fetus I could understand, but being so far along? You'd expect *something*. Some sort of morning sickness, *some* kind of sign. I'd had zilch.

Now, I could feed you some bullshit story about how seeing the heartbeat made it all click into place, and that was the moment I decided to keep the baby... that it was this huge life-changing revelation. The clouds parted! The sun was shining! Heaven and earth stood still! But that would be a big fat lie.

All the heartbeat did was confirm that I really *did* have a huge decision to make. It was no testing error; no case of mistaken pee- the pregnancy was very, *very* real.

It wasn't until about a week later when I was still scratching my head about the whole confusing predicament that it hit me. The estimated due date given to me was my mother's birthday. I had never even put that together before.
There were just too many weird things about this pregnancy to ignore. The seemingly impossible conception date (since we'd been remodeling the entire month they claimed it happened. Aka: no sex), having zero symptoms, finding out about it on Friday the 13th, and now the day that the baby was supposed to be born landing on my mom's birthday? All of that couldn't just be a coincidence.

Just as I was about to second guess all the things I was reading as "signs"-the money from my Mom's estate that we had been waiting for and needed for the house came through.

Suddenly it was as if a huge weight was instantly lifted off of my shoulders.
I didn't have to make any decisions- because it was clear that the decision had been made for me:
I was keeping the baby.

Now all I had to do was find a way to tell all of my friends and family.

# The Preggo Blogs-
## A humbling, yet horrifying experience.

Even though I was somewhat of an unwilling participant in my 2$^{nd}$ pregnancy, it opened up a whole new world of blogging to me.

 While pregnant with Holden I never really had any friends. I just sat mostly in my room like a sorry, rapidly expanding lump with no one to talk to (other than the message board of Moms who at times only seemed to tolerate me), and no outlet for my frustrations.

I never got the opportunity or the idea to blog during my first pregnancy- only to look back in retrospect and laugh at how awful and bitchy I was.

Now I had the chance to fully broadcast that awful bitchiness to the entire world! People had no idea what was coming once I was able to unleash in real-time.

Everything I went through, everything I felt (no matter how ridiculous) was posted as it happened. There was some good, some ugly, and a lot of disgusting. Blogging is already a therapeutic tool in and of itself. You can vent, laugh, and collect your thoughts, among other things- but when I was pregnant the blog saved my sanity.

From anal swabs to small cold hands crammed in my no-no bits, to uncontrollable explosive diarrhea. All written and published for the unsuspecting world to read, fueled by intense hormones and massive amounts of milkshakes, washed down with gallons of grape soda.

This is a collection of blogs from my 'oopsie' pregnancy; starting with my admittance to family and friends that I was 'with child', to the 3 trimesters and everything that went with them. Including the ups and downs of gender disappointment and the unexpected birth story.

One may want to show the next few chapters to teenage girls as a form of birth control. Everyone else? I hope you can laugh, cringe, and smile along with me looking back on a very confusing and interesting time in my life.

The last time I told my Dad I was pregnant, we were out at dinner at a nice restaurant. My Dad, my step mother, Thomas and myself- planning our wedding.
Impeccable timing I have!

I had to tell him that if we didn't scoot up the date of the wedding, there was no way in hell my dress was going to fit.

It took him a while to get it (read: my step mother had to clue him in), but once he finally did catch on he was clearly not happy. It became a very tense dinner to say the least. He wished we'd waited a longer amount of time before getting pregnant, a few months, and maybe even a few years. Holden was planned, but we hadn't expected it to happen *so* soon. My Dad wasn't the only one shocked, Thomas and I were too, so I understood where he was coming from…but didn't expect him to be quite so ambivalent about it.

I did NOT want him to have a severely negative reaction again!

Telling him I was pregnant yet again, but with an unexpected and unplanned pregnancy when Holden was only one and a half years old? How could he *not* react negatively?

My friends? Their reactions were even worse the first time around than my Dad's (and much more vocal).

While a few had given birth after I had Holden, *no one* was crazy enough to have two. I was crossing into uncharted forbidden territory- but the truth had to come out. Being over 2 months along by the time I had decided to go on with the pregnancy didn't give me a hell of a lot of time before it would be obvious without me saying a word.

How exactly could I expect others to be excited about a pregnancy that I...well... wasn't?

The second time around didn't go as smoothly as I had hoped- but does it ever?

Thomas and I went out and bought Holden a "big brother" t-shirt to wear to my niece's 18th birthday dinner that the entire family would be attending. The hope was that maybe we wouldn't have to say anything at all, and people would just get the hint and figure it out for themselves. Leave it to me to put the burden on a toddler to tell the world he would no longer be an only child.

The only one who noticed was my niece. Her jaw nearly hit the floor, and after a few minutes of repeating *"does that really say what I think it says?"* she calmed down enough to ask if anyone else knew. When she heard that she was the first, she wanted to start pointing out the shirt to everyone, but she kept quiet for our sake... but more likely because she wanted to see members of our family's faces as they realized just what Holden's shirt was announcing.

Throughout the entire dinner we waited and waited for someone, ANYONE else to notice. No one did!

The whole family ended up going back to my step sister's house for cake and ice cream. Still we were just hoping for someone to read Holden's shirt and make the announcement for us, because Thomas and I are both pussies and feared extreme disapproval… but once again- no one did. That day, being oblivious was an airborne illness.

It wasn't until I was wildly gesticulating at Holden's shirt that my step mother, once again, took over yet another situation that seemed like a lost cause and says to my Dad:
*"Just tell her congratulations and that we hope it's a girl this time!"*

My Dad, the king of oblivious.

He actually thought we just bought the shirt because it was on sale and happened to fit our slightly massive child. I could not believe someone, my Dad especially, would think we'd put our kid in a "big brother" shirt just because of the price. Bless his heart. I do love finding a good deal, a pretty thrifty bitch I am. I clip coupons and everything, but putting my 18 month old in a shirt that proclaims *"I'M THE BIG BROTHER!"* when I'm *not* growing a spawn in my stomach? Not even saving a few bucks could convince me to do that! All the questions we'd be sure to get would not be worth a handful of change. How cheap did he think we were??

If you've ever watched TV shows about pregnancy, be they real or scripted, you always see this HUGE fuss made about it. Parents crying, people screaming and clapping, and generally being SO overjoyed by the promise of a new addition to the family that they just can't contain themselves.
That didn't happen to us. No, *I* may not have been excited, but I had wished for everyone else to be to help *me* get into the spirit… and when they weren't? It made me even more of a miserable hormonal pregnant bitch tan I already was.

3/1/09
# No Biggie?

In the wake of a huge announcement, you'd expect to get reactions out of people, right? Phone calls, comments, emails, the works.
Happy, sad, angry, neutral, doesn't matter which way the reaction swings- you still expect to get SOMETHING, *right*??

I guess I thought when everyone found out I was pregnant with #2 so soon after Holden, there would be a bit of a freak out. I myself sure as hell freaked out... but there was nothing. An email or two, one text message, and that was it.

What does that mean? Does it mean that I have grown so far apart from most of my friends that they just don't care what happens to me anymore?
It certainly can't be that people just expected me to become a baby factory, because no way in hell is that happening. One oopsie is enough for me to take extreme precautions once this one pops out.

It's just odd to log into my email and social network accounts after announcing another baby is gonna be popping out of me in a matter of months and hardly anyone even bats an eyelash. Or perhaps they're busy talking shit behind my back like people have the tendency to do (ahem, DAD).

Maybe I should look on the bright side- no one saying anything means I don't get any emails or comments saying *"WTF WHY?! GET AN ABORTION!"* because *those* types of emails are not fun to get- and I've gotten a few in the past.

It's kind of like someone talking shit about your mom; only YOU can do that. When someone else does you suddenly feel incredibly protective, and a rage begins to build inside of you that makes you want to punch them in the face. I feel the same way about my accidental fetus. Plus, i'm growing the damn thing, so I feel even more attached to it

You think you figure out who your real friends are once you pop ONE kid out and they stop coming around...try getting knocked up with a second; then they really start dropping like flies.

I hope they get pregnant with triplets.
 And then blow their snatches out.
YES, EVEN THE DUDES.

And don't go blaming my attitude on pregnancy hormones, sometimes you just feel like being a bitch.


# 3/8/09
# Family Non-Reactions

My family... is a strange one.

You tell them something sad, they just kind of shrug their shoulders, internally smile that it didn't happen to them, and move on. You tell them something exciting, they give you a strange look and struggle to get out a "congratulations", and move on.

There are a few exceptions in my family, but the majority doesn't give a crap about anything that happens to you unless it has to do with them. Don't misunderstand- they *love* family members, just have a strange way of showing it sometimes (read: not at all).

That's the thing with family; when it comes to relatives, they're pretty selfish. Let's not get angry about it, it's a fact of nature. We as humans tend to take advantage of the people we know aren't going to go anywhere. Family can't exactly divorce you. They can be mad and hold a grudge (as mine loooooooves to do) but they'll still be your family, now and forever. You'll still see them at family functions, they'll eventually come around again, and you'll end up being on good terms- so why not crap all over them just because you can?

Friends can come and go as they please; they have their own family to shit all over. Blood is for life.

I'm getting away from the point.

I did not expect my family to be jumping for joy about the new pregnancy. Holden was PLANNED and they weren't even excited about him, so an *unplanned* pregnancy? I expected to be stoned (and i'm not talking about getting high).

Going as far as to point fingers will end up getting me in trouble, so I'll just list a few reactions I have received so far... but to be totally honest, most of my family- who I know has heard through the grapevine- hasn't even bothered to say anything to me personally about it. Could it be because I didn't tell them directly? I didn't tell ANYONE directly. No one is special here.

Back to the focus:

**Reaction #1:** Blank. Then asks if i'm going to get my tubes tied after this one.
*Wow... just... wow.*

**Reaction #2:** Says nothing to me, but I overhear them discussing it, and telling *others* to congratulate me.
Gee, thanks! HEY, I'M THE ONE WHO'S PREGNANT! TALK TO *ME* ABOUT IT. THEY CAN'T TELL YOU ANYTHING ABOUT ME OR MY UTERUS.

**Reaction #3:** Shock. Pure shock. That is all.
Not even a fake congrats? I'll take a fake congrats over

nothing.

I could go on, but I think we all see where this is going.
Don't take this as pure complaining... it's only a LITTLE bit of
complaining. I'll use the pregnant card in every area I can: cut
a preggo some slack!

My friends may hate children and never want any of their own
but they at least can muster up fake congratulations after the
shock has worn off.

I don't need real excitement or congratulations, hell I don't feel
either of those for myself; it's just kind of common decency to
do it for others though, isn't it?
Unless someone's popping out their 10th kid and can hardly
afford or control the 9 they already have- aren't congratulations
*always* in order?

Just wait until I do get really excited about this pregnancy. All
hell will break loose if no one else follows suit. You don't cross
an angry, fat, swollen preggo. That is always a bad idea.

# 10 The Belated First Trimester Blogs

While my situation with pregnancy #2 wasn't quite worthy of an episode of *"I didn't know I was pregnant!"* it was definitely a monumental difference from when (and how) I got pregnant with Holden. Back then I was using ovulation kits, charting my vaginal temps (it's just as uncomfortable and awkward as it sounds), and taking pregnancy test after pregnancy test hoping and praying for a positive result.

Considering that I never even thought of the possibility of being pregnant, none of those things ever happened the second time around.

Finding out at 7 weeks along instead of 3 weeks doesn't seem like a big time difference, but in the land of pregnancy where the entire ordeal is only 40 weeks long, with the first trimester being 13- you can easily miss a lot.

Some women might consider that a lucky break. Having no idea I was pregnant meant none of the sickness, vomiting, or exhaustion that most experience from the time of conception well into the 2$^{nd}$ trimester, but I definitely had my own problems to deal with.

While I may not have spent my mornings with my face firmly planted in the toilet bowl, I was attempting to cope with a pregnancy I was incredibly unhappy and unsure about, friends who didn't understand, and a lot of other normal yet horrible things that go hand in hand with pregnancy: Extreme bloating, gender speculation (more like obsession really), Braxton Hicks, and the dreaded Preggo Brain. Did I mention I also caught the stomach flu from Holden? I think the 14 hours straight I spent puking and shitting simultaneously more than made up for all

89

the mornings I didn't spend feeling nauseous because of the new occupant in my womb.

All of this while attempting to take care of an incredibly ornery toddler in the thick of potty training; it was *a lot* to handle.

To try to make the best of the situation, I attempted to follow the exact same pattern I did with Holden. I put on a happy face, and even joined a new MomSpace message board for other women due the same month as me (a decision I would later regret). My thought was that maybe being in the presence of a group of expectant mothers that were genuinely happy and excited to be rapidly expanding with baby, would in turn help to make me happy and excited to be expanding as well. I may have had a rough start with the board I'd joined while pregnant with Holden, but I'd found it to be invaluable as far as advice goes. Over time I'd even come to think of it as a second home- and had even become co-host of the board. I'd made what I had considered real friends, and those that didn't particularly like me had either stopped coming round or had gotten used to me. I'm an acquired taste… like beer. I get better with repeated tries. The MomSpace message board went from being a place I needed only for help, to a place I actually enjoyed visiting. If I could have that for this pregnancy? I'd be set.

Just in case of drama, I went in armed. This time around I had my not-so secret weapon: the blog. Which, on a side note, also showed me just how WRONG, yet so hilariously right I was when I wrote pregnancy blogs so far after being pregnant the first time? It's funny how that worked out.

3/10/09
# Bye-Bye Bellybutton

Before I found out I was pregnant, the ONLY thing I ever noticed about myself that I thought was a tad *off* was my bellybutton.
I looked down and said aloud *"hmm… that looks a little shallow,"* but my bellybutton has really never been quite the same since my pregnancy with Holden. It got the short end of the stick when it came to stretch marks; one going up from the top, one going down from the bottom. It's like a damn compass.

Currently, I am just shy of 10 weeks pregnant, and my bellybutton is history. It's gone.
Even when i'm not full of gas, water, and air, it's flat. Right now, at the end of the day, it's sticking out like a turkey in the oven that's done.
DING!
Well, I ain't ready to pop another baby out, and bellybuttons aren't supposed to pop out this early!
Mine never really did before, even at 39 weeks along with Holden. Only when I sneezed or strained did I get an outtie, otherwise it was totally creepy, flat, and almost seemed sheer. I avoided touching it in fear my intestines would come spilling out... or Holden would… or both.

If i'm hardly showing, how is my bellybutton gone *already*? Am I carrying this tiny little bean higher? Are my insides already making way for this little turd to forge its hostile takeover?

It's now that I really wish i'd changed my bellybutton ring the second I found out about the pregnancy, because currently I have the regular old metal one in, and when bellybutton decides it's time to poke out- it gets a nice little indent from the bar in it. UNCOMFORTABLE to say the least. It's actually downright painful.

Putting in the plastic maternity belly ring is not pleasant; you have to thread the stupid ball yourself. Not a fun thing to do when your button is already poking out and you literally have to work around it to get the thing secured.

Now I guess i'm just waiting for the linea negra to show up and I'll be almost completely grossed out with myself. My dark little line is crooked and i'm so damn pale that it's *really* not cute on me.

Oh the joys of pregnancy! Bring on the leaky tits and cankles!


## 3/11/09
# I don't think I want to know

When it comes to finding out the gender of my growing...
*fetus*... you'd think I would want to find out ASAP.
With Holden, I could not WAIT to find out. We even went as far as to schedule an early determination ultrasound with a 4D studio about 45 minutes away to find out what, if anything, he was packing.

When I found out that Holden was a boy, I was crushed. Tears welled up in my eyes and I had to struggle my hardest to hold them back, I really had my heart SET on a girl. Thomas and I honestly only ever wanted one child total- and we never pictured that child as a boy. The pregnancy with Holden was so rough that I wasn't sure I ever wanted to go through it again, and I was pissed up until the moment he was born that he had a penis.

Once the horrors of child birth had finally made their way to the back of my mind I thought, *"Ok, we can try it again someday"* and I thought we'd attempt the Shettles method of conceiving. Sex farther away from ovulation: girl, closer to ovulation: boy.

Obviously things did not go as we had planned them, and I find myself 10 weeks pregnant with a baby I had no 'choice' in trying to conceive. And I mean that as in: I didn't get to try out the Shettles method. I have NO idea when I ovulated, when I implanted... or even when I had sex- I'm still slightly convinced I never did.

While I feel like it's sort of destiny that I have a little girl (due to the fact that this baby is due on my mom's birthday, was a complete shock because we didn't have sex to where the sperm would logically be able to live long enough to fertilize, etc. etc.), knowing my luck? This baby will have TWO penises. I feel jinxed.
The absolute last thing I want to do is once again get my hopes up for a girl and have a boy. This time, though, I don't think we're going to even consider having more children. Two is one thing, but THREE? I just don't think so. This is my last shot to have the little girl I always wanted, so how am I going to feel at 20 or so weeks if I go into an ultrasound and find out this baby is a boy? Devastated.

Of course I know i'm being selfish, people always say you should just wish for a "happy and healthy baby" but *come on*! I've never known someone to not get their hopes up on one gender or the other, *especially* when you plan on it being your last child.

I can't help but to feel the way I feel. I want a girl- what's so wrong with that?

So what do I do? Do I just not find out to avoid the disappointment and anger throughout the rest of my pregnancy if this baby happens to be a boy?
Or do I give birth and be pissed and happy at the same time?

I'm probably going to end up finding out at 20 weeks like you're supposed to, just to be able to prepare (I hate being unprepared) but i'm struggling with all the 'what if's.

As far as old wives tales predicting gender? They're bullshit. Almost EVERY SINGLE ONE swore Holden would be a girl, and he is *obviously* not.

The only thing that rang true was the fact that I carried low, but i'm 5'9" and long waisted- I don't think it's *possible* for me to carry high.

Being the glutton for punishment that I am, I went and looked anyways, and most of them claim this baby will be a boy. Blah.

If they claimed Holden would be a girl and he's a boy, does that mean that because this one is claimed to be a boy, it will be a girl? Who the hell knows? I should stop looking altogether. Their judgment has the same damn odds as flipping a coin. 50% accuracy is pretty good when you look at it that way, but everyone is that 'accurate'- it can only be one or the other!

There is one thing i'm putting a little weight behind. After Holden was born, last year I believe, I emailed a "psychic" and asked when i'd be pregnant again and what gender the baby would be.
She responded with *"In the coming year you will find yourself pregnant with a healthy girl."*
At the time I laughed and thought *"BULLSHIT! No way am I getting pregnant next year!"* and look at me now. Odd coincidence, yes?

Regardless of what any of those dumb gender predictors say, or what anyone tells me about how I should just want a healthy baby regardless of gender; my feelings are still the same. If this baby is a boy I will be totally crushed (and totally pissed

94

considering we have sold practically ALL of Holden's clothes).
I'm most likely going to go through the gender ultrasound with
my hands over my eyes like i'm watching a scary movie.

3/13/09
# Ch-Ch-Ch-Changes

Ohhh pregnancy- you mysterious bitch!
It's sort of like puberty in a way: Constantly confusing;
everything is new and weird and you're always thinking *"why
am I getting that, there?"*
Only, instead of getting pubes and boobs- you're getting a
ginormous belly and milk filled sacks where those boobs used
to be.
The boob part is cool with me, not so much turning into a
walking whale that waddles like a penguin with a shit in its
pants.

I've been told about a million times that *'every pregnancy is
different'* which makes the situation even more of a mind fuck.
You'd think that since you've been through it once before (or
however many times) that you'd know exactly what to expect
and when because it happened with the last pregnancy.
Wrong.

This pregnancy is about as different as my pregnancy with
Holden as can be. It's almost baffling to me, as nothing is
happening as I thought it would.

Where to begin?

**Morning sickness.** With Holden, my morning sickness started
around week 2- before I even knew I was pregnant-but kicked
into full swing at week five. I never puked; it basically felt like
a perpetual hangover, from morning until lunch time. I just felt

95

nasty constantly. It continued until I was around 17 weeks along.

This new pregnancy, I had MAYBE 3 days of actual 'morning sickness,' where I felt like puking when I looked at my breakfast plate, but I thought it was because I had a few drinks the night before. This must havee been at around 4-5 weeks preggo. For a week after that I felt a little gross in the evenings, but now I feel practically perfect, better than ever even.

**"Showing" or "Bloating".** I can recall being bloated with Holden, nothing near the amount I am now. I feel absolutely enormous.

The weird part is, I was showing more in my pregnancy with Holden then I am with this pregnancy, still. Aren't you supposed to get bigger earlier the $2^{nd}$ time around?

**Return of the Porno Boobies.** My boobage during my last pregnancy was short lived, but I loved every second of it. At the time I was pissed that I'd gone out and spent a small fortune on bigger sized bras that just a few short weeks after giving birth I couldn't even dream of fitting into.

Luckily I kept those bras, because here I am, 10 weeks pregnant, and can't fit into anything but my pregnancy bras. I love boobs as much as anyone else, but DAMN they hurt. I fear if they stretch out even more than the previous pregnancy, they'll end up looking like sad little bacon strips after I give birth.

Since I am only 1/4 of the way through my pregnancy, everything else is yet to be determined. I have no clue what to expect, if anything at all. Will morning sickness start kicking the shit out of me next week? Will this baby go ninja on my insides like Holden did? Will I have horrible god awful Braxton Hicks from 26 weeks on? Will my blood pressure skyrocket?

I hate surprises. I'd love to squeeze out of this pregnancy

unscathed and not have it as rough as I did with Holden, but I have this sneaking suspicion that it's not going to go as smoothly as i'd like. It's just waiting to creep up on me… and I am not excited!

## 3/19/09
# Iron Pills: Not a Preggo's best friend

According to my OBGYN, something like 60% of all pregnant women are slightly anemic. Personally, I think my anemia is inherited (if that's possible), as I can always remember rubbing gold on my face and it leaving black trails behind (Try it; you'll see what I mean if you're low on iron).
I was put on iron pills with my last pregnancy, and don't have too many horrible memories of them. They didn't make me sick and I took them whenever I wanted. Even though they were a little bit constipating- they weren't anything a banana wouldn't clear right up (who says bananas stuff your butt up??)
Sure, they turn your poop dark creepy colors and make it feel like sandpaper pushing its' way out of your ass, but other than that, no harm. They got rid of my headaches so I really couldn't complain much.

Figures, this time around I would once again be labeled as "slightly anemic" and prescribed iron pills. These are *not* the same ones I recall taking a few years back.
These say that I can't take them with food. I have to wait TWO HOURS after eating to take them. Who says i'm not eating every two hours? I'm pregnant and HUNGRY, damnit.
That I can deal with though.

The horrid, god awful, mood altering constipation I cannot.
The head nurse suggested stool softeners as soon as she said I had to be on these stupid things, but judging from previous experience I didn't think i'd need any help- and at first I didn't.

97

Things were still moving along pretty regularly. After a week, it started becoming irregular, and a few days after that, it went to nothing; a total standstill of my colon.

Could this have been the cause of my first Braxton Hicks contraction the other night? Possibly; I think it was more dehydration from chugging a soda in record time, but who really knows.

After not pooping for an entire day (totally not like me, especially while pregnant), I didn't sleep very well at all, and I woke up the next morning in some pain. I can't be positive what constipation pain feels like since I've never had it, but I imagine it doesn't feel good, similar to how I was feeling- so I called the OBGYN office. I always get stuck talking to the head nurse about my pooping situation and this time she suggests an enema.

UM, NO THANK YOU. I am not putting anything up my butt, I don't care if it IS just water... it ain't happenin'!

I decided the best plan of action for me would be to chug water all day long. Being dehydrated can lead to constipation- so why not flush the shit out of my system, literally?

Didn't work; still no poop, and by the end of the day I started to *really* feel like I needed to go.

The worst feeling in the world is having to shit, sitting down, and having nothing happen. You can feel it in your lower intestine, but it doesn't budge. Not even gas; complete and utter dissatisfaction.

So once again last night, I went to bed feeling bad, and woke up feeling even worse. It basically feels like someone punched me in the stomach repeatedly.

Today was a new day though. I hadn't taken my iron pill in something like 3 days, because why take something if you can't shit, and the pill you're taking is the cause of the non-shitting? Once I dropped the kids off at the pool, I figured i'd take it again, and then rinse & repeat.

After breakfast, I got that oh-so familiar feeling. This time, instead of being disappointed, I was relieved, twice... if you get what i'm saying.

Unfortunately, my nurse was wrong and it did NOT relieve the pain, i'm still hurting. So now I don't blame the poop, I blame the baby. Baby is trying way too hard to make room and hurting my insides. Thanks a lot baby!

Under any normal circumstance, poop is supposed to be this HUGE relief; I am sad it was not for me. I built it up to be this HUGE deal, thinking to myself
*"Ok, I'll poop, and I'll feel 150%!"*
Psh. I feel more like 45% right now.

Now I have to decide whether or not to take another stupid iron pill and possibly get stuffed up for 3 damn days, starting this whole vicious cycle all over again.


3/27/09
# Little Doubts

To take my mind off the ridiculous bullshit happening (or NOT happening) in my life, let's focus on my womb fruit shall we?

Every day I get these weird little thoughts in the back of my mind that tell me this is some huge joke. I'm not pregnant- I just eat salty foods and get bloated after meals!

Over 12 weeks pregnant with my second child, and still no symptoms that I can pinpoint and say *"Yeah, I'm definitely pregnant"*
I'm smaller than I was with Holden by about half. I don't count the after-meal-super-bloat as 'showing.'
No morning sickness, no round ligament pain, and no baby

dreams.

Ever since that horrible bout of braxton hicks and 2 days of pain following, any little feeling of pregnancy I had disappeared.

It could be because I am approaching the "safe zone," a.k.a. the second trimester, but those little thoughts keep telling me *the baby is gone... or maybe it never even existed in the first place.'*

Hell, the appointment when I found out I was pregnant was on Friday the 13th, with an impossible conception date, and a due date on my late mother's birthday, *and* my next appointment is April 1st, better known as April Fool's Day. Are they going to tell me this whole ordeal was some huge practical joke?

Ever since I found out that my appointment was on April Fool's Day, I had this feeling that something WEIRD was going to happen. It would fit perfectly with this pregnancy's strange trends thus far; tons of weirdness, so what's it gonna be?
Baby with 2 heads? Baby disappeared? Phantom baby? Ghost baby? Were they showing me videos of someone else's ultrasound?

It's not like i'm begging for morning sickness, it would just be nice to have some kind of confirmation from my body that I *am* in fact pregnant. The boobs are nice, but that's not enough for me.

Maybe this kid needs to start knocking around my uterus like a soccer ball and that will finally put my mind at ease, it's just very confusing not to have any of that "mother's intuition" I keep hearing about. What I've got is a pokey bellybutton and painful boobs; yay me!

3/28/09

# Shenanigans!

Yes, I said it. I officially call SHENANIGANS!

Last night while reading my blog, Thomas pointed out that my weird little fetus-widget that grows as my actual fetus does, had changed from a wiry bird-looking thing to a more fleshed out bird-looking thing.
Since I hadn't noticed, I decided to take a look for myself, and that was when I saw something out of place.

Something was *not* right with my fetus-widget.

Upon further inspection, I came across something highly disturbing.

So you tell me:

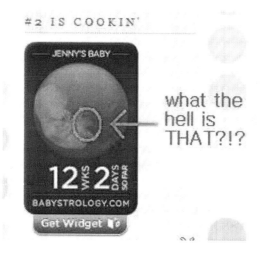

I apologize for the clarity. Paint has, and will always SUCK
ASS, as do my editing skills

My fetus-widget has what appears to be a red STUMP where
its' foot should be!
That can't be right! Why would they give my fetus a stump for
a foot?! I certainly didn't put that in the specified parameters
while creating the thing. It didn't even have a box for *"what
malformation would you like your fetus to have?"*
Even if it did, I don't think I would have chosen "RED STUMP
FOOT" from the list of options.

This just isn't normal. By now, my little parasite should have
two feet, customized with ten toes, maybe even toenails. A red
pointy stump? I think not!

Disturbing, isn't it? I'm highly confused... and now i'm curious
as to what's going to happen with the next fetus-widget change.
Adding another eye to the side of its' head? Fusing its' fingers
together? Chopping off the other foot only to leave a red ugly
stump?

What's next? Stop these shenanigans evil fetus widget!

# 11 The Second Trimester Blogs Part 1:

Gender Disappointment

Most women have to wait until 20 weeks along to find out the gender of their baby. I lack the patience those women possess.

I couldn't bear waiting that long to know (as much as I dreaded the result), so I scheduled an appointment with a private 4D ultrasound studio (I highly recommend!) at 15 weeks 5 days. Why? Because it was the *only* appointment available for months... and because I was obsessed with knowing the gender.

This part of my pregnancy is such an important story to tell not only for the pregnancy itself, but for my life and for other moms- that I felt the need to stop and take the time to better explain what I went through. It's also the first time I really ever felt attacked by complete strangers because of my blog, over something I had written and felt strongly about.

Since giving birth I have found that a *lot* of other women had gone through gender disappointment, some much more intensely than me, but felt like they couldn't tell anyone because of the fear of reactions from others. It's frowned upon by the majority of the snobby online mommy community to not be happy about whichever gender you get "stuck" with.

I was not so fearful in opening up about it on the blog, but did understand that people shaking their heads and calling you names because you didn't get the gender you'd wished for was a very valid fear- because it happened to me, twice.

I made it no secret that I *really* wanted a girl. After hoping and praying for one the first time around and getting Holden- I had my hopes up even higher on having a girl with the 2nd pregnancy. Holden is awesome, but two of Holden and even a Saint would lose their mind.

All the sadness and doubt about being unprepared to bring another baby into the world were all forgotten... as long as I wasn't pregnant with another boy. I know it sounds crazy, I even feel ridiculous just typing it, but that is how my mind was functioning at the time. If I kept a pregnancy I didn't want- it was only fair to give me the gender I *did* want, right?

It didn't help that, as I mentioned before, I was finding 'signs' everywhere I looked.
My mind decided to wander a *little* too far to the crazy side. You can get away with a certain amount of neuroses while pregnant, but there's a very thin line between a normal hormonal preggo, and just plain bananas. I crossed it, y'all.

I became consumed with finding signs that I thought were pointing toward me having a little girl; signs I honestly thought were coming from my Mom. Not that it would be the first time I was convinced I felt her around, but I think it was more than I *wanted* her to be so badly, and wanted to be having a girl so intensely that I got carried away.

When you want something SO much, you can turn just about anything into a sign that you're going to get it, just in order to keep even the tiniest shred of hope.
Every time I heard Journey's *"Open Arms"?*
That was my mom. And for the month before I found out the baby's gender, that song bombarded me everywhere I went. That had to be her trying to tell me something!

I like to think of it as pregnancy hormone induced delusions... or perhaps my brain's subconscious need to balance out the massive amount of testosterone already pumping through my house.

When I thought of what would be important to go into a book on my personal experiences, and all the things parents might think or feel, but feel like they can't say- this was one of the first things on my mind. And while I put it out there for everyone to see without a second thought, it didn't come without consequence; story of my life.

Because of the following blogs, I had my first brush with a group of Moms gunning for me simply and solely because they thought I was a terrible person and parent for not being happy just to be able to *get* pregnant in the first place. Unfortunately, it wouldn't be the last time.


4/10/09
## Nerves

The closer my "big ultrasound" date gets, the more nervous I become. This *huge* part of me still doesn't want to know the sex of the baby in fear that it will be another boy.
Is that selfish? Yeah, maybe, but I think i'm entitled to be.
An unexpected, unwanted pregnancy, that I wrestled back and forth with whether or not to even keep... that I ended up making a (in my opinion) selfless decision to move forward with and make the best of, because it had to have happened for SOME reason or another? Yes, a little selfishness from me is expected.

I'm afraid of walking into that ultrasound, lying down on the table, and getting scanned only to see another penis. I don't know how I'll react. I didn't cry when I found out Holden was a boy, but I was visibly disappointed. Another boy? When I didn't want another baby? When all I ever wanted was one girl, total? When I definitely don't want 3 children? I have no idea what's going to happen.

By now, I had really hoped to get over my issues with having another child and be super amped about it. Everyone told me to give it a few months to set in, and it would feel like I had planned this child for years.
It still doesn't feel that way. I know it's still early, but I WANT to be excited about this baby and i'm not. Sometimes I feel excited, and then I start thinking about how close in age this baby and Holden will be. I think about how I don't want to have to share my time with anyone but Holden. How I don't want him to have to compete for my attention. How my practically non-existent social life will fade into oblivion. How I don't think I can do it or handle it, and any feeling of excitement washes away.

That combined with really not wanting another boy since this will almost definitely be our last child, makes it very hard to be anything but a big ball of nerves. And I know it makes me selfish, to want what I want and nothing else, to know I won't be truly happy with another boy (and I worry I still won't be truly happy if it's a boy, even when 'he' is born)... but it makes me real. It makes me human. It makes me honest. I'm not going to lie to myself and shove this all down, not talk about it, not get it out- and end up with some serious form of Post-Partum Depression. That's the last thing my children need.

I need to vent, to feel my feelings, regardless of how right or wrong they may be. I can't help any of that.

I think these are feelings a lot of expectant moms feel. Worry, disappointment, fear.
They just never say so because they worry about being judged by others, being told they're a bad mom.
Trust me, I got told so many times when I was pregnant with Holden and pissed he was a boy that I should *"just be happy he's healthy regardless of gender"*, and that shit would piss me

off beyond all belief. Of course I hoped he was healthy- I can't hope for something else, too? I was mad up until the minute he was born.

Would I change his gender now if I could go back in time? No. Absolutely not.

If this baby happens to be a boy, I would hope that when I look back on it, I will feel the same way I do about Holden...but a HUGE part of me doubts it. A huge part of me thinks I'll still be angry. I'll never get that mother-daughter bond I've always dreamed of having.

Every day I wish for this baby to be a girl. Is that wrong? I don't know, maybe. It is what it is, can't change it. And the feeling most likely won't subside until that gender scan happens and I find out for sure which one this baby is.

To be totally honest, even though i'd feel relief if this baby is a girl, I'd still feel ALL the other things I've been feeling up to this point in my pregnancy. I'd still wish this was 3+ years later.

I think it all boils down to the fact that I had no control over this situation. I didn't expect it, I didn't plan it, and I didn't want it.

It all boils down to fear.

I haven't had very many people tell me that they think I can do it. No reassurance, all doubts. All people knowing this wasn't planned, and I think doubting in their minds if I'll be able to pull it off. All people thinking i'm insane for going through with it, whether it is because of money, or because of Holden.

If even just one person said to me, *"You're a good mom. You can do this"* it would make all the difference in the world. Unfortunately, even some of the closest people to me have *never* told me that i'm a good mother. I know that I am, but in a situation such as this, where I doubt every decision I make, some support would be nice.

Off to go stuff my face, again. At least food supports me! I sound like a lard ass.

A week later, the hammer dropped. I found out the baby I was carrying was none other than another bouncing baby boy. I'd actually love to tell you that I went totally feral and screamed and threw things, because that would make for one hell of a story… but that didn't happen. Not even close.

I shed a couple of tears, went to drown my sorrows at a pizza buffet to comfort my fat self- and then took to my blog.

All I posted was a picture of the "money shot" from the ultrasound, with the title *"Where are you now, mom?"*
Not a proud moment of mine.
I was just so angry and disappointed that I didn't even know what to say, but my lack of words allowed other people to come and attack me in the comments section of my blog.
*"You should be thanking God!"*
*"Quit complaining!"*

Kicking a hormonal pregnant woman while she's down is not the smartest of ideas. I had to stick up for myself and any other human with real feelings that wasn't afraid to not only feel them, but to express them; and of course, for myself, because I was heated.

## 4/23/09
## Save it

Every 75 posts or so I get a ridiculous, offensive, completely absurd, and of course anonymous comment (or two) that I feel the need to address. Being that I am in a royally rotten mood, and I got one of those comments on my blog yesterday, today is the day to address yet another one of those comments from a moron who obviously knows nothing other than their own deluded excuse for an opinion.

Telling me I should feel "blessed" because i'm fertile myrtle would be like me telling someone they should feel lucky to have a mother, because I don't have one anymore (which I've only done once as a joke, and haven't done again). It is a rude and horrible thing to say to someone who feels unfortunate, or unsure about their situation, just because it isn't how YOU would react. Guess what, you aren't me- and i'm not someone who is having trouble with their mother. I do not judge those who want to complain or vent, it is their right, regardless of what I've been through or how I feel.

Will me feeling 'blessed' about being pregnant again make those who have trouble getting pregnant more fertile? Will it make their fertility problems any less difficult? No? Then why lie about how I feel? Just as they didn't choose to have problems getting pregnant, I didn't choose to have NO problems getting pregnant. If I could give my fertility to someone who has been trying for a long time unsuccessfully, I would. I can't though, so what's the point in being dishonest about how I feel?

If you want to go and put your bullshit opinions on someone, find a girl who's drinking and doing drugs, blatantly ignoring all the things you aren't supposed to do while you're pregnant. Aren't those the ones you should be complaining about and throwing bibles at?

What? Because I wanted a girl it makes me a horrible person? Yeah fucking right. It makes me H-U-M-A-N.

I have never and will never compromise or lie about how I feel to make an anonymous commenter on this blog happy. I am who I am. I feel how I feel. I make no excuses about it, and I do not feel bad or ashamed about feeling the way that I do.

Get off of your high horse. Try putting yourself in my shoes for one second- an unexpected pregnancy that you're not ready for. You can't, because you haven't been here. You also don't know how it feels to have wanted a girl your entire life and to get 2 boys instead, and possibly not being able to have a third for about 100 different reasons. You're trying to tell me you wouldn't be disappointed? Even slightly? If you said no, that you wouldn't be- you're a liar. A big fat liar. And if you truly believe you would be completely happy and satisfied, and not even the tiniest bit sad regardless- you're most likely lying to yourself. Being disappointed is completely natural. It's why books, articles, and reports have been written about being sad when you get a certain gender and how to cope- because it is COMPLETELY normal; typical even.

In the end, the disappointment will completely fade, and I will look back and not change this baby to a girl for anything in the world. Same as I feel with Holden. It's not about how you feel in the beginning, it's how you react, cope, and deal with it. And talking about it, writing about it, venting about it is the healthiest thing to do. You most likely won't read any more blogs about how this baby is not a girl, because guess what? I got it out and now i'm done whining about it.

Throwing your Christian beliefs at me doesn't work because I am the least religious person you might ever come across. So telling me I should *"thank God for even being able to get pregnant!"* means nothing to me. I respect all religions, and the right to believe in them- but to throw God in my face to try and make me feel like I am a bad person sickens me. I may not practice religion, but I know for a fact that it is not Christian to be judgmental towards someone you don't know, or to use God as a weapon. You don't know anything about me but what I CHOOSE to write on this blog.

Oh, and when my child gets old enough to understand logic and reason, i'm not going to lie to him and say he was planned. There's nothing wrong with him knowing he was unplanned (it's how you word it, mistake= bad, unplanned= good) and that

110

I wanted him to be a girl. Kids aren't stupid unless you treat them as such. I refuse to shelter him from every negative thing in the world and have him go into total shock when he realizes life isn't like Candy Land.

I've said it before, and I'll say it again- if you don't like my blog- STOP READING IT. Go the fuck away. I certainly don't want you here, or your ridiculous opinions. They are not welcome or appreciated- as I don't write this blog to please anyone else. Take your sour grapes and shove'em; 'cause at the end of the day i'm still gonna feel the same way and your stupid comment isn't going to change anything. I don't have to justify myself to anyone, especially when I don't feel like i'm doing anything or feeling anything wrong.

The funniest part about that whole situation and that ridiculous blog was that after writing it, I felt 100% better about having another boy. I still can't say that I was excited, but I wasn't angry or resentful like people were assuming I would be. Bitching: It's good for the soul.

Even today, when it comes to gender disappointment- I believe all of the things I wrote...Well, the sane parts anyways. There is absolutely nothing wrong with being disappointed. It is natural to want a certain gender and to be bummed when you don't get it. And if you pretend not to feel it, it will bottle up inside of you until you're as big as a house, about to give birth, and sobbing into a pint of Baskin Robbins with contractions 6 minutes apart about not getting the gender you wanted.
 Feel it, vent about it, and move on. That penis won't magically turn into a vagina in utero or vice versa!

I will give this piece of advice: As much as it's ok to wish for a certain gender, don't ever get your hopes set on one or the other. Don't buy those stupid piss tests from the drug store that can *"predict the gender of your baby with 97% accuracy!"*

111

because you'll most likely end up in that 3% where it's wrong. I've seen it happen time and time again, and it's not pretty.

Most importantly, don't let anonymous internet morons bully you into feeling bad about your feelings. I'd have to go a couple more rounds with a handful of them to really cement that into my head.

Who knows, maybe my mom really was trying to contact me- I was just interpreting it all wrong.

# 11 The Second Trimester Blogs Part 2:

*Bacon boobs, pubic hair, and explosive diarrhea*

Although I may have narrowly escaped morning sickness in the first trimester, I was paid back in spades once the second trimester got into full swing. In front of me was a hefty load of new obstacles to tackle and emotional roller coasters to ride and attempt to overcome.

While I don't think I ever felt one shred of regret about my decision not to terminate the pregnancy- it would be stupid for me to sit here and try to convince everyone else and myself that I had miraculously become happy about it overnight. I still wasn't. There was a perpetual and overwhelming fear of the future, and a complete uncertainty of what it would be like. Add pregnancy hormones to that and you've got a delicious recipe for disaster.

If there's one thing I was absolutely sure of, it's that there was no turning back now. So I did my best to act sane for a moment, and tried my hardest to stay busy and push all the fears to the back of my mind. My body had a hell of a lot of other plans for me- as did Holden and his full swing into the terrible twos. Such a sweet child, but so much attitude; how can so much fit into such a little body?

In the short span (which felt like an eternity to me) of 3 months, I had to deal with aches and pains in places I didn't even know existed, toddler cursing, potty training, uncontrollable diarrhea, and still being pissed about another penis growing inside of me; all made even worse by the sweltering summer heat outside, and the disgusting amount of sweat dripping from every pore on my body. Write this down: Do not plan on getting pregnant when your largest months will be in the summer, you will be a damp, roving landbeast, and small children will take pictures of you to post on the *"People of Wal-Mart"* website, or run from you screaming in a state of sheer terror. Kill it! Kill it with fire!

I even had an internet crazy threaten to call CPS on me because of a blog post about my cat scratching Holden. Yes, CPS over a *cat*. Blogging can lead to some crazy situations.

## 4/8/09
# So much for Second Trimester improvement

According to all the books and all the websites, the exhaustion nausea, cramping, and all other 'icky' feelings that being pregnant causes are supposed to subside by your second trimester. You're supposed to start "GLOWING", have oodles of energy, and be *happy* to be pregnant instead of miserable and pukey.

Now, that wasn't totally the case with Holden, as I had all-day sickness until probably 17-18 weeks, but every other disgusting side effect went away once the first trimester finally ended. When night time rolled around I felt pretty good. I was sleeping better, eating better, and feeling better.

Leave it to the bass-ackwards pregnancy of today to completely buck the trend. No morning sickness the first trimester? Well then, we'll make it so you're completely and utterly exhausted in your second trimester, for absolutely no reason at all!

No joke, it is physically hurting me to be awake. It's not as though i'm staying up until all hours of the night- I've actually been going to bed HOURS earlier than usual because it's become impossible to keep my eyes open past 11:30pm. Still, I wake up and have to drag myself out of bed and find myself yawning all damn day, falling asleep on the couch, and constantly being achy and tired.

I don't get it! What the hell does my body have to be so tired about? Especially when not only do I sleep from 11:30pm-7:30am, but I also take a 1-2hr nap with Holden every afternoon! You'd think I would be wide awake and not able to sleep at night from all the sleep I *am* getting.

And if you're wondering, no, I've never been the energizer bunny. Waking up early is not my thing. I am not a morning person in any sense of the term. Still, I had more energy before getting pregnant... and surprisingly more energy in my first trimester than I do now. Makes no sense, right?

It's not fun; it leads to me turning into angry mommy. Being tired equates to having little to no patience for all the evil things Holden does all day. We didn't get along today because of it, not at all. Next thing you know I'll end up going crazy, seeing dead girls in my hallways, and busting down the bathroom door with an axe.

*HEEEEEEEEEEERE'S JENNY!*

You'll know to alert the authorities when this blog turns into nothing but pages and pages of *"All work and no play makes Jenny a cranky mommy."*

# Sugar & Spice

Has anyone ever watched that movie? The one about the bank robbing cheerleaders with the pregnant captain?
I think I've seen it probably 15 times; it's just one of those movies that doesn't get old.
From that movie, I learned that preggos puke randomly and fart uncontrollably. The puking I knew about- everyone knows that most pregnant women spend a good portion of their day barfing, but the farting was a new revelation. The first time I saw the movie I must have been under 15 years old, so I thought perhaps the gas was exaggerated for comical purposes. Oh, to be young and optimistic!

Now, for me, the puking thing is not so true. I've never had to stop while shopping and barf into a potted plant, though I don't doubt that it happens to others. I've actually never puked once during either pregnancy- unless you count having the stomach flu and retching for 15 hours straight… but I don't think that counts.

Uncontrollable gas? Yeah... Didn't get so lucky in that department. While it's not as bad now as it was in my first trimester, where I was tearing ass nonstop for the first two hours I was awake, it's become more random and embarrassing over time.
For the record, I do not fart in front of Thomas, just can't do it. I just can't bring myself to lean to the side, lift a cheek off of my seat and *BRRRPPPPPPPPPP.* That's a game changer right there.
I'll tell him when I have to poop, or even that I AM gassy, but he will never hear the sound of my butt trumpet if I have any control over it.

Thomas claims he can't make his disgusting farts silent. I call bullshit, as I have become the master of this art. It's really not that hard to just squeak one out- and no- the silent ones AREN'T always deadly (thank goodness).

The only time this doesn't hold true is when I get painful gas; I know you know what i'm talking about. The sharp twinge and rumble of impending doom, ring a bell?

Those are nearly impossible to make silent, and they come out sounding like a machine gun.

*THRRRAP AP AP AP AP AP*

Funny to talk about, not so funny to experience while trying to hide from your spouse.

When Thomas isn't home though, it's free reign. Open season on farts!

Like Holden cares if I let a few loose? Please. He sticks his face in the cat's ass a few times a day; i'm pretty sure he has no idea how to distinguish between good and bad smells.

I let one rip, and he just looks over and gives me a little smile. He enjoys my gassiness. His makes me laugh, but my eyes burn, equal tradeoff I suppose.

I will be more than pleased when my intestinal issues subside. Oh how I wish Thomas' would go away right along with mine... but I think his are a permanent fixture in life. How did I get so lucky?

## 5/20/09
# Incompetent Uterus

Is it possible to have one? I'm not really sure, but I feel like of the uterus world- mine is the one sitting in the corner eating paint chips and banging its' proverbial head against the wall. It just doesn't GET why it has to do all the hard work. It's always angry about something, always paining me and bothering me and causing me to lose sleep, simultaneously pissing off the rest of my body. Basically me in uterus form; I blame the uterus for my severe bitchiness.

I really think if it weren't for my uterus, i'd be one of those happy preggos you see in all the gigantic hanging pictures in maternity sections of stores. Glowing, smiling, prancing through fields of daisies, and having a happy attitude toward pregnancy in general.
Instead, i'm irritable and angry, and it takes me 2 minutes to get my ass out of a chair- not because i'm big- but because my uterus refuses to let me do it any faster or it contracts.

If I want to compare it to something more relatable to those who have never been pregnant, I guess i'd say it's like having a big nasty splinter in your foot. You leave it there long enough and your body gets angry and attempts to push it out. It gets infected, red and painful- *that* is what being pregnant is like for me. My body is trying to reject a foreign object... only it's being freaking STUPID because my BODY is the one growing it. Did I tell the egg to implant? Did I beat it with a stick until it complied? No, no I didn't. My uterus has no right to bitch.

Trust me, i'd prefer to be the happy preggo- but being utterly uncomfortable all the time sort of prevents that. Any wrong movement, any kick from the baby, even him getting the hiccups causes a nasty braxton hicks contraction; even earlier than I got them with Holden. I do NOT want another pregnancy like I had with him. The braxton hicks I can learn to live with because I know that they aren't doing anything other than just being annoying, but if along with the braxton hicks comes the high blood pressure, bed rest, swelling, headaches, dizziness, and medication to 'stop labor' that makes me shake like a crack addict in need of another hit... I think I'll go totally insane, and that's only if I'm not there already.

My uterus sucks, plain and simple. It sucks, and it's stupid, and I hate it! SO THERE!

Now, off to go watch the end of this horribly long and cheesy American Idol finale. It's the little things, y'all.

5/21/09

# Whoaaaa- we're half way theeeerreeee!

140 days down, 140 more to go!

I seriously cannot believe that I have been pregnant for 140 days already. ONE HUNDRED AND FORTY. Unreal. It doesn't even feel like half that long. Pregnancy drags along and flies by at the same time. It has found the rip in the space time continuum and is taking full advantage.

At this point, I think most pregnant women would be getting excited about the impending birth of their child, saying *"yay! halfway done!"* but I seem to just get more nervous as the time ticks away. 20 weeks is still a long way to go when you really break it down and think about it, but I wish I had MORE time. More time to potty train stubborn ass Holden, more time to spend alone with him, more time to mentally PREPARE myself for having two little boys around the house, more time to sleep in, or sleep at all- because I know for damn sure I won't be getting any once the baby arrives. I just want more!

I'm definitely not freaking out like I was in the beginning of this pregnancy, but I wouldn't go as far as to say i'm 'ready.' I'm not sure there's really such a thing as being fully prepared to have a child. You never know what the kid is going to be like, what their temperament will be like, how well they'll eat or sleep, or how you'll handle all of those things as a parent. Sure, parenting comes pretty naturally, but babies are CONFUSING- and that's putting it lightly. It took me a very long time to figure Holden out, and to this day he still baffles me at times.

Someone needs to invent an all-encompassing instruction manual for a baby. Step by step directions on what to do, what baby needs, and WHY baby is crying. That would be awesome; whoever invents it will make BILLIONS.

I suppose now I should just enjoy the time I have left before I become a mommy of TWO... damn that's a scary thought. I should probably also enjoy these mega-boobs baby has given me, because I know they won't last long after I pop him out.

Oh, and I should ESPECIALLY enjoy not having a period or pain in my crotch from physically giving birth. I really *reaaaaaaaaally* don't look forward to that.


## 6/16/09
# Personal Grooming Habits

Let's get right into it- it's not the 70's anymore. I wasn't even alive in the 70's, so the thought of a full on bush scares the living hell out of me.
Even still, what you do with your personal area is your business. Typically the only one who sees it should be you, and your significant other, and on occasion your OBGYN. If you want to let it grow like a crazy cave woman when it isn't bikini season, that's totally your prerogative- but I'll let you in on a little secret...
When you go to your OBGYN, they have a little check-list to mark off about your personal grooming habits. Yes, I was horrified when I found that out too.

"Shaven/Unshaven," or it might say "Groomed/Ungroomed," or even "Trimmed/Shaved/MONSTER BUSH!"

Whichever end of the spectrum you choose, if you walk in and haven't weeded your garden since Britney Spears was still claiming to be a virgin, they'll be checking off an embarrassing little box about you.

No, no one's going to see it but them- but it's still a little bit humiliating to know there's a file in a drawer with a box checked off that your cha-cha is a big hairy mess.
That might not be enough for you to do anything about what you've got goin' on- but the thought of anyone looking closely at my nether region makes me keep everything maintained properly. Personally, I don't even like being unkempt when NO ONE is looking at it, feminist is *not* my style.

I've heard a lot of women say that when they're pregnant- they just don't care about what goes on *'down there'*
*"They're doctors, they have seen it all before!"*
Yes…yes they have- but that doesn't mean they don't laugh about it with their nurses. I have friends who are nurses and I have heard stories about you and your cavewoman bush.
From the "spider nipples" story, to all kinds of harrowing tales about feeling like they were weed whacking in the jungle when trying to pull a kid out of a hairy cooch. Chances are, if you let your area go crazy, your nurses will be giggling about you behind your back, or cringing; maybe both.

I don't care if I have to go at my no-no bits with a razor blindly over my huge stomach- just like I did with Holden- things will stay spic & span.

You might get a cut here or there, will probably even miss some spots- leaving it looking like a patchwork quilt- but do you really want to be the spider nipple caveman cooch lady?? I don't!

6/23/09
# "You're gonna poop on the table!"

It's that time, once again, to address those pesky rumors and myths you read & hear about pregnancy. The ones that freak you out, scare you, make you never want to have children- you know the ones i'm talking about.

I in no way consider myself the 'master' on childbirth and pregnancy knowledge, but seeing as this is my second time around in a not so long period of time, I think I know enough to at least confirm and dispel a few of the major ones that constantly pop up in conversation.

Let's get down to business (oops, I forgot, already did!)

**Rumor #1:**
*Your boobs WILL get saggy if you breastfeed.*
**Fact.**
Sorry to say, it's true for the unfortunate majority of us. BUT- they'll also get saggy if you *don't*. Pregnancy is going to change your boobs regardless of what you decide to do with them once you pop your kid out.

Due to the fact that your boobs grow during pregnancy and have a bit of time to get used to their larger size, once they deflate and get rid of all that milk- unfortunately they aren't going to snap right back to sitting at full attention on your chest.

Mine definitely lost fullness after Holden; they weren't even big for very long anyways. I might not necessarily call them 'saggy' by the standard definition, but comparatively? Yes. I call them 'sad.'

What I can't say for sure, but what I think is true- is the longer your boobs are full of that milky goodness, the more saggy they're going to be, so it could be if you breastfeed they'll end up being *saggier* than if you didn't just due to that fact alone. The only reason I assume this because I saw my mom's boobs after breastfeeding two kids, not a pretty sight.

122

Then again, there is a small group of people who just aren't affected by the growing and shrinking boobage. Some people go right back to normal (probably the very young people), and some get to keep their larger size permanently (which is lucky or unlucky depending on the person). For the most part? Get ready for your boobs to drop like the Times Square Ball on New Year's Eve. Sorry!

## Rumor #2:
*Your nose will widen and your feet will grow during pregnancy*
**Fact.**
My nose didn't widen until I started retaining water in my face, MAN was that attractive, and I definitely didn't believe the rumors until it happened to me. It DID, however, go back to normal after I gave birth and shed the water weight.
As for the feet? Up a full size during pregnancy and they've still yet to go back down to normal. I had huge feet to begin with. Now they're sort of caveman-esque: flat wide and long; even though they've decreased in size a little (it only took a freaking year). I'm still holding onto all of my shoes in hopes that one of these days these flappers will shrink.

## Rumor #3:
*You will poop on the table during vaginal delivery.*
**Myth *and* Fact!**
I say that because while it CAN happen, it does NOT happen to everyone! Even if it does, your doctor and nurses aren't going to tell you. They'll just scoop that shit up and take it away without saying a word. My doctor seemed to be a glutton for punishment and was *constantly* telling me during labor to *"Push like you're taking a poop!"* and I kept replying *"But I don't want to poop on the table!"*- It's just that serious.
From what I am told by others in the room, I didn't. Big sigh of relief.
If you do happen to pass a log during labor, the only person who's going to care is anyone you let in the room (other than medical staff) who happens to watch while it occurs. I can't even imagine the nightmares that would cause to see what

would likely be diarrhea coming out of someone, along with blood, baby, and fluid.

**Rumor #4:**
*Once you're in labor, you will stop being shy about who sees your va-jay-jay.*
**Fact.**
I am the best example of this. I do NOT like going to the OBGYN and having my cooch examined. The first time was scarring to my psyche. I made sure I found a practice with an ALL female staff because the thought of a man digging around up there horrifies me. I don't even like Thomas staring at it. He's lucky I let him in the room during Holden's birth, that's how uncomfortable I am with multitudes of people staring at me while naked.
Once active labor began, all of that went out the window. My friend who had just came to visit and was unlucky enough to show up right as i'd gone into labor? Stuck in the room. I wouldn't let her leave. I'm not sure how much she saw, but I can tell you I didn't care at that point.
Somehow my room was the supply rooms for the whole delivery area, so nurses were coming in and out constantly that were not my nurses, and they did NOT pull out that privacy curtain to block the view into my room from the hallway. Did I care? No. I just wanted my damn epidural.
This doesn't mean i'd invite my entire family into the room to view the birth, that's SERIOUSLY pushing it. I think giving birth is a little more of a private experience than that- but I definitely lost a lot of inhibitions once my pain level hit *"TWELVE!!!!!!"*

**Rumor #5:**
*Vaginal birth will stretch out your vajay and you will be "loose"*
**Myth!**
I'm screaming it, MYTH! MYTH MYTH MYTH! I don't know where this rumor came from, but it is NOT true in the slightest. I've talked about it so many times I'm nearly blue in the face,

yet still this rumor swirls.

Your "hole" is like a piercing hole, it'll close back up. Just like if you don't have sex for a really long time and once you do it's almost as though you're a born-again virgin; your vagina will not remain huge and flappy, whistling in the wind and gathering cobwebs

## Rumor #6:

*If you're young, your body will 'snap back' right after giving birth!*

## Myth!

Hate to say it, this just isn't true. Not for us mere mortals anyways. I was only 23 when I had Holden, which I think is relatively young.. and while I am told I did not look as 'bad' as some people do post-partum, it took a lot of work and a *very* long time to look even remotely like I did before getting knocked up.

The weight? Sure, maybe it'll come off more quickly the younger you are, but that doesn't mean you're going to have a tight stomach and be completely rid of the cellulite and water weight. Getting your stomach muscles back up to par takes a while unless you're a celebrity and have hundreds of thousands of dollars (and a serious Madonna complex) to waste on a personal trainer who will kick your ass for 8 hours a day, and a nanny to take care of your brat while you're at the gym. They're the ones that made you fat! Screw them!

What it boils down to is that you can NOT believe everything you hear or read. Even if it is true, it might not happen to you. Even if it *didn't* happen to your friend- you may not get so lucky. Pregnancy ain't easy, and no one comes out completely unscathed. You're growing another person IN you; it's not supposed to be child's play. If it were…well… we'd all end up looking like the love child of Rumer Willis, Paris Hilton, and Mickey Rourke *post*- face melting plastic surgery.

7/7/09
# Leaky Faucet Syndrome

I've said it before and I'll say it again: pregnancy is a bitch! So many things you'd never expect, all bundled up into one 9 (technically 10) month period.
If there's one thing I can say for it- it certainly does leave you guessing. If you like surprises... weird, gross and sometimes disgusting surprises, pregnancy is definitely for you.

This is where any man should overt his eyes. I'm pretty sure you don't want to read this, and i'm pretty sure the woman in your life you may have knocked up, or will knock up in the future won't want you to know the gory details of what I am about to write, either.

Around the halfway point in pregnancy, you'll start... *leaking*. And i'm not talking about from your boobs, although it's possible; usually you'll just get crusties (aka colostrum). But yes, leaking.

The first few times it happened while I was pregnant with Holden, I kept wondering if maybe I was peeing myself and just didn't know it. Had I lost that kind of control of my bladder already?? Impossible!
After a while, and a few pairs of pants leaked through like a nervous 1st grader, you realize that while it could definitely be pee, maybe it's not. You may find yourself letting a little go when you sneeze, cough or laugh; it's a different feeling all around. Not quite the same as the full on bladder releasing, pants wetting sensation.
You begin to wonder: *"Is my water breaking? Is this what water breaking is?"*

Only one time in my entire pregnancy, was the amount expelled enough for me to actually get up the nerve to call the doctor (that along with regular braxton hicks) who immediately sent me to L&D to be checked (yay! more poking and prodding!) only to find out that it was *not*, in fact, my water that had broken; just me and my leaky bladder.

While other parts of pregnancy are annoying and uncomfortable, I find this one to be one of the grossest & most confusing (next to losing your mucus plug, but that's another story for another time).
There are quite a few women who will just stick a pad in their underwear and go on their way- but I refuse! One of the biggest perks to pregnancy is NOT having a period, and NOT having to use all the products that go hand in hand with having a one, so mucking up the blissful bloodless 9 months with a pad? I'll pass, thank you very much! I'll suck it up and change if I have to. My area is uncomfortable enough at the moment without shoving some cotton in my underwear, having it chafe my already swollen bits, and then walking around with an even more pronounced waddle than usual.

7/9/09
# The third trimester is looking bleak

It has to be some kind of weird role reversal; my first and third trimesters seem to be getting their wires crossed.
The first trimester is supposed to be miserable, filled with nausea, exhaustion, and a general feeling of *"bleck"*.

While the third trimester is definitely not said to be a cake walk- being that you have a huge belly to lug around and swollen feet- a lot of women really seem to enjoy it.

If you've been following the blog for a while- you'd know that my first trimester was the easiest of all, especially considering I had NO earthly idea I was even pregnant until almost 2 months into it. No morning sickness, no fatigue, no nothing.

As my doctor would say: My pregnancies never go by the book!

Technically, I have a week until my third trimester (most people say it starts at 28 weeks), and while my second trimester has been not so fantastic, the third is gearing up to be even worse.

Suddenly, every other night I find myself intensely nauseous to the point where I have to stop doing whatever i'm doing, and brace myself for impending doom. I try to breathe my way out of it, but end up making a mad dash to the bathroom- as fast as a huge pregnant woman can run anyways. I'm not really a puker if you catch my drift.

Nothing I eat sits well in my stomach anymore. I've had trouble keeping ANYTHING I eat in there for more than about 45 minutes. It's not as if i'm eating things that would generally make one's stomach turn (taco bell, spicy foods, alfredo sauce), it's regular things like sandwiches and cereal that make my stomach twist, clench, and ball up into knots. It's not pleasant; my poor toilet never saw it coming. Hours spent hunched over my gigantic belly, sweating and crying, all while explosively shitting in waves. If that's not a way to flare up those hemmies, I don't know what is.

Combine that with the ever-intensifying and more frequent braxton hicks, and toes that turn bright red and look like overstuffed sausages after a few minutes of standing, and the third trimester is beginning to look like a crapshoot.

Maybe I'll get a reprieve and somehow, magically, next week all this nastiness will clear up. I sure hope it will. It's the worst to be as big as a house, sick, and whiny. Not that whining can't be fun from time to time, but it's a really consuming hobby when you're doing it 12 hours a day. Just look at Holden- been so whiny lately that he wears himself out into a 3 hour nap.

128

Although I guess I can't complain much about him taking a huge nap, it's always a welcome break in this house.

# The Third Trimester Blogs:
## Beginning of the end, and a new beginning

The final trimester in an unexpected pregnancy, or any pregnancy really, is a very stressful (or maybe exciting) time for a woman. You never know quite how to fully prepare yourself for a child, because you don't know what they'll be like once they're outside of you. And as much as you'd like to focus on the impending birth, your body goes through so many rapid and uncomfortable changes in a handful of months that time may just get away from you.

For me, that was definitely the case.

I was honestly the most miserable preggo on earth, and while the thought of no longer being full of a baby who could kick harder than an MMA fighter sounded like a tropical vacation, it also meant having a pink screaming baby in the house keeping everyone up all night, shitting itself, and vomiting all over me.

If I had to choose the lesser of two evils, I'd go full term-HANDS DOWN! Who wants to take a cake out of the oven half baked, anyways?

At this point in the recap of my pregnancy, it sort of feels like I've left Holden out- as though I shipped him off to *some "Big Brother Boot camp."*
The truth is- that aside from typical toddler crap and a few choice stories I'm saving for later- he was *incredibly* well behaved.

What I assumed was the beginnings of the dreaded 'Terrible 2s' must have been gas or something he ate. The kid was practically an angel.

He easily could have made my third trimester an absolute living hell if he so pleased. He could have torn the house apart, smeared shit on the walls, screamed in my face non-stop, threw himself on the floor, banged his head into walls, the whole 9 yards... but instead, he let me veg out on the couch and brought me books to read to him.

Trust me; it was a much needed and much appreciated break, because the pain I experienced in my 2$^{nd}$ trimester only got worse in the 3$^{rd}$. A LOT worse. Tenfold even. The zapping pains I felt in my lady bits that my doctor so lovingly referred to as "Lightning Crotch" made it so that I could barely walk. When I *could*, it looked like I'd been riding a horse bareback for 6 hours straight. Rolling over in bed at night? Forget it! That caused such sharp pain that I'd let out audible yelps.

Regardless of whether my body was going to complain about it or not, I had to make sure to spend as much quality time with Holden before the baby came. After that, he was no longer my only child, and to him- no longer "the baby", and thereby the only one getting all of Mommy and Daddy's attention.

Holden got dragged to all kinds of ridiculous appointments and non-stress tests because toward the end, go fig, my blood pressure spiked out of nowhere. He got dropped off at my brother's house so I could get monitored at the hospital. He had to deal with my ridiculous mood springs and near panic attacks about Braxton hicks contractions and whether or not they were the real thing or just a tease per usual. He had to sit and watch as I cried and hyperventilated on the toilet because I was so sick *all* of the time, thinking I was going to crap my intestines out. He listened as I debated with others about how far along I was and how big I was compared to the number of weeks I had left. I liked to think I was gigantic, while others would

132

continually tell me I was *"all baby"*, with a handful of people telling me I looked ready to pop two months before go time. He gave me puzzled looks as I got frazzled by internet moms arguing with me and each other about everything from breastfeeding to who would be the one to give birth first. He watched as I grew to the size of a water buffalo, but I'm not sure he ever fully understood exactly what it meant, even if he could point to my belly and say *"baby!"* He even tried to help as we scrambled to switch the office into a nursery and started placing things like a swing and a vibrating chair in strategic places around the house. He was not so pleased when I told him he could not sit his fat ass in either of them.

Holden really went through the pregnancy with me, every single painful step- he witnessed them all… And I have to say, he took it a lot better than I did.

To top it all off, due to my lack of friends, I had to basically plan and throw my own baby shower (and find one friend I could rope into hosting it) *and* throw Holden's 2nd birthday party, which to me would most likely be the last one he'd have alone since the baby was due just 3 weeks later. No way in hell could I throw two birthday parties in a month; learned from experience that it's hard enough just to get people to come to *one*.

Holden's last birthday party all to himself needed to be huge and special; it had to be the best birthday ever. That wasn't going to be an easy task to accomplish while barely able to even function, and I certainly didn't want to push myself so hard that my water broke in the middle of the damn party. What a way to ruin a birthday that would be!

While a possibility, I didn't think it would actually happen. I was more convinced that the baby would be as stubborn as Holden and have to be forced out of me by induction. I actually panicked about being induced again; it was such a horrible experience the first time, I never wanted to relive it. While

133

going into labor during Holden's birthday party may seem like the worst thing to have happen, to me at least, it was a hell of a lot better than Satan's evil mistress: Pitocin.

I've digressed- back on the subject now.
Getting all of the above done before baby-time with my body objecting to every move was not an ideal situation. I was busy mentally and physically, when really all I wanted was to sit in a cold pool and soak my fat swollen self.

In the end, the parties turned out just fine- much less eventful than I thought- but I can't say the same for the rest of the third trimester. Of course my mind and its constant state of wandering was always coming up with the strangest, most random thoughts, only adding to the madness.

I like to think that even in a pinch, we managed to pull through and check everything off of our list of things to do- but the stubborn child in my belly decided to make an unexpected arrival just to throw one last wrench into our plans. I should have seen that one coming.

7/17/09
# That foul orange drink & the joys of the third trimester

When you reach the third trimester of your pregnancy, you enter a whole new realm of discomfort and awkward situations. It's not just your body making you blush at the most inopportune times (uncontrollable gas, peeing when you sneeze, etc.), but your doctor will have a series of not so fabulous, and slightly atrocious things for you to do as well. Really, why do they have to make it worse than it is? We're swollen, we're tired, we've gained an asinine amount of weight

that we aren't very pleased about already and as Oprah would say: *our va-jay-jays are a-painin'*!
Adding more to that just seems cruel and unusual.

Get used to it ladies, because your nether regions are going to be poked, prodded and stared at more often, and by more people than your standard second rate XXX film.

Before all of that though, comes the dreaded glucose test (for gestational diabetes). I had the joy of drinking my disgusting orange concoction today. If you didn't think it was that bad, or if you thought it was tasty- good for you! For some reason, I just can't stomach that crap. The first time with Holden wasn't TOO bad, but later in pregnancy I was made to take it again and not only did I heave multiple times throughout it, but the night after the second test, I had an intense sugar crash involving sweating, shaking, and eating half a bag of grapes to try and not feel like a crack head feening for another hit.

It's Pavlov's Theory of Conditioning that already had my brain thinking this time around was going to be just as bad as that last time with Holden, because it was foul. I didn't heave this time, but I sure wanted to. I think the worst part is the fact that you not only have to chug the disgusting ,rotten, melted popsicle tasting liquid in 5 minutes or less, but that you can't drink ANYTHING afterwards... or eat anything… or chew gum… or even a mint.
Did I mention that the weather outside felt like the inside of a fake leg? Absolutely sweltering; my body was not pleased.

Today marked the first appointment of my 3rd trimester. You go from having an appointment once a month, to every 2 weeks- and most of those appointments you'll be told to drop your pants, and then have fingers shoved into your hooha to make sure you won't be going into labor any time soon. Yay! Just what I wanted to complete my day!
This is also about the time where most women start packing on a ton of weight. It slows toward the end of pregnancy, but the

end of the 2nd trimester to the beginning of the 3rd? Whale Watch 2009.

As I've mentioned before, I've been trying not to turn into a roving land beast like I did my last pregnancy. I exercise 5 days a week, I generally eat healthy (aka: I'm not stuffing my face with McDonald's milkshakes every single night like I did with Holden.) To me, it *looks* like it's working. My hips have definitely gotten bigger which makes my ass the size of a Mac truck, but there are no rivers of cellulite, and my maternity pants aren't getting snug yet- go me! Right?

Wrong.

Hopped on the scale today and i'm up 10 pounds in the past month. WHAT?! HOW?! WHERE?! While of course I wasn't pleased, it solidifies my theory that regardless of what I do or don't eat- i'm going to gain a ridiculous amount of weight because *that's* what my body wants to do; sadist.

I love that the nurse told me to *"watch it"* (my weight)... Bitch! What do you think I've *BEEN* doing? People really don't listen. If it's not by the book, it can't be true to them.  Put on some weight? You must be cleaning out buffets every night! My doctors seem to understand that things aren't always as written in medical text, but not the nurses. Kiss my "fat" ass!

I told the nurse about how my stomach has been evacuating its contents on a regular basis lately, and can you guess what she gives me?

A sample cup.

*For poop.*

This NEVER happened with Holden, but I guess me telling her I can't stop crapping is cause for concern (I've always been a poopy person, inherited from my Dad; thanks Dad!)

The thought of having to catch my crap in this tiny little specimen cup... and then NOT refrigerate it and bring it in when they're open horrifies me. What if I have to go #2 at 5pm the previous day? I have to keep my container-o-shit on the bathroom counter until then??

Man, being pregnant is a blast!

Next up on the awkward pregnancy checklist? Group B Strep test. Or in layman's terms- ANAL SWAB!

The hits just keep on comin'

## 7/19/09
# Strange Realizations

There are times where I am sitting around, doing nothing particularly special, when a weird thought enters my mind. Out of nowhere, I get smacked with an overwhelming feeling of creepiness- because the thought I'm having *is* creepy... but only because it's true.

Being pregnant in itself is an odd thing. I mean, come on- we carry our own young? We have the ability to *actually* create, grow, and birth our own children? Am I the only one who thinks along these lines?
It seems like most women just *say 'Yay! New baby!'* and go on their merry way; Blissful, nonchalant, carefree.
Meanwhile, i'm sitting here thinking things like:

*Weird, i'm growing an actual human inside of me.*

From there it wanders on to:

*Weird, i'm growing a living, breathing, hiccupping, yawning, kicking, stretching human.*

And really it just goes downhill, fast:

*A tiny naked little human. There's a NAKED little human inside of my stomach.*

Right here, my brain should just cease and desist, because I am officially totally and completely weirded out. But it continues in a downward spiral.

*A naked little human inside of my stomach with a penis. I'm technically growing a penis in my stomach...*
*A penis that's peeing in my stomach..*
*So - this naked little human i'm growing is swimming in his own pee, and probably rubbing his creepy baby penis all over my insides...*
*I have to push this naked little human, with a creepy baby penis, through my birth canal and out of my va-jay??*

Seriously- WHO ever thought having babies was a good idea?

Oh well…
At least I never lost my sense of imagination.


7/20/09
# I would do anything for love… But I won't let you do that!

I've brushed upon the subject of personal grooming while pregnant before, but now it's time to get down to the dirty. Let's face it- when you're pregnant, and you can't see around that ginormous bulge (if there weren't a baby in it, i'd call it a FUPA) protruding from your stomach to be able to *really* feel as though you're being thorough down there, it can get a bit frustrating.
I've tried the 'lift and look-around', and I've tried to just blindly go at it- and that is what I will continue to do. Some effort is better than no effort!

138

Oddly enough, it has been suggested to me on numerous occasions to let *Thomas* do the work for me.

Sure, it'd help me not have to try and squish, bend, and squeeze myself into uncomfortable positions in order to do it myself-but...just... NO!

It's not that I am what i'd consider shy or bashful- but i'm not a NAKED person. I don't like being naked at all, not even in front of just myself. I don't walk around my house naked, dance naked, sleep naked, it's just not my thing. Hell, I even wear a bra to sleep because I don't like my jigglies flopping around all willy-nilly like i'm some hairy pitted hippie (plus i'm paranoid that letting them do so will curse me with droopy-tit-itis.)

I've just never been comfortable letting it all hang out. My mom always said my Dad wanted to be a nudist, not something I *ever* wanted or needed to know, but I definitely didn't take after him in that area.

Going to the OBGYN for the first time? Scarring. I like to keep my parts to ME, especially in harsh fluorescent lighting.

So to think about Thomas, even though we *are* married, being about 2 inches from my girly-bits while they are almost *comically* swollen (c'mon, if you've been pregnant, you know exactly what I mean) with a sharp razor in bright lighting? That is something I will PASS ON!

More power to you if you're comfortable enough to let your man do the dirty work for you- that just doesn't work for me.

There's not only the fact that I don't want anyone who isn't a licensed professional (aka my doctor) inspecting my area with a fine toothed comb, but that I think I would be in a constant state of terror that he'd slip and cut off something important. The thought alone makes me shudder. That area is hard enough to groom on my own without making a mistake every now and then; an inexperienced person- such as a husband- down there with a blade? I can only imagine the amount of blood and razor burn i'd end up with.

Again I say- Pass!!

Would I return the favor? Hmmm... I don't know that shaving balls is up my alley of expertise. Seems like more trouble than it would be worth! Loose, saggy skin? That's just asking for trouble isn't it?
I MIGHT, and I mean *MIGHT* wax them, if he asked nicely... and only because I know it would inflict ridiculous amounts of pain and make me laugh.

8/19/09
# Your boobies, your business.

In honor of National Breastfeeding Awareness Month, I thought i'd take some time out from writing about poop and braxton hicks to discuss breastfeeding.
Well, not so much breastfeeding, but the peer pressure surrounding it.

I'm no breastfeeding enthusiast; I don't do it- and my reasons are my own. I don't really feel as though it's anyone's business but mine as to the reasons behind why I 'chose' formula. At the same time, I would never try to convince someone to formula feed over breastfeeding.
If you wanna whip out a tit to give your kid a snack, more power to you! I think it's fabulous, and I actually think it's quite ballsy (especially if you do it in public.)
If you choose to pump, bottle feed, formula feed, whatever- as long as your kid is happy and healthy I really have no negative opinion on the matter at all.

Unfortunately, others do not think along the same lines. The judgment and peer pressure that will come to a woman who chooses to formula feed over breastfeed, REGARDLESS of whether it was a choice or another reason (no milk production, medication, whatever) is intense. And it bugs me to no end. When I had Holden and went the formula route, there were a lot of dirty looks, stink eyes, and condescension. From nurses in the hospital, to lactation specialists, to our first pediatrician; it seemed like *everyone* had something to say about it. The worst offenders were granola crunching hippy moms, and older generations who have that mindset of *"Well, I know better than you because I raised kids 20 years ago! AND I walked 20 miles to and from school every day, uphill both ways in the snow!"* I'm not saying ALL breastfeeding moms are this way. Most of my friends who have kids breastfeed, and they could care less what I do or don't do, but all those negative Nancys get to you after a while. Making you think you're doing something wrong, that your kid won't be as smart or as healthy, that you won't have as close of a relationship with your child; they'll throw the whole book at you.

Why? I'm not sure. I don't know why it matters so much that someone else isn't lending out their boob as a 24 hour diner.

Now that Holden is older and off of formula, to me, all those negative things I was told about it in the first place, and how breastfeeding is the *only* way to go seem ridiculous to me. Take one look at Holden and you'll see that. Happy, healthy, is RARELY sick, and I consider him my best friend (which I haven't decided yet whether that is sad or sweet, but that's beside the point.)

While I've already gotten some crap about the decision not to breastfeed this time, people can't use the same scare tactics on me as they did before- because all I have to do is point at Holden as proof positive that formula is not "THE DEVIL!"

My mom let me snack on her boob and i'm *always* sick, my immune system sucks ass, and I wouldn't exactly consider myself smarter than someone who was formula fed by any means. And she and I did NOT have a close relationship (not until I was 18 and out of the house anyways )

Basically, what i'm saying is that you're not going to ruin your child by opting not to breastfeed. Bad things can happen regardless of what you do, all depending on the kid, the situation, the genes, and about a billion other factors.

I get so mad listening to other formula feeding moms getting crapped all over for not being a booby buffet, regardless of their reasons. While i'm sure it happens the other way around too (staunch formula feeders pooping on breastfeeders), I think formula feeders get the shit end of the stick for the most part. What you do with your boobs is your business- no one else should ever think they have the right to weigh in on that. But...But...
*"Breast is best!"* don'tcha know?
No, I don't have to hear whispers behind my back about pulling out a boob in public to feed my kid, but they don't have to hear that they're ruining their child by *not* doing so.

This whole rant started because of an innocent comment a friend made about boiling bottles and then receiving a boat load of *"YOU NEED TO BREASTFEED INSTEAD!"* comments in return. Who says that boiling bottles automatically means that she isn't breastfeeding? And did she *ask* for your opinion on what she is or isn't going to do with her tits? Are you going to tell her how exactly, step by step, to raise *her* child next? While you're at it, would you care to comment on her sex life and how the positions she's using are all wrong?
'Cause she totally asked for advice on that, too.

In the end, it all comes down to that moms need to respect other moms, period. It's gotten out of control how high the wall has been built between formula feeders and breastfeeders, for no good reason at all other than haughty-taughty opinions and people thinking they know what's best for you and your baby.

Your boobs are your boobs, your children are your children-
and what you do with all of that is up to you. End of story!
Can we just leave it at that, put the claws away, and stop the
shit flinging? No one cares what the other thinks, so why even
bother?

To quote an incredibly over-used and annoying saying: *'Can't
we all just get along???'*

8/28/09

# Yep that seals it- I hate being pregnant

Yes, I know, *"poor poor fluffy!"* and the whole *"I should be
grateful to even BE pregnant"* type complaints and arguments
that will be running through certain people's heads... at this
point- I don't care!

I'll say it loud and (not so) proud- I HATE BEING
PREGNANT! And i'm pretty sure pregnancy reciprocates that
feeling.
I am seriously not meant to carry children; at least my body
doesn't seem to think so. My pregnancy with Holden was
miserable for 75% of it; this one is quickly growing to about
95%. I can't even remember the last day where I felt even
*relatively* good.

Today I think takes the cake on the scale-o-miserable. It started
out pretty good. No incident with breakfast, I exercised a little
(while avoiding ANYTHING that would irritate my pelvis- that
ornery bitch), ate lunch without a problem and then took a
quick nap with Holden.

As soon as I woke up things went downhill fast. Not only was
my pelvis hurting so badly that I could hardly hobble myself

off of the bed- but I knew as soon as I got Holden to the bathroom after he got out of bed that I was going to be sick. And not just sick... but *SICK*. The kind of sick where you're sweating, shaking, clutching the toilet and praying your intestines don't come spilling out of your ass.

Since it's happened to me so many times before (but always after Holden's in bed for the night and I can evacuate my bowels in peace), I thought I might cut it off at the pass by chugging water to rehydrate myself and maybe, just MAYBE, stop it before the floodgates had a chance to open.
Yeah, not so much.

Being that sick when you're home alone with a toddler is never a good thing, especially since Holden has had a fascination with shoving his fake food as far into his mouth as it will go the past few days; can't exactly watch a toddler when your ass is glued to the toilet. I decided as I cried on the pot while trying to keep an eye on Holden that this situation just wasn't going to work out.
I sent Thomas a frantic text message to come home immediately, which he did... but Thomas works 45 minutes away, even in very little traffic. Being a Friday with bad weather, it could have been a hell of a lot longer, so in keeping true to my typical nature, I started to panic.

I got myself off of the toilet and sat on the couch, trying my best to breathe through the pain and drink more water than my stomach was allowing- and that's when the chain reaction began. Whatever was going on inside of me seemed to irritate my uterus to its breaking point. Painful braxton hicks began coming one after another, and having the braxton hicks irritated baby into doing barrel rolls, front flips & karate kicks.
That's when I decided to give in and say *'Fuck it! I can't do this!'* and called my brother, who only lives a few minutes down the street, to come and keep an eye on Holden while I made runs to the bathroom (no pun intended.)

Go fig it took him just as long to come over as it took Thomas to get home, and by THAT time- I had nothing left in me to poop out. That didn't stop the delightful Mr. Braxton Hicks from coming every 5-10 minutes, which made baby even angrier; so while they both missed my poopcapades, I was glad to have people there to distract Holden.

Even hours later as I sit here and type out this blog, the braxton hicks haven't let up. Most people would probably have called their doctor by now, but I know better. They aren't increasing in intensity, I feel no pressure down below- this is just how my body chooses to react to being pregnant and all the hormones that come along with it, and i'm SO DONE DEALING WITH IT.
Give me just ONE day minus the pelvic pain, violent poops, and baby doing barrel rolls and I seriously won't complain ever again. ONE DAY, that's all I ask.

My body is an angry anal retentive landlord and would love nothing better than to evict this unruly child-tenant.
Come October 1st, I'll be totally on board with that idea. For now, I just wish they'd learn to get along and leave me alone so I can get through the rest of this damn pregnancy in peace, and then *never* have to do it again.


9/2/09
# Mmm, Placenta!

The first time I had ever heard of anyone taking a placenta and EATING IT was years back when Tom Cruise was in his "couch jumping" phase and Katie Holmes was popping out their weird alien child. Of course he'd be the one to talk about it as if it were served up as a delicacy in a 5 star restaurant. The mention of the act alone was enough to make me shudder.

When you venture into the realm of mommyhood, you are introduced to all kinds of weird notions, potions, and ideas to help with all sorts of different things that may ail you- so the subject crossed my view more often, but never enough for me to think that this was commonplace in anyone's household. Cleaning up exploded diapers, being puked on, and bleeding for 13 weeks straight… none of that prepared me for this craze to pick up and to start reading about it everywhere I looked.

Now, I've done my research on this whole "eating your own placenta" thing... and yes, it *does* have its benefits. It can help with the 'baby blues', postpartum depression, and the cramping you experience after birth as your uterus desperately tries to shrink back to an acceptable size, but EATING something that came out of your snatch?? Really??

Making it into a delicious Placenta Parmesan? Drinking the veiny vile thing as a smoothie, or baking it into a creamy casserole?
Sorry, but I am highly disturbed by this notion. I think i'd much rather pop a Zoloft if I were feeling down than try and gag down my own uterine discharge.

Placentas are not appetizing, y'all. Have you ever seen one? If I ever even attempted to taste this delicacy of sorts, all that would cross my mind is the memory of after I gave birth to Holden... and trying to "pass" my own.
I felt the doctor TUGGING the umbilical cord, which was detached from my baby but not me, because the placenta is attached to your uterine wall (and when it TEARS off, that's why you bleed for so long; open wound on your insides.)
When it finally came loose, I felt a large sense of relief and heard a huge SLOSH sound. That was my veiny, bloody placenta plopping into a bucket.

And women EAT this thing?? They put it in the freezer, and pull it out to mix up in smoothies? Or cook it like a tender, juicy steak?

Placenta, with a side of fetal membranes for one, please!

From what I've read, the most common (and by far least disgusting) way to ingest yourself is to have a midwife dry the bitch out and put it into capsules.
 Placenta pills! Guaranteed to take your blues away!

Call me closed-minded, but there's just no way in hell I could ever swallow a pill full of something that was leeching off of my body for 9 months, and then came plopping out of my snatch in a big bloody mess.
Technically, wouldn't that be like... eating yourself out?
Just sayin'.

Sorry ladies, but I won't be joining you in this cannibalistic craze! No matter how good for me it is. Mommy could never get me to eat lima beans; you're sure as shit not going to get me to eat my own bloody sack of nasty.

## 9/21/09
# Float like a butterfly, swell like a bee-sting

So far in this pregnancy, we've covered many uncomfortable topics from practically pooping out your intestines, to eating placentas- but there's one topic I feel we haven't delved far enough into, that I think *every* pregnant woman should be aware of.

You may have heard that when you get pregnant, your nose will widen for 'mysterious reasons'- the reality is that it's just water retention. That's not the point though, my point is that your nose is NOT the only thing that's going to... *widen*. And i'm not talking about your ass from that pan of brownies you just inhaled all by yourself (although, that's true too). I'm talking about something far more embarrassing and far more personal.

Have you guessed yet?

That's right, your VAGINA. I said it!

Better learn to live with the idea now, because even before *you* start to get fat- your hooha will. It's like one of those old cartoons where the anvil falls on the characters hand, and it swells to five times its' normal size and begins to throb- that will be your nether region for *months*.

It's not pretty (are vaginas ever pretty?), and it's definitely not the most pleasant of feelings to experience.

Once you begin to get used to having the vag of a woman 4 times your size, it starts to hurt. Pregnancy never lets up.

Imagine your va-jay as a professional boxer, only not a good one, and it's being put up in a Payperview fight against the likes of Muhammad Ali. Somehow, it manages to last a couple of rounds, but that's not before taking about 500 shots straight to the kisser. THAT, my friends, is how your poor, comically swollen vagina will look and feel for the last few weeks of pregnancy.

Maybe if you get lucky, instead of your kid deciding that the nerves to your legs are fun to play with- he or she will play with the nerves to your snatch instead, giving you the wonderful sensation of "lightning crotch." It's pretty much exactly what it sounds like: shooting pains right where it matters.

Don't worry your pretty little heads, your kitty will eventually go back to normal a couple of weeks after birth, and when the extra swelling from THAT goes down- you will have a new found appreciation for your un-swollen, non-aching private area. At least there's *one* upside to the whole situation, right?

148

9/25/09
# No...That'll just make you shit

If you've ever been pregnant, and gotten to those final horrible weeks like I am in right now- i'm sure your friends have dispensed a ridiculous amount of advice on how to get your child out of you naturally in order to help end your suffering.

From just popping an herbal supplement, to drinking tea, to some things that will have some side effects, I've heard them all- and have known people to try every single one.

Here's the thing- there is NO sure fire way to get your child out of you unless he or she is ready and raring to go. As much as you want to believe all the hype, they're kind of like old wives tales. They might work for some, but for most: sorry, you'll have to wait- miserably- like the rest of us.

Still, if you want to be informed on a few of these child-popping aides, i'm more than happy to share them with you and let you decide for yourself whether you want to try them or not.

Let's start with the harmless.

**Evening Primrose Oil**
You can find this in your local Wal-Mart in the vitamin section. Pop a few pills per night and it's said to help soften your cervix, which is necessary in order to go into labor. It won't push you into labor if your body isn't ready, hell, it might not do anything at all- but it's natural and harmless so giving it a shot won't hurt you. You can even poke holes in a few (as told to me by my friend), and stick them up your cooch, getting them to the horse's mouth, so to speak, a lot faster. I've yet to

get that desperate.

## Sex
Ahhh yes, good ol' sex. But not just ANY sex, mind you. Your husband or significant other has to leave a *deposit*, which is another way to soften your cervix. WAIT- there's more. He's not the only one who gets to have fun during this process, because you need to get off too in order to reap the full benefits. Sex, or more specifically, an orgasm, can help by releasing a hormone called oxytocin, which causes the uterus to contract. Has this worked for either of my pregnancies? Nope, but I know plenty of women who swear by it. Maybe they were just so excited that anyone would touch them with a watermelon under their skin, and more ass cellulite than an 80 year old grandmother of 12, that they jumped the gun on claiming it's the be-all end-all in getting your baby out of you.

## Raspberry Tea
There are people who believe this will help to induce labor, but from everything I've read that's pretty much a complete myth. What it WILL help with is your labor, and your recovery; so really, it's still worth it to drink it- and it's tasty! It can ease contractions, keep you from hemorrhaging during labor, and help your cha-cha heal more quickly.

## Walking
I don't know how many times I've been told to *"go for a nice long walk"* to try and bring labor on. I've seen women do it on those evil baby shows, but they're IN labor, so it's just helping move things along after they've already started. Movement in general can help get that baby down into the birth canal, putting pressure on your cervix and possibly pushing you into labor. I've found that all it does for me is make my feet swell and my pelvis hurt, and trust me- I have attempted walking MILES in the past to no avail.

## Nipple Stimulation
Just like it reads. Get some lube and rub those nips, ladies! It

has the same effect as sex; the stimulation releases oxytocin into your system and brings on contractions. Awkward? Yes. More effort than sex? Absolutely. But if you just can't manage to let your husband poke you in your fat and uncomfortable state, this is the way to go.

Some aides I've been told to try but can't find the reasoning behind? Spicy food, pineapple, and eggplant parmesan. Not all together mind you, I can't imagine that combo tasting very good.

And now for the **"try at your own risk"** way to induce labor.

### Castor Oil

There are plenty of women who will swear up and down that castor oil will send you directly into labor, and others who will tell you to stay the hell away from it. If it doesn't get that baby out, what it *will* do is make you nauseous, crampy, and make you shit so much that you'll be crapping out food you haven't even eaten yet. It might be more of a constipation cure then a way to induce labor in all honesty. All of that shitting could potentially send you into labor, since those areas are so close together and the increased action down there could irritate your uterus enough to get to business, but I personally wouldn't recommend it.

Labor is bad enough without lacing the toilet in intestinal goodies right beforehand, and God forbid during. It's no wonder doctors wear splash guards on their faces while delivering babies!

Most of these remedies become more "sure fire" once you're past due, but even then it's not a guarantee. Not even being stuck on a pitocin drip is a guaranteed way to go into labor (I have two friends who it didn't work on at all). Unfortunately, when it comes to labor, we just have no control when or how it will happen, or how much it will hurt. Sucks. I think if we have to tear our insides apart in order to bring new life into this world- we should get at least a little bit of a say in how it's going to happen, maybe even when, but nope! That would make too much sense.


9/29/09

# Single Digits and what could be my last day as a mommy of 1

I'm finding it incredibly hard to believe that there are only 9 days left until my due date, and sooner rather than later I will have two small children in this house to take care of. Most of me is still in a state of denial about the whole thing. I don't think that it's fully hit me that i'm *THISCLOSE* to bringing another baby into this world. I'm not sure it will actually hit me until i'm lying in that hospital bed ready to push- that's when the overwhelming feeling hit me with Holden... and the reason why all of the pictures taken of me after his birth look like my face is melting, because I spent basically the whole time sobbing hysterically. Just couldn't believe it was over and that I actually had a baby.

Tomorrow is the appointment that has been a black cloud over my head for the past week. After my last appointment where the nurse noticed that my blood pressure had become elevated, the word "induction" started being thrown around. So what's it gonna be? Induction? No induction? I have no idea what's going to happen when I step foot into that exam room. There are a few things that could get me sent over to L&D to pop this kid out tomorrow. If there's protein in my urine, i'm pretty sure there's no skating out of an induction. While i'd be disappointed, I realize how serious that could be so i'd have to accept my fate and deal with it. High blood pressure is another thing my doctors just aren't taking lightly this time around due to my history from my last pregnancy. I could try and argue, and if my blood pressure is elevated again i'm definitely going to try my damndest to at LEAST barter by having them strip my membranes. If that doesn't work, THEN I'll agree to an induction in a few days and see if they'll go for that. I don't want to put baby's health at risk, but I also don't want to be induced.

One thing I haven't even really considered happening is that *somehow* I'll have dilated to a 4, and around these parts, a 4 with no contractions means you get sent to the hospital and stuck on a pitocin drip. I highly doubt that will happen. I just don't think this kid is going anywhere in the next few days, but I suppose anything is possible at this point. I've been shocked by this pregnancy way too many times to count, so I really can't rely on anything to happen or not to happen at this point. I think my jaw would hit the floor if they told me I was that dilated though. I never had a 39 week appointment with Holden, so I have nothing to base any kind of educated guess on.

I'm just hoping that for ONCE, things go my way and my blood pressure will be fine, and I'll be able to convince the nurse to strip my membranes to help coax this kid out of me naturally, and then be sent home to wait for things to get moving. I'm still really wishing for an October baby, and I don't think I'll be going into labor tonight or get moving so quickly tomorrow that he makes an arrival before midnight of the 1st rolls around... but again, you never know!

Cross your fingers for me and maybe some toes too. Tonight might very well be my last night at home as a mommy of 1.

––––––––––––––––

# The Birth Story
*Sometimes an Epidural just isn't enough*

Turns out I was right- because just a handful of hours after writing that blog I went into labor. Parker Cadence was born September 30th, 2009 at 9:50am; eight days before his due date. Just like my positive pregnancy test, it was definitely not what I expected. He of course couldn't wait ONE more day until October to avoid me having two kids with September birthdays.

This is his birth story, written while still in the hospital and slightly under the influence of some fantastic pain killers.

10/1/09

## Making you long for a Pitocin birth

I took the time today while Parker was in the nursery getting his tests run and his foreskin snipped (OHHHH BAD MOMMY!) to write out my entire lengthy birth story for everyone's reading pleasure.

I seriously thought no labor could be more painful or more insane than my labor with Holden. Leave it to this birthing experience to prove ALL of that wrong, and literally having me saying *"I wish i'd just been induced!"* mid-contraction.

I sort of had a feeling that something weird was going to happen on September 30th. I really don't know why... but it may have something to do with that both Thomas and I have birthdays on the 30th of a month, and I always joked that this baby would 'complete the trifecta.'

155

I never really expected Parker to make it until October because of how enormous I was, but at the same time, as you all well know- I had a sinking feeling he'd have to be FORCED out- so I was doing everything in my power to do a little 'forcing' of my own.

Evening primrose, pineapple, spicy food, pelvic rolls on a yoga ball- you name it, i'd either tried it or was trying it.

On Monday night I got really sick for no reason, yes, *that* kind of sick. This had happened a million times before, but for some reason this time felt different. I guess because afterward I didn't get much sleep, spent the rest of the night tossing and turning, and the entire next day continuing the cycle of poop. Yes, i'm a poopy person on any given day, but even this was pushing it.

Not to mention, the past few days Holden had broken out in a mysterious case of hives that we could NOT find the reason behind- perhaps he knew what was about to come??

Tuesday night Thomas' friend, who happens to be a Benedictine Monk in Nebraska, was in town so we all went out to get Thai food. I don't know where, but i'd read some kind of comment from someone joking about how Chinese food is another one of those things said to induce labor. Thai isn't Chinese, but it's close enough for government work. Before he left, he gave my belly a good rub (magic Monk hands??)

I felt fine after dinner, wrote the blog post joking about how MAYBE Parker would get out before my appointment on Wednesday where induction had been mentioned (the appointment I had been DREADING), and went to bed.

Thomas usually is still fiddling around on the computer at that time of night, so I stayed awake waiting for him. Why? I'll delve into TMI (my favorite thing to do) and say I was hoping to get some sex out of him, not that I was in the mood, but thinking maybe it would help my cervix soften up since at every appointment it had been "long and hard." Plus, I figured labor was pretty much imminent at this point with how far along I was, and if recovery was going to go anything like Holden's, we might as well get SOME in before I put up my "*I just blew my crotch out*" force field for however many weeks it would take to stop aching and bleeding.

I think I must have dozed off a little, because it was around 2:00am when I woke back up and suddenly remembered that i'd wanted to try the good ol' *'sex to get baby out'* method. We didn't even START getting into it when I had what felt like two nasty braxton hicks. Since it wasn't unusual, I just ignored them and went about my business. I assumed it was because of how I was laying, that would have made sense with how irritable my uterus had been the entire pregnancy.

Immediately after doin' the dirty, I started feeling a little funny. I got up to go pee, got back in bed, and got hit with a contraction. Notice I say contraction and not braxton hicks- I knew this one couldn't JUST be a braxton hicks. This was the kind of pain that made me clutch the bed hard enough to make my knuckles turn white. About 6 minutes later, I had another. Thomas was already back asleep (must be nice to fall asleep so easily) so I woke him up and said:
*"Um, Thomas.. I think I might be in labor"*- I don't think that's something I've EVER said before. I always think it's false, and that line of thinking has always been right.

We didn't start timing them right away, but the longer I laid still the more they hurt, so I got up to walk around the house, post on Facebook because i'm a loser, and even filled up Holden's sippy for the morning (I had the thought in my head that I wouldn't be around to give it to him, so I had better start getting his things ready).
I then laid back down after maybe 8 minutes or so of pacing the house and not feeling anything (except a little discouraged) and not even a minute went by when I had another contraction, then one more immediately after. THIS was when we decided it might be wise to start timing them.

After about an hour and a half of them being anywhere from 4-8 minutes apart and painful enough for me to have to focus my way through them (but still not painful enough to where I couldn't carry on a conversation), I called my doctor. Of course, she said to go ahead and make my way to L&D to see what was going on.

Thomas called our friend Nicole who had offered to watch Holden, we felt so bad waking her up, because it must have been around 3:45am at this point.
We rushed to pack my bag and the rest of Parker's bag.
I think Nicole got to the house around 4:30am, and off we went.

At that point the contractions were a solid 5 minutes apart. They hadn't gotten a LOT more painful, but still pretty nasty. I now understand why in baby shows, the laboring woman yells to "SLOW DOWN!" over bumps and around turns- they were hell on my uterus.

We get to the hospital, get into our room and hooked up to the monitors, and then the attending nurse checks my cervix. She had asked where I was at my last appointment, to which I responded 1cm and hard.

*"A loose 1, and a little softer"*

I was totally devastated. All those hours of contractions and NO progression (i'd been 1cm for almost 3 weeks). I was afraid i'd get sent home, and all the excitement and waking Nicole up would end up being for nothing, so of course the tear factory started and I whined a little about it, but continued to hope that this was the real thing.

Be careful what you wish for, because while we're answering the MOUNTAIN of weird questions (the hospital literally had just gotten an entire new computer system the day before) the contractions went from painful to

158

*"ok, I need to really focus and breathe in through my mouth and out through my nose and NO! DON'T speak to me right now!"*

This next part is a little fuzzy, but I remember the nurse leaving to update the doctor and having me lay on my side because surprise surprise, my blood pressure was elevated, and that's when the contractions went from bad to worse. I was still focused and was managing to get through them, but it was becoming tough to do so.

By the time she came back in the room I can remember yelling through a few of the contractions *"I NEED HELP! I NEED TO GO TO THE BATHROOM!"*

I *really* did. Since arriving, i'd pooped probably 5 times already. Embarrassing, yes, but if you want to look at it in a positive light- it ensured that I wouldn't be pooping on the table during delivery.

The nurse comes back in and checks me again, and i'm now at 4cm and almost fully effaced. She was shocked because it literally happened in less than an hour.

She says that I can now have Stadol (a pain killer to 'take the edge off'), and disappears for what felt like FOREVER. During that time I pretty much lost it. I was thrashing around the bed, yelling, and even started sobbing like a little bitch during some of the contractions. I had begun to lose all control of my labor.

I have no idea how long she was *actually* gone, probably less than 30 minutes. When she comes back, she has me sign MORE paperwork, and then hooks me up to the Stadol drip and some fluids (I was feeling dizzy and dehydrated by that point, wonder why??) and asks me if my pain level has increased since the last time she checked my cervix. DUH! YES!

She checks me again, 6cm. Another look of shock. I warned her that this happened with Holden's pregnancy, and once the process started it did NOT slow down for anything. She immediately requests the epidural.

My contractions at this point are still getting worse with every passing second. Some are still 5 minutes apart, but i'm having a lot that are literally back to back, not giving me a break to really compose myself.

By not compose myself, I mean that I was making a total ass out of myself, because I could no longer tolerate the pain at ALL. Inaudible yells, screaming almost incoherently that I couldn't do it, punching the bed, you name it. We were in a hospital that prides itself in religion (Its name is Mary Immaculate, so you can imagine. Nuns used to roam the halls) so I actually *didn't* curse, much to my surprise. I found other creative ways to scream about how much pain I was in: *"HOLY CHRIST!"* was one of the main ones. Fitting, don't you think?

I don't know who it was, where she came from, or why she showed up in my room- but this strange woman (who I assume was a nurse) appeared by my bedside and was seriously *The Preggo Whisperer*. She somehow talked me through some of the worst pain I've ever felt. She told me to relax my muscles, sink into the bed, let my shoulders go and not be scared of the contractions. This helped SO much, just having someone there coaching me through (poor Thomas looked absolutely petrified, and while he's a good hand holder, I don't think he knew what to say to help). Of course when she left, I pretty much lost it again. The Stadol only helped for about 10 minutes and then, once again, the pain of the contractions increased.

I got checked yet again while we waited for the anesthesiologist- and i'm at an 8 and fully effaced. At that point my nurse gets worried and tells me *"You're progressing so quickly, i'm going to warn you that your epidural may not work."* She cringed while saying it, probably fearing a punch in the face.

You don't tell that to someone screaming in pain about to push out a baby! More tears started pouring out of my face (eyes and nose), and thoughts were sprinting through my head that I was literally going to die. The pain I was feeling was FAR worse than ANYTHING i'd ever felt while being induced with Holden. Sure, those contractions made me cry like a baby and hyperventilate, but NEVER did they make me sound like a dying wild forest animal, or cause me to start punching random objects around me.

My doctor (who had been in and out a few times, a NEW doctor, mind you) comes in and attempts to break my water, no dice. She asks me if i'm *sure* it hasn't broken already because she can only find a little bit of fluid. I tell her (probably in broken English) that I really have no idea because I've been pooping and peeing so much since i'd arrived, but I didn't think it had.

The anesthesiologist showed up REALLY quickly (this usually doesn't happen. They are slow), maybe 10-15 minutes after being called, if that, and then starts another huge stack of paperwork I have to try and sign mid-contraction.

I hate all the paperwork, understand it's necessary, but all I could think about at that point was getting my lovely epidural and *finally* being able to relax. I literally looked down and begged Parker, through my stomach, to PLEASE slow down so that it has a chance to do its job.

She puts it in and then we wait... absolutely no change in my pain level. She puts an injection into the epidural of pain killer (which I think is normal), still no change. *Another* injection, and she starts testing my left leg for numbness by rubbing a cold washcloth in certain parts. I can still feel that it's cold.

I see another injection go into the line. Wouldn't you know it- no change.

I think this repeated itself a few more times, all the while i'm panicking, and in turn start crying even harder, making an even larger ass of myself- this epidural is *not* going to work and i'm going to have to give birth naturally. I was not prepared for that! I would have taken birthing classes, practiced breathing techniques, something!

*This can't happen- it will kill me! I'll die! I'm dying!*

161

Just when I think it can't get much worse, the anesthesiologist decides that moving my laboring ass around might help kick all the drugs she's pumped into me to kick in. She has me lay on my left side, the pain returns on the right; has me lay on my right side, the pain moves to my back; gives me another injection, no change.

Literally, *nothing* helped. The pain just wouldn't go away. She offers to take out the epidural and start the whole process over to see if that would work (and I can tell she feels absolutely horrible), but we're all pretty sure at that point that i'm just too far along, and it isn't going to work for me because there's no time for all that medication to catch up with the amount of pain I was in, and with how fast I was progressing. Most women who get epidurals are more along the lines of 4-6cm, not 8cm going on 9.

Right then, at that very moment- my water broke. It wasn't a wimpy break either- it went everywhere. Just kept leaking and leaking, and i'm in the middle of a contraction, crying *"my water is breaking! Still breaking! I'm still leaking! It's getting everywhere!"*

My doctor comes back in and checks me, no shock- i'm fully dilated- and decides to have me start pushing. I don't think Parker was at the last station but she figured we should give it a try anyways.

I get an oxygen mask, because my hyperventilating is not helping to get me or Parker who was quickly plowing his way down my birth canal enough of it, and the room starts to transform. Lights coming out of the ceiling and the stirrups coming out of the bed, only this time it didn't horrify me like it did with Holden. What did was that she asked Thomas to get in on the action by holding my leg back. This did NOT happen during labor with Holden. Thomas stayed by my shoulder throughout the entire birthing process, and I was very grateful for that.

He grabs my left leg and that's when I realize that I am

completely numb from the waist down; *COMPLETELY NUMB*.

I can't feel my contractions, I can't feel my doctor poking around my hooha, nothin'.

Bout time, right?

I think it was around 9:10am when I started pushing, but again, everything is really fuzzy because of how crazy it got in such a short period of time.

I'm so numb by this point that I have no idea HOW to push. I think I'm trying, but can't figure out if it's actually doing anything. My doctor keeps telling me to *"push like you're taking a big poop!"* (must be a favorite line of all doctors), but I can't feel anything down there but a teensy bit of pressure where she's yanking on me.

*"Are you having a contraction?"* she asks
*"Is that your finger i'm feeling?"*
*"Yes"*
*"Then no. I don't know. Am I?"*

I honestly think I did most of my pushing in my face instead of my ass. I'm lucky I didn't break all of the blood vessels in my eyes.

I'm feeling pretty damn good by that point, the pain is gone, my legs are high up in the air, and i'm cracking jokes about my doctor being in the "splash zone" and she says *"well, you must be feeling better!"* No shit, Sherlock! No more face melting screams and boogers dripping out of my nose from crying so hard, she was right.

Thank GOD the epidural decided to kick in.... I wish it had kicked in sooner, but at least it did *something*.

After about 30 minutes of pushing, I for some God awful reason decide to look down, and can see Parker's head (and also Thomas' sheet white face, I told him not to look!) emerging.

I do three back to back pushes when my doctor tells me to wait. The cord is around Parker's neck; from over my belly I can see her unwrapping it. The hot sting of new tears and a knot in my stomach hit me like a freight train. He doesn't look pink at all. She gets the cord unwrapped and I guess I must have looked away when I felt the INTENSE urge to push, and gave him the final shove- he came flying out into her arms (yes, literally).

She sticks him on my stomach and asks for the bulb to clear his airways. No one knows where the bulb is. Parker wasn't crying. I look over at Thomas and just feel like breaking down, I could tell he was worried too. When she finally finds the bulb, which felt like an entire year, she does about 5 squeezes and like music to my ears, Parker cried. At that point I cried too, but not because I was sad, not the same painful cries I'd been letting out for the past few hours, but because I was so happy that he was ok.

Thomas manned up and cut the umbilical cord after MUCH debate about the subject (it squirted), and then Parker was taken across the room to make sure he was really ok, and for his apgars and measurements and all that fun stuff. I didn't even get to hold him other than those first few seconds on my stomach, just watched him longingly from across the room.

My doctor then informs me that I have a tear, once again pulling my attention back to my poor vagina. Something like a 2nd degree?? I don't know much about tearing, but she says it wouldn't have happened at all if it weren't for the 2 episiotomies I got when I gave birth to Holden. THAT is where I tore! Great! I had to go and tear scar tissue, way to make recovery even more painful.

While she's stitching me up, at the same time she's also trying to get the placenta out of me, telling me to push (as if I hadn't just done enough of that) and yanking on the umbilical cord. I can't really push at that point because not a single bit of feeling had returned to my lower half. I had nothing better to do at that point, since I couldn't help pass the placenta, couldn't hold

Parker, and I had to wait to be stitched up, so what left was there to do to keep me occupied than texting?

I started sending messages to everyone. Imagine their faces when they were asking what was going on and I respond with: *"I literally just popped him out."*

I think the process of stitching & tugging took a good 30 minutes, and once the placenta went flying at my doctor (and watching Thomas' face as he is once again be repulsed by what he's seeing) - we were all done and I FINALLY got to hold my baby. Felt like an eternity, but I was so happy at that point I didn't care anymore

I didn't get feeling back in my legs for the better half of two hours and when I did, and had to stand up to pee (they wouldn't move me to my recovery room until I did), blood went EVERYWHERE. It looked like a scene out of a horror movie; there was blood all over my hospital gown, down my legs, between my toes, and in a trail following me to the bathroom. I laughed, Thomas looked ready to faint. I think he may be scarred for life.

I honestly am not sure if I can do, or ever WANT to do the whole pregnancy/birthing experience *ever* again.

I am pretty happy with the result though. So far, Parker is an angel (other than the projectile tar shit he did all night), although I won't be counting those chickens just yet because Holden didn't turn into a reflux monster until he was 3 weeks old, but I'll take 3 weeks of bliss!

Holden is ambivalent at best about his new baby brother. They met today for the first time and after a few kisses, a snuggle, and calling him *"best friend"* he was over visiting us in the hospital. I think things will go pretty smoothly once we get home- which will be tomorrow! Thank GOD because I am about to SET THIS HOSPITAL BED ON FIRE.

I am not going to get bed sores, so STOP ADJUSTING AND MOVING EVERY 60 SECONDS!!!

# 14 Table for 4, please.

After a few very long and boring days, and some incredibly restless nights, I was finally sent home from the hospital- new baby in tow. I'd spent most of my hospital stay alone because Thomas and I didn't really have anyone who could watch Holden 24-7, and he'd never been left for more than a few hours at a time, so it just seemed more comfortable to have Thomas stay home with him while I stayed with Parker. Not ideal, but you do what you gotta do for your kids.

If you think bringing your first child home from the hospital is confusing, try #2. I know it seems like it should be the other way around. I should have been a veteran! I should have known exactly what to do and what to expect! This should be a piece of cake! I am a pillar of parenting knowledge- a new baby is no match for me! I can DO this!

My brain must have taken the day off during that specific pep talk. I'd managed to black out every horrible moment from the first days home with Holden as to save myself from remembering the sleep deprived insanity, so I really couldn't exactly recall what it was like. As much as I had dreamed of one, unfortunately there's no instruction manual for kids. You're no longer surrounded by doctors or nurses who can be to your room in less than 60 seconds to answer any of the ridiculous questions you may have regarding your brand new bundle of confusing. You can't just press a button or pick up a phone and say *"Hey, don't you need to run some tests? Can you come take my baby so I can sleep?"*
Those options are no longer available. It's the Mommy show! Limited commercial interruption! Every day all day!

I was more panicked than I'd ever been, and that was a hard hurdle to jump. So many questions running through my head, none of which I could answer by my lonesome.

How is he going to sleep? Is he going to wake Holden up? Is Holden going to do to him what my brother did to me upon being brought home from the hospital? HITABABY!
What if Holden has to pee while Parker is eating? What if they won't nap at the same time and perpetually keep each other awake and we ALL go crazy? And how can I do everything by myself without popping a crotch stitch?

These were questions I had stupidly never really sat down and pondered until reality decided to bitch slap me while we were checking out of the hospital (which took HOURS.) It was a long, hard, stinging bitch slap.
Thomas brought Holden to come and pick Parker and I up, and it was at that very moment that it hit me just how intense this was going to be. With Holden getting into absolutely everything in the hospital, wires and monitors and pressing every button he could find, and Parker being none-too-pleased that I was shoving him into a car seat, I was instantaneously overwhelmed. And that was only in the first five minutes.

Bringing home a new baby, whether it be your first or your fifth, I would liken to quitting smoking. Bear with me here.

Once you quit, you have to basically re-learn the parts of your life you routinely had a cigarette before, during, or after. With a new baby, instead of taking something away- it's *adding* something new and equally as frustrating. Everything in your life that was so easy and comfortable to do has to be totally re-learned and re-arranged around your tiny, red, screaming bundle of joy. Which adds even more questions to the plethora already scrambling your (or maybe just my) fragile mind. Can one brain handle so much at once?

How will I eat if baby is crying? How will I bathe (and for me it was 'how will I bathe 2 kids at once?'), and how in the HELL can I ever take two kids out grocery shopping at once, when one kid is enough to test even the strongest will?

It's essentially a total nightmare trying to work all of that out when you don't really have a clue what you're doing, or if what you *are* doing is right.

Parenting is just one gigantic guessing game. Since no two kids are alike, no specific set of advice will ever work for everyone. None of it ever makes sense, no matter how long you've been a parent. There are always new and even more confusing questions. Having two to take care of that are two years apart? That only heightens the fear that you may very well lose your mind before you ever even get close to figuring it out.

Adjusting to life as a mommy of two was pretty much exactly how I thought it would be, hard. It was a long adjustment period for everyone, and of course, my life never fails to add a few extra bumps in the road.

There were some good days and a *lot* of rough ones… and a few I'd prefer to pretend never happened at all. What really helped me get through it was to get the kids on a schedule. I may have seemed like fascist dictator mommy for a while, but when both the boys and I knew what to expect and when, it made the days run a lot more smoothly. I don't give out a lot of parenting advice that I think people should *really* take to heart-but that is the one I will spew to anyone willing to listen.

Above anything else, the best thing that can happen is for your little crotch blossom to start sleeping through the night (as opposed to screaming through them). Once you get more than two consecutive hours of sleep in a row, you feel like an entirely different person with a brand new grasp of sanity.

More importantly, selling your kids on Craigslist or joining the traveling circus won't seem so appealing anymore.

Parker was generally a pretty normal baby. Totally insatiable when it came to bottles, slept most of the day every day, and was up all night every night- as to be expected. A few days in, it became very clear that he had reflux, BAD. Just like Holden, but something I thought karma would allow me to avoid with a second child. How fair is it to have two children with a disorder that causes them to wail like a banshee all day and night?

With Holden we could at least stop the screaming with a pacifier. Parker was not so easy. He refused EVERY pacifier we tried. Over 7 different types and he wanted nothing to do with any of them, so that left a lot of open mouthed screaming fits. We went through 3 different medications and a lot of completely sleepless nights before finding the right combination to soothe him.

I was pleasantly surprised (and unbelievably relieved) with how easily Holden made the transition into big brother mode, he didn't pull what my brother did on me when I came home from the hospital (slapping me in the face). He instantly took to Parker. Showered him with snuggles and kisses, and brought him toys that Parker was way too young to play with- but it's the thought that counts, right? There was even a time where Parker was in the swing, fussy, and Holden thought Parker would be happier with his boppy, so he picked it up and placed it on top of him, over Parker's little face. Good intentions, bad in execution; Parker could have been smothered.

Who Holden chose to take his frustrations out on was me, and *only* me. That kid seemed to hate me for months. He would scream *"DON'T LEAVE!"* to Thomas in the mornings when he had to go to work, refused to hug me or really come anywhere near me, and to really put the icing on the cake- completely reverted on potty training- much to my (and my flooring's) chagrin. All the work we had put into it for the past year was totally undone. Piss and shit all over the house, turds hid in corners and toys, urine soaked bed sheets and poopy pants for 6 months straight.

It was a long hard road to get life back in some kind of semblance of order after giving birth to Parker. I expected it to be bad, but not to the extent that it was, which is really just my luck. The pain in my crotch wasn't quite as intense the second time around, but taking care of two kids- one of whom was mobile- all while bleeding profusely and aching from my nethers was *not* what I would call a simple or enjoyable experience. I bled for 10 weeks straight (not so terrible when compared to 13 with Holden), but as to avoid another 'oopsie' baby, once that seemingly never ending red river dried up and my first real period came (it's like being a prepubescent all over again), I promptly went on Depo-Provera, the birth control injection -BIG MISTAKE. That damn shot caused me to bleed for another 7 MONTHS. That joke men always tell about how they *"can't trust something that bleeds for a week straight and doesn't die"*- what does 7 months of bleeding mean? I was the walking dead; a postpartum zombie!
It was a game of dominos I was playing, and I was the biggest loser ever. Once I felt like I got one thing in my life under control, something else spiraled out of it.

The kids and the bleeding achy crotch may have been difficult, but they were only half of the problem (and that's probably not even the right word to use).

I didn't breastfeed or even attempt pumping this time around. My lovely, wonderful, size D preggo-boobs deflated like an old beach ball less than two weeks after giving birth; there was no hope for milk production. The ta-ta's were clearly empty and sad looking, but somehow one of them managed to not only get clogged, but infected as well. Seriously, worst luck ever! My stomach after popping out two kids in 2 years? Squishy, loose and floppy. I had a serious case of what I like to call 'waterbed belly.' You stop moving, it keeps going. For my entire life I'd been what most people would consider thin, so seeing my stomach in that kind of disarray was a bitter pill to swallow.

Yes, I was relatively fluffy after having Holden, but I'd also gained more weight during that pregnancy- and only looked about 2 months pregnant after giving birth to him instead of this time where I appeared to be 6 months along post child popping. I felt downright nasty, body and mind. The first week or two home I had a serious case of the baby blues because of how overwhelmed I was with all of the life changes. With how Holden reacted to me, I worried he would never let me hug him again, that he would hate me forever, that I'd ruined his life, and ruined our relationship permanently.

I can't lie- it was one of the most difficult processes I've ever gone through. If it weren't for all the hair I was already shedding thanks to postpartum hair loss, I would have torn it all out on my own.

Watching the boys together made every disgusting and humiliating thing happening to my body a little more tolerable, though. There was one time I can remember, where I laid Parker on the couch on his boppy- screaming bloody murder- in order to go and make him a bottle, only to have him abruptly stop out of nowhere. When I rushed back into the room, assuming that he'd taken a nose dive off the couch and was screaming face down into the carpet- I found Holden lying on the couch next to him, one arm wrapped around Parker, and the other stroking his head. It had completely calmed him down. That one moment honestly made it all worthwhile. The pain, the bleeding, the shit hidden in strategic places around my house- none of that mattered, because my little boy loved his baby brother. That meant absolutely everything to me. My snatch may have felt like it was falling off, and I may have been bleeding enough to sponsor an entire blood drive alone- but my babies loved each other. What could be better than that?

As much as the stress and the pressure…and the profusely bleeding, angry vagina were killing me (aside from the spontaneous lovey-dovey brother goodness), nearly pushing me over the edge- I do have to say that it never left me searching for interesting blog subjects. There was always something new, something weird, or something to bitch about, and I'm *damn* good at bitching.

## 10/2/09
# Postpartum Memory Repression

Now that I am officially in the 'postpartum' stage, I am realizing there are a plethora of things that I pushed *waaayyy* to the back of my mind from the last time I was in this same position. Things I probably should have remembered so that I could be prepared for how ridiculously miserable postpartum is. I can understand why I did it; there are things you just wish you could forget. The things that have been seen cannot be unseen- but they *can* be repressed.

I like to keep other people informed so that they aren't as shocked/horrified/embarrassed as I am- so I'll let you in on all the things i'm re-experiencing that I had long since 'forgotten', that may humiliate me, but will be helpful to you.

Not that I think vaginas are beautiful things to begin with- but MAN are they ugly after giving birth! Obviously they're swollen, that's no surprise, they basically just lost a tag-team fist fight between your child and your doctor. What I didn't remember is that your little bits become discolored and resemble sliced roast beef for at least a few days if not a few weeks, effectively ruining Arby's sandwiches for life. You just can't look at them the same way ever again. Now that you don't have a huge belly in the way, there's no way to avoid seeing it either.

You won't be the only one looking at it, either. I forgot about the enormous amount of people that come into your hospital room once you've expelled your spawn, who want to take a look at your stomach, your boobs, and your vag , and then they tell you they *'need to check your pad'*- HORROR.
While you can probably get used to people staring at your va-jay, you never get used to someone telling you they want to inspect your bloody pad... or teach you how to wash your swollen beef-curtains.

Speaking of huge belly, that thing will still be large and in charge. It's not going to disappear just because you hatched your crotch fruit. You might have shot five pounds of fluid out of you while giving birth, but there's a hell of a lot left in there to expel over the next few weeks; not to mention your poor angry uterus, now empty, and still a thousand times its normal size, has to contract (PAINFULLY I might add) until it's back to normal. Chances are you'll still look 6 months pregnant. It's not pretty. I knew i'd be fluffy, but I didn't expect to still look "with child."

The stitches, thank God, don't feel as bad as I remember, although I might change my mind on that tomorrow. It helps that the hospital I delivered at gave me some fabulous numbing spray for my goodies to help with the soreness.
What I conveniently forgot was just how much blood continues to drip/gush/flow out of you after birth. Ew. And I forgot just how disgusting it feels to be sitting down or standing, or doing nothing at all, and to *feel* it doing so.

It's like not being able to control peeing ... WAIT, that will happen too! You thought tinkling yourself during pregnancy was bad? Try the near complete loss of bladder control afterward. This time around it's even worse than my last post-partum experience. For your own sake, I'll humiliate myself here and tell you that since I've been home (which has only been for about 4 hours now), I've already peed all over the floor in the bathroom before getting in the shower because I just couldn't stop it. I couldn't hold it at all. Once it started, it was going to finish whether I liked it or not. I then proceeded to cry in embarrassment, and had to call Thomas in to help me clean it up. That's love, folks.

Exhaustion should be a given, but I never remember how completely exhausting the days/weeks following giving birth are, and sleeping in the hospital really doesn't happen. It's not home, people are constantly coming in and out, and you have a new baby who makes strange noises that will inevitably wake you up once you actually *do* start to doze. All I want to do is sleep but with 2 kids (one of which wakes up every 3 or so hours to eat), being 'well-rested' is a thing of the past.

Your postpartum mind and soul may be filled to the brim with joy and happiness due to your new addition, but your postpartum body will feel like pure and absolute hell, and nothing that happens *to* it or comes *from* it should be shocking. From pissing yourself, to having the hugest swollen feet you've ever seen... it's going to take a *long* time to get back to normal, hell, it might *never* get back to normal.
Expect the unexpected, and especially the unwanted.


10/15/09
# What a day!

After today, I am fully convinced that the days that aren't full of screaming, crying, and general brattiness, will be filled with other strange and semi-horrifying things, much to my dismay. Days of calm laziness are now fantasies.

Everything started off relatively normal, as it usually does. Breakfast went pretty smoothly, and then Parker woke up for his morning feeding. I took Holden to the potty early, as to make sure he wouldn't piss his pants while I was busy with the baby... and the power went out. It came back on momentarily only to go out again a minute later, and stayed that way for another two hours.

For those two hours, both kids were awake, and both wanted my undivided attention. Parker was perfectly happy as long as he wasn't left to his own devices, and Holden brought me book after book after book after BOOK to read... in the dark.

After the first hour, I set Parker down on his boppy and went to take care of a few other things, and when I came back he was out cold. Happy day! He didn't make me rock him to sleep like he has for the past week!
He stayed that way for a while, and seemed to wake up peacefully, but was squirming quite a bit.

When I went to pick him up, immediately I knew why he'd been so restless by the smell permeating from his rear end. Curses! I loathe baby poop. Toddler poop I can handle, it's a solid mass, but you never know what lurks in the depths of a baby's diaper.
I carted him off to the nursery only to be even more horrified by the actual poop itself than the smell (I have learned over the years to breathe through my mouth, a lot less dry heaving that way).
It was a lovely forest green with a pasty texture. The worst part? The power was still out, and it was a rainy day, meaning there was zero sunlight in the house. Basically, I was trying to clean up a blowout in total darkness. Try and tell me that's easy to do!

Six wipes later, I was pretty sure I had him all cleaned up, when I realized he'd also pissed all over himself while I was struggling to clean the poop off of his pecker.

After that mess was *finally* taken care of, it was bottle time. He ate about an ounce before trying to pass out on me, which is an ounce and a half less than his past few feedings, so I tried my best to keep him awake to get him to eat a little more. In hindsight, this was probably a bad idea.

He didn't want to go to sleep after he was done (surprise surprise), so I tried to 'entertain' him the best you can entertain a newborn. Patty cake, tickling his feet, talking to him, and then it came.

The entire bottle I mean; all over him, all over me, out of his nose and his mouth. Lucky me, I was wearing the ONLY pair of pants I have that fit, and it's cold outside… and now they were drenched in warm, stinky baby vomit. It didn't seem to bother Parker, thank God (Holden would have been flipping his shit back in his reflux heyday), but it did mean we both had to change clothes.

I was sure that incident HAD to be the last of the disgusting things to happen to me today, why am I always wrong?

After his next bottle, he once again didn't want to sleep. I was bracing myself to be vomited on when his ass started making the scariest noises I've ever heard. Farts so loud, so wet, and so guttural, I panicked and laid him on the couch with a burp rag under him waiting for liquid shit to come spraying out of his clothes. The sharting didn't stop for a solid 3 minutes.

When I was sure it was safe, back to the nursery we went. I had to psyche myself up to remove his diaper, I was sure it was going to look like his ass threw up, and I in turn would hurl.

It wasn't as bad as I thought it would be. Yellow, seedy, and a little wet. It wasn't until I started wiping him down (and had already moved the dirty diaper out from under him, because he kept attempting to put his feet in it) that the playdoh fun factory action started. Half solid baby excrement pouring out of his ass, all over the changing table. I really can't even describe beyond that what was coming out of him, but it was *not* pretty. Even Holden, who was in the room with us at that time, had to remark that it was *"nasty"*, followed with a *"stinky butt!"*

177

What's a day if it isn't full of vomit, putrid farts, and runny baby shit?

I'm crossing my fingers, hoping that Thomas gets a tiny little taste of what I went through today. Kid is currently farting like the winner of the baked beans eating contest at the county fair, so I think *something* might be brewing.
Ohhhh please! It would make my day. Maybe even my week.


10/24/09
# Hemmies

If you're familiar with this blog, you know when I say "hemmies" that i'm not referring to the kind that make your engine go VROOM, i'm talking about the kind that dangle from your ass.

Yes, hemorrhoids. Thank your lucky stars if you've had a vaginal birth and haven't been plagued by them, you are one of the few.

Unfortunately, I think it's hard not to get them while pushing, grunting, and forcing a child out of your vagina. Especially when your doctor and all the nurses are encouraging you repeatedly to push from your ass, as if that's where babies come out of. All of that straining is bound to make your butt angry, and you won't know just *how* angry until you're trying to take a poop after giving birth, and cringing in pain because it feels like you're shitting razor blades.

I won't go as far as to specify whether or not I have them (I do have SOME pride left), but i'm sure you could make an educated guess.

Just because you don't feel hemorrhoids on the outside of your sad, strained little hole does not mean you don't have them. You may come to find out that hemmies can be internal as well as external, and the internal ones are no walk in the park either. No, they may not hang out of your anus and cause discomfort when you shuffle along because they're rubbing all around in your crack with every move you make, but you'll *definitely* feel pain when you go #2, and horror will wash over you when you peek in the toilet and it's full of blood. That's always a little unsettling.

I've had some fellow mommies tell me that their evil hemmies hurt more than the aching crotch they have from giving birth. How *anything* could hurt more than that baffles me, and makes me feel deeply sorry for anyone who has them that bad.

Some tips: Tucks medicated pads, baby wipes (or just flushable wipes if you want to go and buy something different than what you wipe your new baby's ass with), and stool softeners will become your best friends. Or you could take some dreadful sounding advice I heard- and if you have external hemorrhoids- *push them back in*. ACK!

We women already have to get fat and lumpy, get hideous stretch marks, bad skin, unmanageable hair, mood swings, stitches in our vajays, and an achy crotch among other horrible things in order to bring a child into this world- do our asses really have to suffer as well? Cut us a break here!
Pooping should be a time of relaxation and relief. Not cringing, painful squirming, and ass bleeding.

11/9/09
# Holy Infected Boob, Batman!

*"You learn something new every day"*

Typically, I love learning new things about kids, pregnancy and all the horrible, wonderful things that go along with it. I feel more knowledgeable, and always have something interesting to write about.

This time is not one of those situations.

Yesterday my boob was killing me, I thought from Holden catching his ear on my nipple in the early morning while I was attempting to, sleep and he was attempting to steam roll me... *wrong*. Holden just called my attention to pain that was already there and hadn't noticed yet since i'd just woken up.

All day my boob was killing me. KILLING me; sharp pain, aching pain, swelling, tenderness. It was just not a good boob day all around. All days should be good boob days.

It wasn't until I went from feeling mildly sick (flu like symptoms), to getting chills and feeling like absolute death that I decided to get ready for bed, and while doing so I took a look at my paining boob.
I knew it was swollen, but at that moment I noticed that my nipple was severely misshapen, so I decided to give it a poke... and was greeted by a large lump right under the surface of my skin. Me: glutton for punishment.

I don't know about you, but when I feel a lump in my boob my mind immediately jumps straight to thoughts of breast cancer (which runs in my family), and so I started freaking out.

The first thing I did was text my friend who just finished nursing school a few months ago and asked what in the living hell was going on with my boob.

Through the night and the next morning we started going through symptoms and all sorts of things that could be the problem, and she mentioned that it might be Mastitis, which is an infection of the breast.

I went to Parker's MomSpace message board (with other moms who gave birth this past September) and their consensus was the same as well: Either Mastitis or a clogged milk duct.

Leave it to me to have something wrong with my boob that typically *only* happens to breastfeeding moms. Having milk in your tits can cause all kinds of ridiculous problems, yes, but I never did!

I leaked about TWO drops total and then my boobs deflated and started looking sad again weeks ago, so getting a clogged milk duct or an infection was never something that even crossed my mind. I never even considered it a possibility, and had actually never even heard the word Mastitis before.

I was still a little unsure about this being actually mastitis until I was about to get in the shower and noticed that the whole boob is now red and inflamed. Combined with being misshapen and swollen and you have a severe case of FRANKENBOOB. It is not a pretty sight, y'all.

The only upside to this is that if it IS in fact mastitis, it means I don't have swine flu- which I was beginning to think I had because of how sick I've felt lately- because mastitis will give you flu like symptoms.

Swollen, ugly, inflamed boob AND flu symptoms? SCORE! I really knocked it out of the park with this one.

The super-mega downside? It could get bad enough to where it abscesses and has to be drained.

Boob draining???

Quite possibly the last thing on earth I would EVER want to have done to me. Even thinking about someone TOUCHING my boob right now makes my stomach turn... and it's gonna have to happen because I moved up my 6 week postpartum checkup to have this thing looked at before it gets that serious, which means relentless, not so gentle poking at my already sore boob.

I get the feeling it's pretty bad already considering nothing I've read has talked about a LUMP in the boob- so it's more than likely that there's something nasty going on in there.

Yep, as much as I like to sponge up as much random mommy info that I can, this would never make that list.

Take care of those boobs ladies! You do NOT want one of those suckers getting infected- use my horrid experience to your benefit. At least it will do some good for one of us.

## 11/22/09
## SpongeHolden PottyMouth

In the past I have written at length about how younger toddlers won't pick up on curse words (or at least won't attach to them) if you don't give them value - assuming you aren't walking around your house repeating them all day long.

Make a word seem like a big deal, and of course they're going to want to say it over and over, but just say it in passing and you're pretty much set. They might pick up on it and say it once, but if you don't freak out and let them know it's a dirty word, a toddler will typically lose interest and move on to something that gets a reaction out of you (words like mommy and daddy, because we cheer those words on when they first learn them).

Positive or negative reaction, doesn't matter- they'll take either one.

All of that holds true... up until your child decides to become a human mockingbird.

Babies are always sponging things up- absorbing every little thing they possibly can and learning massive amounts of new things per day, but when they hit around 24-25 months (could be sooner or later depending on the kid), instead of just repeating single words here and there- they literally begin to repeat absolutely everything that happens to slip out of your mouth in entirety.

Not even just things you say all the time (Holden's favorite for a while was *"OH MY GOD!"* just because I say it so freakin' much), but even the most random uncommon things you can think of somehow manages to sink into their spongy little brain and regurgitate back out. Even weeks later, you might not remember you said it, but they sure do. And they even remember the correct context to use it in.

This is when cursing around them really becomes a problem; A quite embarrassing problem.

Holden's memory is SO insane and specific that he has memorized practically all of his books (and he has books as far as the eye can see), random commercials, logos from stores and fast food restaurants, all kinds of crazy things, so I know there's no getting away with cursing in his presence anymore.

Since i'm home alone with the kids all day, I don't really have much use for curse words. I won't lie and say they haven't slipped out; like when I stub a toe or drop a cup- the most likely reaction from me will be of the 4 letter variety. Thomas has a serious issue with cursing around Holden; a SERIOUS issue. It's a hard habit to break when you've been doing it for so long without ever having to watch your mouth, but the guy almost NEVER filters himself, even when I remind him multiple times per day.

So now unfortunately, Holden is a potty mouth. A FOUL potty mouth. In the past 2 weeks alone, he's walked up to an 8 month old and said *"you're being a dick!"* (he also calls *himself* a dick when he's getting in trouble), dropped toys and exclaimed

*"God damnit!'* or *"damnit!'"*, and I swore I heard him call me a bitch one time...but I could be mistaken (I sure as hell hope I am) because that word is not used in that kind of context in this house, if at all.

I was totally fine with being called *"stinky butt"*- that is cute and childlike. Bitch? No no, not ok.

Curse words might not be your ONLY problem though- they certainly aren't ours. Any questionable phrase you might say in passing can be used as a weapon by a 2 year old.

Everything you say needs to go through a sanitizer before it comes out, which sucks. I've never been one to filter myself, but i'd personally prefer to avoid the dirty looks from judgmental strangers in public when my kid is running around calling people dicks and yelling *"DAMNIT!"* at the top of his lungs, so I'll do what I have to do to nip this in the bud.

It's times like these when you miss your kid ignoring your conversations and just babbling gibberish instead of clinging on to your every word, phrase, and action, and then repeating them for the world to hear. Don't even get me started on how Holden knows parts of the Beyonce *"Single Ladies"* dance from watching just *snippets* of the video a handful of times.

12/7/09

# How Rude!

Today I heard through the grapevine that someone called Holden "rude."

STOP THE PRESSES!!!!
GASP!
A two year old... *RUDE??* No freakin' way!

I don't have the wool pulled over my eyes, nor do I wear rose colored glasses. Holden has an attitude, there's no doubt about that- but he's a TWO year old. Isn't being two years old synonymous with attitude and defiance?

For someone to call a two year old 'rude' and act like it's some kind of shock or surprise, or *anything* out of the ordinary for his age is absolutely ridiculous to me.

They don't call it the "terrible twos" for nothing.

You would think this comment came from someone who has no children, and has no idea what they're talking about, since it's such a stupid thing to say...

Unfortunately not. This person has three children. THREE. It should be safe to assume that said person would and *should* have intimate knowledge of just what kinds of attitudes children can and *do* tend to have, and therefore name-calling a two year old for actions that are normal for a two year old to have just wouldn't happen- but no.

People are stupid, point blank, no matter how many kids they have.

Friends have come over and been highly embarrassed by their child's actions when they're snatching toys, throwing fits, and not wanting to share or play nicely, but I've never seen that as anything other than absolutely normal. That's just how little kids are. Especially at such a young age, they haven't learned to play *together* yet. They haven't learned to be able to share. Sure, I get embarrassed by the same things when Holden acts that way, but I've never thought that made him a bad kid or "rude"- just a normal run of the mill toddler.

I'm not above thinking mean things about other people's children- but when I do it's because their kid was abnormally misbehaved. Hitting, spitting, biting, pulling hair, screaming and throwing fits over absolutely nothing- those kinds of things are what I cringe at.

In Holden's defense though (even though I don't think he needs

185

to be defended for something that comes with the age he is), the person name-calling him has only ever met him once, for about 30 minutes, at a late lunch when he should have been napping, sitting in a highchair next to another kid who was hoarding crayons he was too young to play with that Holden wanted.

Even then, in no way could Holden be considered "rude." A little obnoxious? Sure. He wanted those damn crayons. He didn't hit, he didn't cry, he didn't scream… he really wasn't all that badly behaved when it comes down to it.

It also needs to be said that this person, for reasons unknown to me, dislikes me. So really, they have a problem with me- and have taken to name-calling my 2 year old son instead.

How low do you have to be to talk shit about a child because you don't like their parent? Pathetic, really, and this all coming from someone who openly admitted to not being able to discipline their oldest child because of the 'tude she gets in response. Yes, this person *really* has room to talk.

The mean and vindictive part of me hopes that person's precious under-two children grow to be total and complete monsters, hitting and screaming "NO!" to everything they may tell them to do- so they get a *real* idea of what a 'rude' child is.

Don't ever assume that your child is going to turn 2 and be a perfect little angel; it's not gonna happen without a lobotomy. They all have their moments, no matter how well behaved they are for the majority of their days. If you see a 2 year old freaking out in the store, don't roll your eyes and call them a brat, or think that they have suck-ass parents, 'cause chances are- sooner or later- you'll be put in that same situation with your small child throwing an absolute shit-fit in public, and won't appreciate the rolling eyes and hushed whispers around you.

Oh, and don't be a bitch! That one's key.

12/30/09
# My uterus doesn't take kindly to threats

My uterus seems to have serious issues with authority. It doesn't like to be told what to do or when to do it. Doesn't conform to uterine norms or follow any regular pattern.

Perhaps my uterus thinks it is James Bond. Stealthy, sneaky... likes things shaken and not stirred. Believes that rules are meant to be broken. Rebel without a cause. The ultimate in defiance. Queen of the fake out.

I want a little girl, it gives me two boys; one of which was planned, and one that can only be described as immaculate conception. Then again, knowing my uterus- it could contain a hyperbaric chamber that can keep sperm alive for YEARS just to release them when I least expect it. PREGNANT! Take that!

My first pregnancy: evil uterus allowed me to get 8 hours into an induction with NO action whatsoever. It was then that I was informed that if I did not go into labor, i'd be put on Cervadil, then back on Pitocin- and if THAT didn't work, it'd be C-section time.
I begin losing my shit, of course- and BAM: active labor. Five hours later Holden was born.

Pregnancy #2: the night before the appointment where I was positive i'd be sent for an induction due to my high blood pressure, I go into labor. Get to the hospital where i'm informed that i'm only 1cm (where i'd been for weeks.) Once again I panic, thinking I'll be sent home- and shit hit the fan. 3.5 hours later- Parker was born.

And now, just as my doctor gave me a prescription to start my stupid period, since it's been 3 months since I gave birth- my uterus decides to revolt yet again. I take the prescription in to the pharmacy that night, planning to pick it up the next day (yesterday), and just as we're thinking about leaving to go and get it, guess what starts? Yep, my period. Out of nowhere. No cramps, no nothing. Now my lady parts feel like they're going to fall off if I stand for too long, my back is killing me, and my uterus is aching... probably doing a victory dance. At least I don't have cramps, I guess.

My wily uterus has grown a mind of its own. It won't be told what to do! My lady parts are only the first stop on the road to world domination.
Or maybe, just maybe... it's my brain *willing* my uterus into action.

If only it had that kind of power over my weight loss!


1/3/10
# Toddler ogling

One thing that I absolutely cannot stand, cannot get over, makes me grit my teeth and knuckles turn white, is when random strangers come up and ogle my kids.
I'm not talking about the *"Oh how cute!"* maybe coupled with a *"Hi there precious!"* directed towards the lil'un. That is normal and completely acceptable; I do have some irresistible children. Everyone likes to hear that their miniature human is cute- and the best way to hear it is when it's short and sweet. Get in, get out, no problem.

There have, of course, been times where it has drug on too long for my liking, causing extreme awkwardness and a strong uncomfortable feeling (plus it's annoying), but more often than not, since a baby is nothing but a lump that *might* smile at you and that's about it- the chances of someone hanging around them for more than a minute or two are pretty slim. Not to say it DOESN'T happen, there are a hell of a lot of weirdoes out there, but usually the interaction is short and relatively harmless.

As Holden gets older, the strangers seem to be more adventurous, and don't know when to either walk away or shut the hell up.

I miss the phase where any stranger who walked up to us and tried to even speak a single word to Holden was brutally rebuffed. And not by me, but by him; instant scream fest. I didn't need to make up a reason to walk away; those were happy times. People tend to get the hint when a child seems to find them utterly terrifying.

Now that Holden is at the age where he can communicate with people in coherent English, they seem to think he's fair game. Open season on toddlers. No more are just passing comments on how cute he is, or asking *me* how old he is; I don't even exist anymore.
Random ass strangers just walk right up and start conversations with him. It's just plain strange.

Yesterday while shopping with both boys (a harrowing task on its own), an older lady walked right up and started talking to Holden. Did his puzzled and unhappy look stop her? Oh hell no!

There I am, trying to navigate my way through the aisles, and she just won't leave him alone. Talking to him about her family, pointing to some globe she was holding and telling him where they all live and all of their names... pointing to her cheesy grandma shirt and explaining it to him as if he actually cared (he didn't.)
Meanwhile, Parker, who was also in the cart (Holden rarely rides in the cart anymore, but yesterday he wanted to. For once it seemed to be a very bad idea, because on any other day he'd just walk away from this batshit crazy lady) was ridiculously

upset. He was fussing and crying, and nothing I was doing was helping the situation… yet this lady just wouldn't quit. How big does the neon flashing "EFF OFF!" sign have to be???

I had hoped Thomas, who was standing a few feet away looking at drinking glasses (since all of ours have mysteriously found themselves cracked or broken over the past few months), would help me out of this situation by saying we had to go, or even just walking away so i'd have to follow... but no. He seemed to be pretending he wasn't with us and left me to deal with this wackadoodle all on my own.
Thanks for nothing, asshole!

While on this blog I may seem opinionated and assertive, I do try my best not to be rude to strangers, but this woman was working my last nerve. Couldn't she see I was busy? Or that Holden was not interested in anything she had to say? Or that Parker was screaming inconsolably, and she was holding me up from getting the hell out of there? Couldn't she feel the flaming poison covered eye daggers I was shooting her?
Sure, I could have politely excused myself, but that's just not me. I'm not good at polite, especially considering how irritated I was by that point. And let's be real, do you honestly think she'd have let us go?

If you feel like you don't exist to other people when you have an infant, just wait until your kid can *speak*. People no longer care that you're covered in vomit or baby crap, they don't care that you have places to go or people to see (that *aren't* them) - they're talking to your KID, not you. Didn't you know that??

I should have just been rude to the whack-job, because that damn lady decided to shoot ME flaming eye daggers a couple of minutes later when Holden decided to be a total brat and I was disciplining him. So sorry my attempt to raise a normal, house-broken, well-mannered child offends you, psycho!

Next stranger who comes up to me and sparks a one-sided five plus minute conversation with my two year old is getting punched in the throat.

Let's see you try to talk when you can't catch your breath!!!

1/14/09

# Yet another *"what was I thinking?"* moment

For the life of me, I can't figure out *why* I ever considered sleep sacks to be better sleep-outfits for babies than good old fashioned footie-pajamas.

I can still see what appeal they have; they don't have billions of annoying snaps going all the way up both legs, and all the way up their frickin' body. All they are is one annoying tug over the head and they're on. Want to change a diaper? Just pull it up, no obstacles in the way! What could be bad about that?

When you have a baby blob that doesn't love to wiggle and squirm and move all the time, I suppose sleep sacks don't cause any issues. You're feeding and changing them so often that anything expedite the process, and with less screaming, is welcomed and applauded.

Now? I loathe them. They annoy me. I find them a nuisance not only to get on, but to keep Parker in at all.

If he hadn't projectile vomited all over every other footie-pj he has, no way would I ever even consider putting him in an elastic baby dress, but because we don't have very many pajamas for Parker now that he's grown out of 0-3 month seemingly overnight, while cleaning out his drawers I knew I had to hold on to the infernal contraptions just in case the few acceptable pajamas we have managed to dirty themselves all at once. And wouldn't you know it, they did.

I would have had better luck putting him in some kind of jumper with a pair of socks (and if you've ever had an infant, you know how impossible it is to keep socks on them) than sticking him in this nefarious baby sack of doom.

After digging through the 6-9 month bin of clothes we have for him, hoping that at least ONE of them might *possibly* be small enough to fit him without it being some sort of hazard- and coming up empty handed- the only option left besides a crusty vomit soaked footie… was a stupid sleep sack.

Of course, the first thing he did was kick until it had worked its way above his knees. I pulled it back down, he repeated. Our house is only semi-old, but VERY drafty, so it wasn't long before his little toes felt like icicles. I don't like having a cold baby. Babies should be warm and snuggly at all times.
The bunching and riding up got even worse when I picked him up- which I do before his last bottle every night while Thomas puts Holden to bed. So bad in fact, that it became very tempting to hold him upside down and pull on the bottom of the damn sack just to get it straightened out again, because half the fabric had made its way all the way up to his chin, while his knobby knees were just hanging out in the cold air.

All those snaps might be annoying- *especially* annoying when you snap just ONE wrong without realizing it and end up having to re-do the entire damn outfit- but legs that are secured underneath fabric are much better than free flapping in the wind and turning into fleshy popsicles.

I swear, if he frees those bony little legs and gets cold enough to decide that sleeping is an impossible task, thereby successfully whining and crying enough to wake EVERYONE in the house, including my already irritable toddler who enjoys hiding shit in random places when he's upset… I'll burn every single one of those damn sleep sacks, and then do a happy little dance on their ashes! Screw you sleep sacks! To hell with you!

# 15 RSV and the Mean Mommies
## Part 1:
*A sick baby, a confused mommy*

It took a while to get there but I have to admit, life was going pretty good for us... well, besides the potty training regression and toddler tantrums. Once Parker got past the newborn stage where all he wanted to do was cry and fart and we'd finally gotten his reflux under control, it seemed like we were finally getting back to the place we'd been at before the unexpected pregnancy turned our life on its head; and while Holden was still randomly crapping his pants- things were getting easier with every day that passed.
Our house was turning into a pretty relaxing place to be.

It's relatively simple to take care of one mobile child and another who is somewhat content to just lie on the floor and watch- especially when those two kids are what I would call obsessed with each other. There were times when it seemed like I didn't have to do a damn thing because Holden wanted to take over. If he could have learned how to change a diaper I might have been out of a job. Although... he did attempt to help wipe Parker's ass once. That did not go well; it did not go well *at all.*

All of the bliss we had finally found ended very suddenly when Parker was around 3 months old.

It started with what I thought was a slight head cold making the rounds in our house. Neither boy was coughing, but they were

193

both running mild fevers. That was nothing I couldn't handle. 'Twas the season after all, kids just get sick in the winter time. That's the sad and unfortunate truth, and just another reason to add to the ever-growing list of why I *hate* cold weather.

This particular "head cold" seemed to linger for Parker though, after a while I thought perhaps it was an ear infection. Those pesky bitches can give babies cold-like symptoms, and he *had* been tugging at his ear. Not always a positive indicator since babies will tug at just about anything they can get their hands on- but it was something to go off of. Holden had never actually had an ear infection in his entire life so I really couldn't be sure, but it seemed to fit.

It wasn't until Parker screamed for an entire night nonstop after we tried to put him to bed, and had a fever of over 101 in the morning, followed by Holden coming out of his room telling me his *"throat hurt"* that I became concerned. This was clearly not an ear infection.

Thomas and I made the decision to get the boys in to see their pediatrician immediately. It was going to be hard to swing since we were informed that our pediatrician was out, AND it just so happened to be the day I had scheduled to get my Depo-Provera shot in order to avoid another 'oopsie' pregnancy from occurring (an appointment that I'd already rescheduled multiple times.)
That day turned into one of the most stressful and scary days I've *ever* had.


1/15/10
# One of my top 3 'Worst Days Ever'

In years, no day has been worse than today. Today is for sure one of the top 3 worst days ever in my entire life, and is a strong contender for the top spot.

I don't have much time, you'll know why as I go on, so i'm going to TRY and keep this horrific experience breakdown as short as possible- but with everything that transpired- I don't see that happening.

After not being able to find a sitter to watch the boys for my appointment today to FINALLY get the Depo shot, and Parker taking a nasty turn for the worst yesterday- Thomas decided that he would take a very early "lunch" and come and meet me at the ped's office to take the boys and get Parker checked in while I ran right down the street to my OBGYN to get my shot. Seemed like a smart plan at the time- killing two birds with one stone.

We just changed insurance providers, and with the new provider came a flex-spending account (money taken from Thomas' paychecks in order to pay for medical expenses like co-pays and prescriptions.) Thomas put $500 into it so that I would stop having to pay so many RIDICULOUS medical expenses out of pocket. Just like a credit card- it needed to be activated, so he took it to work with him.
BAD IDEA. I needed the card so I could pick up my Depo prescription at the pharmacy before my appointment. Since he had it instead of me, his schedule had to be re-arranged in order to go and pick it up.
Wouldn't you know it- they had no record of my Rx. I call the nurse in a slight panic, and she insists she DID in fact call it in- even had record of what day and time she did so, so she called the pharmacy and gave them a good talking to, and that stupid vial of baby-banning 'medicine' was ready in under 10 minutes.

The Depo shot went off without a hitch. They didn't even give me a pregnancy test even though they had made a HUGE deal about how long i'd waited to call them to make the

appointment, because I might've gotten myself knocked up in the meantime and bla de bla bla.
The shot feels like the one you get when you're a kid and your arm hurts for DAYS, and you can hardly lift the stupid thing up. Remember that? What was it, tetanus?

It seemed to be a good sign- not the pain in my arm- but getting in and out so quickly after such a rough start to the day. I was confident that the appointment with the pediatrician was going to go just as smoothly.
I knew they'd say Parker was sick, considering he had screamed from 2am-7am last night... relentlessly.

He wasn't eating much, but he was screaming a HELL of a lot less this morning, so I figured maybe it was just the cold coming back, or possibly an ear infection- no biggie on either count. Although yesterday I did have this strange feeling in the pit of my stomach that something more was wrong. His breathing seemed weird, but I tried to brush that feeling off.

I rushed back to the pediatrician from the OBGYN and the boys were already in a room- that NEVER happens- so that's another good sign to add to the list.
Thomas and I make the switch off, and a few minutes later the doctor came in, not our regular doctor mind you. At first he was incredibly rude and condescending towards me, I did not appreciate that. I am not an uninformed parent, or a new parent, and I don't like being treated like I know nothing at all.
He checked his ears: perfect. His lungs: clear. Then he checks Parker's breathing... and then re-checks. He says to me that Parker seems fine, BUT, his breathing is abnormal. He pulls up Parker's onesie to get a look at his chest, and Parker isn't breathing through his chest. Instead, the breathing is fast and under his ribs. It was a scary sight to see, and I hadn't even noticed it before. I had noticed he was breathing quickly, but that was it. Didn't seem like a big deal, I thought it was normal for him. He then checks Parker's breathing again. A normal baby takes 30 breaths per minute, Parker was taking 80

(Holden, who also had not felt well was fine, no issues or problems at all, just a cold). This was very concerning, and he immediately sends us downstairs for an X-ray.

We waited an HOUR to get called back for it. I was glad that Parker slept the whole time, but by this point his bottle was getting later and later. Since he'd already been eating so little (even his poor soft spot was sunken in), so I knew he was getting dehydrated and I wanted him to eat. That wasn't gonna happen.

For the X-ray, Parker was all smiles. He didn't like me holding him down, but he was a trooper.
Holden acted like a perfect angel. Sat quietly and played while this all went down. His lunch was also getting later and later.

We got back upstairs and back into our room, and the nurse wanted us to start Parker on a nebulizer for his breathing. Incredibly scary to have to put a mask over his face and watch the sad look in his eyes as he breathed mist in.
Once that's done, she comes back and asks if we had gotten labs done while we were downstairs for the X-ray. Uhh... no, no one said anything about lab work!
So she says we have to go BACK downstairs for labs. MORE lugging Parker, his crap, and Holden around when my arm was killing me from the Depo shot; I was hungry, already terribly exhausted, frustrated, and scared.

Again, there was nothing I could do. He needed the labs, so back down we went. I figured we'd be waiting ANOTHER hour, so I bring out Parker's bottle and start to feed him. Not even 2 ounces in, and we get called back. Great. Had to stop mid-bottle, and he was not happy about it.
I thought the labs would just be a toe prick... ohhhh no. They wanted to get blood from a vein.
I have NEVER had a sick baby, and never imagined Parker would get so sick that they needed to get blood from a vein, so at that point I was about to wig out. They tried and *tried* to find

a vein in his arm, but couldn't find one, and started talking about putting the needle into his head. I wanted to die at that point. My poor sick little baby. They checked the other arm and fortunately found one there. Parker screamed, a LOT... even more when the needle came out.

All this time, Holden was still acting like a perfect angel. The blood drawing room was decked OUT in Spongebob crap, he was in total heaven. Spongebob is the ONE show he asks for by name every day.

Once the labs are done, we go BACK upstairs and back into our room, once again, where I attempt to get Parker to finish the bottle that had been so rudely interrupted. Another ounce in and he vomits the entire 3 ounces back up all over himself, his car seat, and me. He was soaked, and I didn't have any extra clothes for him. I was so upset at that point that I just held him to me, soaking myself in upchuck, and somehow got him to down the rest of the bottle. There was no more spitting up after that. I wasn't happy that he'd only gotten 2.5 ounces in the whole FIVE hours we'd been at the doctor, but there wasn't much I could do about it at that point. I didn't have any more formula with me, because I never in a million years expected to be there for so long.

The nurse has us do ANOTHER breathing treatment, and the doctor says while Parker's chest X-rays came back totally fine- they might want to admit him to the children's' hospital because of his breathing, but he was going to wait for the labs to come back to make the final call. He was confused about the X-rays; he was positive Parker's chest would have fluid or SOMETHING in there to indicate RSV, which was what he thought Parker had.

It was 3:30pm by that point. Holden's lunch is usually at noon, and on any normal day he'd already have taken a nap and woken up. We had no food with us at all, nothing he could even snack on... and he was begging for *something* to eat; no one even seemed to care.

The nurse that took care of Holden when *he* was an infant came in and saw how distressed I was (we looooove that nurse), and offered HER snack for Holden. That woman is the best. It was a pack of peanut butter chocolate crackers, two of Holden's all-time favorite things in one. He was happy, which made me happy, but still sad that he hadn't gotten a full lunch or a nap. I knew he was tired and wanted to go home- so did I. And I had tears in my eyes thinking of my baby being hooked up to IVs and tubes in a children's hospital all weekend. How could he be THAT sick but act SO fine?

The doctor comes back in after Parker's 2nd breathing treatment and we started discussing home care for Parker; giving him breathing treatments at home if I was comfortable doing so. He still couldn't wrap his head around how not only had the X-ray come back clean, but how Parker was smiling and interacting considering how distressed his condition was. He said if we went to the children's hospital, they'd probably send us home because of that.

The labs finally come back: all normal except his white count. It was a little high, indicating a bacterial infection (I THINK). Meaning he was sick, but they couldn't figure out why exactly. Even though all the tests had come back normal, the doctor was still convinced that Parker had RSV, and not just RSV, but Bronchiolitis: a condition caused by RSV that is potentially fatal to infants. Fan-fucking-tastic.

Still, he sends us home with a nebulizer and a prescription for the stuff that goes in it.
They took Parker's temp one more time since he hadn't been on Tylenol all day long: 98.6, crazy. You would have thought it would be high as hell with how sickly he was.

FINALLY, at 5pm, we get to go home. We got there before 11:30am, just to give you an idea of how outrageously long we were there. No food, one bottle, up and down elevators and across corridors, needles and X-rays... Just an all-around

AWFUL DAY.

I picked up chicken nuggets & fries for Holden (which i'd been promising him all day because I felt so bad that he had to sit there and do nothing the whole time) on the way home, and dropped off the prescription for Parker.

We get home, eat, Parker is sleeping, and then Thomas gets home from work. Thank GOD. I was SO exhausted by that point it was unreal. As much as I wanted to let Parker sleep, I knew he NEEDED to eat, so we woke him up. Lots of screaming. He didn't eat much, but it was better than nothing. Of course- he puked most of it back up.

We then went to get his prescription. Can you guess how much it was?? ONE HUNDRED AND SIX DOLLARS, and that's AFTER insurance covered over $100 of it. Holy hell! Thank GOD for the flex spending account or we NEVER would have been able to afford it.

I took Holden into Walgreens with me to let him pick out a special toy since he had been SOOOOOO *sooooooo* good all day, when most 2 year olds would have been flipping their shit. Figures, he picked out a Lightning McQueen matchbox car. $4.50 well spent and WELL deserved, he is obsessed and happy.

Parker was semi fussy and not really eating for the rest of the evening, but he LAUGHED for the first time. He's chuckled plenty of times, but he LAUGHED. A baby SO sick laughing? Insanity, he is SO strong.

I'm still terrified though. I just read a blog last week about a baby around Parker's age who died after being diagnosed with RSV when he actually had Whooping Cough. That poor baby and poor mommy, that thought alone is nearly sending me over the edge. My baby HAS to be ok. I'm really tempted to sleep on the floor by his crib tonight just to make sure nothing goes wrong.

Babies should NEVER get sick; it just doesn't seem fair or

right.

---

That was only the beginning of what would be a nightmare that lasted for MONTHS.

Up to this point, Holden had only been sick a total of two times in his entire life. Once with Roseola, which for all intents and purposes is just a fever and a rash, and once with the stomach flu- which was only a 5 hour long ordeal. Nothing could have prepared us for what Parker was going through, or was *about* to go through. Never really having dealt with a sick child before, I had no clue what to do. I'd felt in the dark when it came to babies and parenting in the past, but never like this.

It took everything I had not to go into complete hysterics, and generally I cry pretty easily. I teared up at an episode of Futurama, so you can imagine how hard it was for me to hold it together. I'd heard about RSV and how dangerous it could be for infants, and even though Parker didn't swab positive for it, it was still assumed that he had it, and we still had to treat it as such.

Honestly, I wasn't satisfied with that. No matter how many days we sat for hours upon hours in the doctor's office getting Parker checked on (3 times per week, give or take), no matter how many different breathing treatments and nasal sprays we tried- he wasn't getting any better. Actually, he was getting worse. *Much* worse.

His breathing went from just fast, to crackling and wheezing. He developed a nasty cough (finally), and with every passing day, he was eating less and less until his intake was practically nothing. I'd had enough of the dicking around from doctors, and after a positive RSV swab (weeks into the ordeal), and a round of steroids one doctor had prescribed to hopefully increase his appetite that did absolutely nothing to help, we were sent to the children's hospital emergency room.

We waited for probably three hours to be seen, and I felt like tearing someone's head off once we were finally called back and the ER doctors acted just like every other doctor we'd already seen.

Sure, he's lost two pounds. Sure, his breathing is bad- but his electrolyte level is normal, so there's nothing we can do, sorry! I must have argued with three different doctors there about it, insisting that there *had* to be something more they could do to help him, but no one would listen. Every doctor who looked at him saw his smile and assumed he was fine. It pissed me off more than I can ever explain.

While I was happy that Parker didn't appear phased at all by what his body was doing (had he been I really don't think I would have kept it together), it also meant no doctor was ever going to take his condition seriously. And I *knew* it needed to be. He needed help, a hell of a lot more than he was getting. Losing two pounds at 3 months old is not normal. Not eating for weeks is not normal. Not getting better is *not* normal.

We got second, third, and fourth opinions, but it was always the same. Out of all of those doctors, not a single one could tell us why he wasn't eating. Most didn't even seem to care. They all just threw prescriptions at him hoping something would stick and told us to "force fluids" by dropper feeding him (putting formula and/or Pedialyte into a syringe and dropping it into his mouth) and eventually, they said, his appetite would return. Well guess what? It never did.

By this point I was totally worn down. Exhausted, frustrated, stressed out and pissed off. I had lost all hope in the medical community and was quickly losing hope that Parker would ever recover. It was a feeling of total helplessness. There was nothing I could do to make Parker better. Having to dropper feed a baby every bottle just to keep them hydrated wears on you very quickly. It was absolutely heartbreaking.

The whole time this ordeal was taking place, I had turned to my blog and the MomSpace message boards for support. I figured there *had* to be someone else out there who had gone through the same thing. *Someone* out there had to have more answers then all the idiot doctors we'd seen.

By the boat load, I got what I asked for... sort of. Advice from everyone and their mother; all kinds of suggestions and comments about what might be wrong with Parker. Some ideas didn't sound so bad, but some were so outlandish and off base that I wondered if people even knew Parker's symptoms and situation before just regurgitating something they'd read while doing a Google search.

I appreciated the support and the fact that so many people cared enough about Parker and about us to try and help us find answers, but weeks of getting 10+ different ideas, possible disorders, and suggestions every single day was beyond overwhelming,

Never in a million years would we have had the time, money, or resources to follow every bit of advice given to get Parker tested for every possibility mentioned to me. We'd already spent our entire flex spending account, meant for the whole year, in less than 2 months, not to mention a ridiculous amount of money out of pocket once the FSA was gone- all on doctors that knew nothing and medications that did nothing. I felt like my head was going to explode.

So what did I do? What I always do: I blogged. A blog I thought was relatively innocent and would be totally harmless, but started a reaction of apocalyptic proportions.

# Part 2:
## Bullying isn't just for kids

Before we get to the blog, let's rewind for a moment to earlier that same day.

I'd been perusing the Facebook updates from 'friends' that had been posted when I came across one that struck me as odd… and somewhat personal; To *me*.

Throughout the time I'd been a member of Facebook, I'd added a number of random girls from the MomSpace board that I may never have even had a real conversation with, but added anyways just to be polite.

This comment from this particular girl struck me as one of those random adds. I didn't recognize her and her name was only somewhat familiar. I figured maybe she was a MomSpace board member back when the board for Holden had just begun, and had lost interest and stopped posting, as most ladies tend to do over time. To see a status update that seemed directed so specifically at me was puzzling.

I can't remember the exact wording, but it said something to the effect of
*"Force feeding is wrong and unnecessary. My baby will eat when he/she gets hungry! Now excuse me while I go and cuddle with him/her"*

Since I had been talking about force-feeding for weeks (which was what I considered dropper feeding to be since Parker wasn't eating it by choice), and had blogged about it on many occasions, and since I highly doubted that anyone else was "force feeding" at the same time, I immediately assumed the comment was meant for me to read and be offended by.

Had I been in my right mind, not having gone through weeks of pointless doctors' visits, more prescriptions than I could count, and running on little to no sleep because Parker's sickness had spread to everyone else in the house (including me), I may have let the comment go. I didn't know the girl, what the hell did her opinion matter? She obviously had no idea what she was talking about, no one who hadn't walked in my shoes could understand, so why even dignify the comment with a response?

Well, I wasn't in my right mind unfortunately- so I did just that. I was upset by the comment, but not enough to be argumentative; however I did let my emotions get the best of me and got a tad dramatic. In a response to her comment, I re-iterated my situation to her, telling her that I adamantly disagreed with her statement, and said that "force feeding" had basically saved Parker's life; as I said, just a tad dramatic.
I don't believe it 'saved' him, not exactly, but it definitely kept him from having a feeding tube shoved down his nose in a hospital bed. That to me was a much worse option than using a dropper to keep a baby hydrated under doctor's orders.

I didn't think anything would even come of the comment. I hadn't intended to start any kind of argument, but when I returned to the computer later I saw that instead of responding to my slightly emotional outburst, she instead had spammed Facebook with *"drama this!"* and *"drama that!"*
After a big fat eye roll, I decided the best thing to do would be to just remove her from my Facebook completely. I wasn't looking for a fight, but clearly she was. While I'm always a fan of a little drama, I typically prefer not to be involved in it myself, especially when I had a sick kid to take care of and a toddler to manage. I like to watch from the sidelines with a hot bucket of buttery popcorn

I clicked the 'delete friend' button and went about my day. I didn't even give it another thought. She wasn't my friend, not in real life, and we didn't have any mutual friends that I knew of- so to me that was that, and it would be the end of it.

It was back to sifting through the hundreds of suggestions for treatments I'd accumulated, and back to where this chapter started- the blog. Two seemingly unrelated incidents would soon collide in a *horrible* way.

3/18/10
# Unwarranted advice train, coming into station!

There are probably 500 ways that this blog could come out wrong and hurt a lot of people's feelings that I certainly don't intend to, so i'm going to preface the entire thing with this:

I appreciate ALL of my friends who care enough to come to me, and talk to me about what is going on with Parker, because NONE of the doctors we've seen have ever *really* cared enough to listen. I love that there are people who take a genuine interest in what i'm going through, who can sympathize, who try to make me feel better, who offer up their advice, and their opinion. Who agree that what is going on is NOT normal and that there *has* to be an answer out there... *somewhere*. It feels nice to know, that although the doctors don't give a flying fart it would seem, that i'm not crazy in thinking that there's clearly something wrong with Parker.

I'm sure you can sense a BUT coming, and you'd be correct- there is a big one.
And here it is:

BUT... there is a line that is drawn in the world of advice, where it goes from helpful to just plain… overbearing in a way. My/our situation crossed that line a LONG time ago.

Parker has been "sick" for so damn long, that I swear I have the same conversation 50 times per day with 50 different people, and while I appreciate that people care enough to ASK and to help me try to find answers- it is so tiring- because no answer is ever the right answer. Everyone has a different opinion, and a different viewpoint. After 3 months, it has become repetitive. And when people think they're helping unfortunately they aren't. They're really only being comforting -which is better than nothing- but it gets downright irritating after a while; and not because of the suggestions in themselves, but because I'm exhausted trying to make them fit and failing instead.

I've done hours and hours and days upon days' worth of research on what could be wrong with Parker. I've looked at hundreds of websites, asked a dozen different doctors, and everything has come up inconclusive. Plus the 3 months' worth of friends coming and telling me what *they* think might be wrong, we alone have basically touched on pretty much everything you can find online.

Over and over I've had to say no, it's not that- I've looked into it, he has none of the symptoms. No, it didn't start when he started solids, it started when he got RSV and has continued. No, he isn't in pain. Yes, his breathing is still abnormal, but no it doesn't seem to bother him. No, it's not that his stomach needs to stretch out- if that were the case, why would he eat big bottles randomly throughout the day and then refuse his bed time bottle?

Trust me; I've been through it ALL, dozens of times. I love that you care enough to try and Google to find something that may fit, that maybe no one had thought of yet- but chances are- I've been there, I've looked there, and we've ruled it out.

I realize you love your doctor, but i'm not going to waste time and money to drive 2 states, 3 states, 4 states away just to go to them and be told the same exact thing- *"There's nothing wrong. Just give it time. "* because I would put MONEY on that's exactly what they'd say. I loved our previous pediatrician, too. Over TWO YEARS with her and no problems until she decided not to do anything but make us wait for 2 months for an unnecessary Cystic Fibrosis test. She always found out what was wrong before that, and after her we've seen 8 other doctors who also could find nothing. I highly doubt yours will be different. I wish they were, OH how I wish they were, but they won't be. Unless they call me up and say *"I know what's wrong with your kid, bring him here and I'll fix him"*- then i'm just not going to waste my time.

No, not even to your fancy Children's Hospital, the one we have here is pretty damn good. It has saved TWO of my family members thus far, and they turned us away without even a second look. Again, I doubt yours is going to be different. They're going to see that his electrolyte level is fine, that he's gaining weight back, his breathing rate is relatively normal, and they're going to send us home. Point blank. It's procedure, protocol, whatever bullshit term you want to give it. It's going to happen everywhere.

So please, y'all, just give me a break for a little while. I love that you care, but really, i'm just done. My brain and my heart just can't take any more right now.
I've sort of accepted that there really is NO true answer as to why his eating is so erratic. I know it has to do with RSV, either lingering effects or something because of it- but NO doctor is going to try to find out why as long as he's gaining weight- and although some of you think I should just let him not eat for 14 hours and *"eventually he'll get hungry"*- sorry, can't do that to him. Not an option. Not ever going to happen.

All there is to do at this point, is wait for the cystic fibrosis test to prove me right when it comes back negative (and who the hell KNOWS how long that will take if it took them 2 months just to get us in for it), and then watch the doctors scramble because they realize that they're all morons and were thinking

the wrong thing all along.
Ohhh I relish the day!

---

That night I went to bed without a care in the world. After getting out how I feel (even if it wasn't an angry rant per say), I always tend to sleep a little better. I didn't even think twice about the blog. It was no big deal to me and shouldn't have been one for anyone else- that's what I thought anyways. That's the problem with not reading what you've written before publishing it for everyone to see- you can't be positive of how it came out, and it seems to be a trend that my words sounded angrier than I'd intended.

Obviously, others did not agree with my original thought of the blog being harmless, because when I got up the next morning and found time to log on to Facebook- it had exploded with mean and incredibly hateful comments. You'd think I'd burned down an orphanage full of underprivileged infants the night before, it was *that* bad.

Going over the massive amount of damage done to my profile, my heart felt as though it would beat out of my chest. My hands were shaking, mind racing, I went into total panic mode. There must have been ten or more comments stating everything from that I was an "ungrateful bitch" to that I was a "horrible abusive mother." Multiple comments from the same people, just to make sure I got the point.

I've been insulted before, internet drama was nothing new, but never by so many random people all at once, and never so specifically about my choices as a parent. In my mind I went over everything going on in my life, and couldn't figure out what I'd done to deserve to be assaulted by relative strangers. The blog I'd written wasn't personal, what the *fuck* is going on?? Had I woken up in an alternate universe?

There was a recurring theme throughout the comments. Two names kept coming up over and over again. One was the name of the girl who had posted the force-feeding status update the day before, who we will call "Tweedle-Bitch," and the other, whom I didn't really recognize, but for all intents and purposes we will now refer to as "Tweedle-Liar." I knew Tweedle-Liar was from the message board I'd joined for Parker on MomSpace, but as far as I knew, there couldn't have been anything I'd done to offend her. No status wars, no arguments, nothing. As far as my memory served, I'd never even chatted with her before.

Allow me to take you on a trip to crazy town, because from here it just gets more and more bizarre... to the point where you may not be able to wrap your mind around what I'm writing as something that actually ever happened.

As soon as I'd finished erasing the majority of vicious comments from my profile out of horror and embarrassment (leaving a few just for proof of what I was enduring)- I noticed a message in my inbox. There were probably a few, but only one really worth making note of because it was from Tweedle-Liar, who I'd seen mentioned in the majority of comments. Apparently, although I couldn't pick her out of a lineup, and couldn't remember ever having a single conversation with her, the blog I'd written the night before was about her and *only* her. Unbeknownst to me, it was a calculated, deliberate, verbal assault; Who'da thunk?

And she was MAD, oh man was she ever! Tweedle-Liar gave me a piece of her mind, couldn't believe I'd 'written about her.' How rude! How terrible I was! How offending! I'd better watch what I say *or else!*

I scratched my head. Who are you again?

Even if I'd written the blog specifically about anyone- it most certainly wouldn't have been her. Why would she think I would waste my time writing a blog about her, a perfect stranger?

I'd soon learn it was because, to put it simply, Tweedle-Liar was (in my opinion) certifiably crazy.

It turned out *all* the comments were from the same group of people- the Moms from Parker's board on MomSpace. Even the girl we are calling Tweedle-Bitch. I was right that she'd been on the board I joined for Holden, and I was also right that she'd dropped out of that board long ago. What I didn't know was that she'd just so happened to join the one board I had for Parker, because she too had a child his age; what an awful coincidence! Just goes to show you how often I visited that second board. I rarely, if ever, posted there- which made it even stranger that not just one, but a group of girls from that particular board that I didn't know, and who didn't know me, would be attacking me on Facebook so savagely.

Apparently after I responded to that very first comment made by Tweedle-Bitch the day before about force-feeding- and then deleted and blocked her as to avoid drama completely- she and some of the other girls from the board on MomSpace kept the conversation going, all agreeing that I was the world's worst mother for following doctor, after doctor, *after doctor's* advice. I figured they'd just do what I did, delete it and move on. No big deal. It's an internet disagreement, who the hell cares? Let it go and move on with your life, no one's going to even remember this in a week.
Unfortunately for me, it seemed that no one else was of like mind on the subject.

The blog I wrote that night was just the icing on the cake for them. While to me it was totally unrelated to the force-feeding comment made by Tweedle-Bitch, it made the pot-o-crazy boil over.

One mad as hell about the comment, another mad as hell about a blog she'd deluded herself into believing was about her joined forces against me. Tweedle-Bitch and Tweedle-Liar: partners in crime!

I know it sounds totally absurd- it still does to me even typing it today. The story I am telling you is my own personal account of what went down next thanks to a silly little blog and one stupid comment on Facebook. I am going to give you the story as I know it to be, what you choose to believe is up to you.

It didn't stop with just Tweedle-Bitch and Tweedle-Liar. They somehow managed to pull a hell of a lot of other people from MomSpace into it with them, hence the full-frontal Facebook assault. Anyone who "sided" with them was in the clear, while anyone who sided with me was deemed a *"Jenny lover"* and would be attacked almost as enthusiastically as they did me.

Not one of those girls who chose to go to the dark side I could ever remember chatting with a single solitary time- but that didn't seem to matter. I was now public enemy number one, and over what? A Facebook comment and a blog? My mind was reeling, are you kidding me? Is this *seriously* happening? People are *this* crazy??

The answer to that is yes, and they weren't done with me after just one round.

To try and stop the madness, I foolishly responded to the message I had received from Tweedle-Liar.
*That blog wasn't about you. I don't know what you're talking about. Calm down! Leave me alone!*

In response to that, I received a message even more deluded than the first, with a lot more insults that I don't really care to repeat filling it out.
I was done. I don't negotiate with terrorists.

I went through my Facebook account settings and deleted and then blocked any and everyone involved in the 'assault.'

*That should be the end of that!* I thought. What else could they possibly do?

Before I could even calm myself down enough to make my hands stop shaking, more messages began flooding in, only this time they were from women I knew; women from the MomSpace board I was co-host of for *Holden*. Women I considered friends, and who never should have been dragged into this mess for any reason.

*"What's going on on the board?"*
*"Have you checked the board?"*
*"Is any of that true??"*

That sick, sinking feeling in my stomach returned. I didn't have to check the board to know what was happening.
Blocking the mob on Facebook and rejecting their comments from my blog (yes, there were a handful of rather colorful ones) didn't stop the mayhem. Instead, it only seemed to light a fire under their asses.

I'll be honest; I was terrified to log on to MomSpace in fear of what I'd find. What could it *possibly* be now?

Being that I'd become co-host of that board over a year prior, it was somewhat my responsibility to handle and get rid of the drama on it. And I definitely didn't want ladies I had considered friends to be pulled into the ridiculous bullshit being spewed by random people. So I logged on... and what I found was shocking.

Due to the fact that I had not remembered that Tweedle-Bitch was a current member of the board at all, I had made a post about being harassed on Facebook by her, without ever naming names. Another comment I thought was harmless that ended up being used against me. You'd think I was on trial, and unlucky enough to get a group of lunatics and naïve, bored housewives as my judge and jury.

Accusations of *"abusing my power"* were made, comments about how I'd spent my family's money instead of using it to get Parker medical care, you name it- it was said about me. And they all insisted that I be removed as co-host because of these things.

I was shocked before, but now I was absolutely flabbergasted… and pissed. How dare they come to *my* board and lie about me by making assertions of things they have absolutely no idea about.

Yes, I'd spent money here and there on what could be considered frivolous things, but all before Parker ever got sick. None of that even matters though, why the fuck should I have had to justify myself to ANYONE, especially some stranger on the internet? It was absolutely *none* of their business what I or Thomas spent money on.

And abusing my power?? What power, exactly? A co-host of a message board owned by a large company has absolutely no power other than to click the "report" button when drama gets out of hand, and to keep things moving when it gets slow. I didn't have some gilded gavel to pound. I was not a Supreme Court Justice. If I'd had any kind of power whatsoever, those chicks would have gotten smashed with the Ban-Hammer instantly, never to post again;  but all I could do was hit a button, sit back, and hope the posts disappeared.  It was unfortunately out of my control.

Luckily, those *actually* in charge of the MomSpace board we all belonged to did not take kindly to harassment and unnecessary drama. They had many rules in place to keep crap like this to an absolute minimum.

Within minutes, all the posts were gone, and the thread they'd been posted in was locked so that no one else could even respond to it. And from what I understood, all the girls

215

responsible for the upheaval were issued warnings (basically a slap on the wrist.)

I was not happy. I had gone from being panicked and confused, to angry, and was now absolutely LIVID. There's only so much drama I can take without the strong urge to lash out and defend myself.
I was clearly being baited, but I knew my limit for bullshit tolerance was about to be breached.

After the message board drama died down once the suspensions were handed out- even though I'd removed and banned the girls from my Facebook- I still had friends who were "friends" with those girls. Through them, the trickling of more insane bullshit started making its way to me.

Through the grapevine I was told that Tweedle-Liar (the crazy who insisted my blog was about her), was threatening that if I wrote *"one more blog"* about her, she'd report me to CPS (child protective services). As mad as I was about the situation as a whole, I laughed at this comment. She would really call CPS over a stranger's blog? *No way.* No one is that cruel.

I didn't know what to make of what she had been spewing all over the internet, but I certainly didn't believe she would EVER go through with it; and if she did, CPS would never in a million years do anything about it!

That is by FAR the most ridiculous and absurd thing I'd read yet, and by that point, I'd heard a hell of a lot of ridiculous and absurd shit.

This "threat" sounded more like a challenge or a power-play by a desperate drama whore than something that should really concern me; and I don't back down from challenges. You tell me not to do something *"or else"* as though you're my Mommy who's going to give me a good old fashioned spanking if I *dare* defy you… it makes me want to do it even

216

more. She may have been acting batshit insane, but I'd dealt with internet crazies a couple of times before- and they've always been all talk and puffed up chests. No real action, just another immature little girl wanting attention because she doesn't feel pretty or special enough in her real life.

I was too caught up in the drama, too riled up and angry to understand that stirring the pot is *not* something you want to do when dealing with whack jobs making threats, so I called her bluff, and I called it *hard*.


## 3/19/10
# Drama gives me heartburn

Will she? Won't she? That's been the question of the day. Probably the most "anticipated" blog in my blog's history, and not for the right reasons- that's for sure.

And you may be wondering why (although I doubt it).

Ahhh, to wake up this morning, get breakfast out of the way, get Parker down for a nap and to log onto Facebook in the small amount of time I had in between, only to find that a rabid pack of hyenas had completely demolished it with hateful diatribe, lies, and ridiculousness. Definitely what I wanted to see! YAY FOR USELESS DRAMA!!!

My first reaction, always, is just to roll my eyes, call these people idiots, and remove them. I do not need or want drama. I do not need to defend myself to ANYONE. I, as well as 9 doctors and a specialist, plus other mothers who have actually BEEN where I am, agree with what I have done to get food into Parker.

So I did just that; I deleted them, and then I came across the e-

mail. The e-mail of the day! Loaded with insults, insinuations, and assumptions, and the best part- a threat!!! Not even a good threat, but a threat that made me smile nonetheless.
It said something like:
*"And you'd better not write a blog about me tonight or I'll email EVERY ONE OF YOUR FACEBOOK FRIENDS to defend myself!!"*
I literally LOLed.
OH PLEASE!! PLEEAAAAAAAAASE write to all my Facebook friends and 'defend yourself', I would literally PAY to see their responses. It would make for an amazingly hilarious blog!

But don't feel all special or anything, because this blog isn't just about you- it's about the entire group of wackos that spammed my blog and Facebook with lies and bitchery today.
Oh, and *you*- I giggle that you think last night's blog was about you, as if the entire world revolves around you and what you say. Guess what?? It wasn't! Nope, not even slightly!

I'm not scared of any of you! I do not doubt myself for one single second, and if you'd actually BEEN where I am, I think you'd have done the same thing.
Don't believe me? Allow me to QUOTE people who have actually gone through what I've gone through, and am still going through (and don't worry, I won't use names. No one deserves to be FLAMED for caring for a sick child like I have been)

#1: *"I hope by some miracle he wakes up some day and just starts eating for you. I think about him every day. You have gorgeous kids, you're a great mom, and don't let internet drama get you down. I can't say I have any clue what it's like to force feed and I have no clue if I'd be able to do it, but it's not my place to judge or pretend I know best. I just wanted to let you know I support you as a mom and sometimes doctors forget that moms tend to know more than we're given credit. I finally feel like the doctors here are at least listening to us so hopefully you'll find a doctor that will listen."*

#2:
*"I've been thinking about you and Parker a lot this month.
We've been crazy busy with therapy, but I read your blog post.
I also left an encouraging comment for you on the post, but it
got denied I think. :-( Big kudos to you for sticking with it and
ignoring those ignorant people. I STILL have to offer liquids
and solids to my son or he won't take them. First thing in the
morning after sleeping for 12 hours you'd think he'd be
thirsty/hungry - but NO. I get him to drink a measly 3 ounces of
liquids and maybe 10 bites of "solids." And it's like that all day
long. *sigh* I have been where you are and I'm still there and
for people to say you're breaking the bond with your child -
they are SO freakin' full of shit."*

And one more, just for good measure, though I could keep
going
#3:
*"Both of my kids have been incredibly sick this winter. We've
seen H1N1, pneumonia, RSV, Bronchiolitis and stomach flu
within 4 months. Child #1 is on steroids twice a day and that
continues until JUNE because now he all of the sudden has
asthma. Child #2 is on $30 formula, Prilosec and is STILL
spitting up all the time. I question every single day if that's
what is right for them, and I can't imagine being ATTACKED
by other mothers WHO AREN'T DOCTORS. I'm not in your
position Jenny, but I can't imagine that I'd do ANYTHING
different. For what it's worth, I think you're doing a great job. "*

Are you Miss Money Bags, who can afford a BILLION
different doctors opinions, really only telling you the same
thing? Doubtful.
 Hey, I wish we could, but we can't, and I don't care what you
think you know about my financials or what I am or am not
spending money on, you know nothing. Period.

Point blank: if you have NOT been in my situation, you have

219

ABSOLUTELY NO RIGHT to judge me. I don't care what little article you read telling you force feeding is "bad", it kept Parker alive. Yeah, that's right, it sure did. If not that severe, it most DEFINITELY kept him from being in the hospitalized and miserable. As a responsible parent, you really expected me to let it get that bad when I had control over how hydrated he stayed?

And you think i'm a BAD parent because of that? Get a LIFE. Spend more time on YOUR kids instead of on a child and a mother you have NEVER met, and know nothing about other than snippets you've read online.

Do you have a medical license? Have you been to med school? No? Then how in the living hell do you think you're qualified at ALL to tell me what i'm doing "wrong" with my child? The doctors I've seen sure don't think so. All NINE of them have given me pats on the back and told me I am doing the right thing, and to continue doing it until the Cystic Fibrosis test is done and we get an answer on that. Unless you're a qualified doctor, you should NOT be telling people what to do or not to do with their children, I don't give a flying FUCK what YOUR baby is eating. Don't you realize that not all babies are the same? My kid is NOT your kid. *I* decide what is best, along with the doctors we have continually seen to get through this process, and none would EVER agree with the crap you're spewing all over the internet. One day, you're going to end up seriously hurting a child who could benefit from force feeding when they are ill because of your unqualified advice.

Oh, and if you're going to *"report me to the authorities"*- at least get your facts straight, because you've been twisting absolutely everything I've said into one gigantic farce. That's the problem with idiots, they only read the things they can pick apart and twist into what THEY want it to say, and then try to tear you down over it instead of fully reading what you've said and having to admit they're wrong.

There's nothing wrong with being wrong. While I don't THINK Parker has Cystic Fibrosis, I am fully aware it is a possibility, even if only a small one.

So here are the facts, for those of you too lazy to actually READ my blog posts in the past, and instead creating an alternate universe for your own sick enjoyment:

1. Parker was diagnosed with RSV. On that day is when he started refusing bottles for weeks.
2. We were told by both the Children's hospital doctors (three of them) AND 3 doctors at our old pediatrician's office to force feed fluids into him to keep him hydrated, because he was eating absolutely nothing on his own.
3. After that, we were told, *by the doctors*, to set goals in consumption for the day in order to get his weight up.
4. Multiple doctors' visits with a number of different practices, specialists, ALL told us to continue what we are doing, and eventually they believed he would get his appetite back
5. Finally, he seems to be getting better, so we don't force feed unless absolutely necessary, which is only when he has a string of 3 days where he eats NOTHING on his own. You really think i'm just going to LET him not eat and get dehydrated?? THAT would be cause to report to CPS, not actually CARING enough to make sure he stays hydrated.
6. Never ONCE did I say he *"screamed hard enough to get broken blood vessels"*, you need glasses. I said he has broken blood vessels and NEVER screamed hard enough to get them.

Did anyone ever think to ask how often I force feed or why? Nope. All the morons just assumed I still do it every day, all day, even when he's eating just fine on his own because I *"want him to be chubby like Holden"*
That is one of the stupidest things I've ever read. Let me get this straight- me wanting him to gain the weight back that he LOST from RSV makes me a bad parent? It makes me have Munchhausen by Proxy? Are you THAT stupid?? Seriously?? Even though NINE doctors have looked at him and know something is wrong and just don't know what?? Oh my bad, I just want him above the 5th percentile when he was in the **75th**

221

before getting sick; yes, I am a TERRIBLE parent!!!

Get this through your thick skulls- I do not force feed unless
ABSOLUTELY NECESSARY. I DO think it was lifesaving
back when Parker would eat NOTHING. When was the last
time I force fed? DAYS ago. That doesn't mean I won't again. I
ABSOLUTELY will if I feel it's necessary, because he is MY
child and *I* decide what is best, along with the doctors (who
again, all NINE agree with me).

YOU, who have no experience, have no right to tell me that I
am "harming" my child. How do you even have the right to say
things like that? What gives you the authority?

So go ahead, *"print this blog out"* and show it to your doctor,
or to Child Protective Services, i'd love to see them LAUGH
IN YOUR FACE because they actually have serious cases of
negligence to worry about, like babies being punched in the
face, not fed at all, abandoned, or shaken, rather than come to a
loving house where the parents care enough to *not* let their
child dehydrate to the point of hospitalization.

And if he's eating just fine, why do I *"complain"* about him
being sick? Oh, yeah, because he *is*. His breathing never went
back to normal, he sleeps for 11 hours and wakes up and
refuses to eat ANYTHING, and now he has a cough again. So
yes, he IS sick, which ALL NINE DOCTORS can clearly see,
and why they are making us have the CF test. There is very,
*very* clearly something wrong, whether it be the lingering
effects of RSV, or something else related to it- and I swear to
all that is holy, if you say MILK ALLERGY one more time I'll
snap worse than i'm snapping now. You don't think I ASKED
the doctors? You don't think I RESEARCHED it and had him
tested? You're an idiot. It's not a stupid milk allergy.

Remove your head from your ass and see reality. Get over your
ridiculous unwarranted vendetta over a blog that was NOT
ABOUT YOU, and go and take care of your OWN children.

Morons. Yes, I said it, you're MORONS. And if you actually, somehow, make CPS believe I am somehow *"unfit",* I will not hesitate to sue the living shit out of you for defamation. Don't try me.

Wait until your child gets sick for half of their life, won't eat, doesn't breathe correctly, and you take them to as many doctors as you can afford (and by the way, we have over $1500 in medical bills because of all the tests, and that's NOT including the $500 we spent from our FSA and the money out of pocket already spent in under 3 months), and are still waiting on a test that will most likely come back negative, and then see what you do.
You'd freak out, not feed your kid, and they'd end up with a feeding tube down their nose. WAY TO GO, AWESOME PARENT! YOU RULE!!! Sorry I can't be that irresponsible, because I LOVE my child and would do anything to avoid that.

Oh yes! Our bond is SO weak that he was laughing HYSTERICALLY while I was feeding him today, so much so that he couldn't calm down enough to nap and it took 20 minutes to get him to sleep. OH NOES! TOTALLY BREAKING THE MOTHER/SON BOND!!!! LOCK ME UP!!!

So suck it. SUCK IT!! And suck it hard.

Oh,

By the way, hilarious that you claim I *"sit on Facebook aaaaaaallll day"* while you tend to your family, when you're all the ones spamming Facebook with my blog URL and writing me lengthy stupidity filled emails, posting about me on your profiles CONSTANTLY because you're *that* insecure, while I was spending time playing with my little ones, dancing to music, and reading books. Way to go, you super supreme mamas!

223

P.S- PLEASE keep linking people to my blog! Oh yeeessss, I love it! It just makes me more money. Thanks, bitches!

P.P.S.- I know you were all sitting around wasting your Friday night that you could be spending with your oh so special family, so I waited 2 hours after i'd normally post a blog to post this one. Have a good night, morons!

P.P.P.S- YAY name calling! I can be just as low and pathetic as you!

---

Ahem, yeah, I'm shaking my head about that one too. I should have known better, especially with reactions to previous blogs I'd written about specific people. I should have restrained myself- what I did was *stupid*, and i'm not proud of the petty nature of the whole thing. I actually had never gone back and read that blog until I went to put this book together and I am definitely not proud of how I reacted, but put yourself in my shoes for a second- would you really be able to sit back and just take being called an abusive mother over and over again, and not say anything about it?

Then again, most people don't have a public blog to take out frustrations on. Sometimes my blog works to my benefit, and other times I take advantage of it, and that ends up being my downfall.

It's a little bit funny to read back on it now, because I find my own anger hilarious- but at the time I *knew* it was not one of my wiser decisions. I fully expected another Facebook assault, or hundreds of blog comments cursing me out. I however did not expect any follow through on any of the threats I'd received. They all seemed so outlandish, so outrageous, and so low- that I didn't think even the meanest of mommies would do that sort of thing to another.

The next morning was a Saturday morning not unlike any other. We'd finished breakfast and were all just lounging around in our pajamas. Thomas was on the computer, Holden was playing quietly, and Parker was fast asleep in my arms as I sat on the couch watching TV.

I'd zoned out on whatever program was on when I noticed a car pulling up outside of our house, not that it's a totally unusual occurrence, as we live on a corner and people are constantly stopping outside and rarely ever to see us. When I saw this particular car though, I instantly got a bad feeling. The car was white, nondescript, inconspicuously conspicuous, and the driver was shuffling around a bunch of papers- the telltale signs of a city or government vehicle. I tried to shake the thoughts out of my head.

*No way, this can't be happening. It's not possible!*

But as the woman emerged from the car, clipboard in hand, I knew it was true:
That stupid *bitch* really did call CPS on me.

At that moment, all of the oxygen felt like it had been sucked out of the room. I couldn't breathe, couldn't move, I was completely frozen in that place on the couch. All I could manage to do was to call out to Thomas and warn him that CPS was in fact at our home (we'd discussed it when the threat took place and both agreed that it was absolute hogwash.)
He called bullshit, and then the doorbell rang. Thomas got up to answer it, walking by me with a grave look on his now pale face.

The front door wasn't far from where I was sitting, but it was far enough to make it hard for me to clearly hear the conversation taking place right outside. I prayed Thomas would get rid of her and she'd go away. He'd tell her whatever she heard was bullshit... or maybe she was just selling Girl Scout cookies, or trying to get us to switch long distance carriers- and we didn't have a land line, so problem solved!

It was hard to hear over the sound of my heart pounding in my ears, but I made out the words *"Child protective services"*, and *"report"*, and then she invited herself into our home.

Usually in situations where I feel cornered or threatened I get upset and the water works begin. I'm a huge crybaby, and it doesn't take much to get me started. Not this time, there were no tears. In their place was a fiery hate filled rage I'd never experienced before. I wanted to jump off of the couch and scream in her face to get the fuck out of my house. I wanted to kick her in the shins and then tear her head off. I realized she was just doing her job, and in situations such as this you're always told not to shoot the messenger, but there was no justification for her to be standing in my living room, and I was finding it increasingly hard to stifle my anger.

She sat on the couch diagonally to my right after introducing herself, and then told me what I already knew, but didn't want to hear:
*"We received a phone call last night that you are abusing your child by force feeding him?"*
All I could do was shake my head. She was sitting right there but I still could *not* believe it, this was actually happening to me.
*"I know who called you. Not only has she never met me, but she doesn't know me, and she's a liar. She's mad about something I wrote online"*

*"You've never met her?"*

*"No. She is a total stranger. This is crazy. She threatened to report me if I wrote about her. I can't believe this"*

226

That's when the woman informed me that every call made to CPS has to be investigated, no matter how ridiculous (and she agreed the call made on me didn't really add up.) You read that right, *every single call*. If you look at someone the wrong way, they can call CPS on you, tell them that you're feeding your children dog food and rat crap, and CPS will have to go to your house to make sure you aren't.

There are late term "abortion" clinics illegally running for *years* that have been reported time and time again with no investigation, but CPS can come to my house the **next morning** based on one phone call from a person who admitted to not even knowing me?

As nicely as I could, even though I wanted to explode, I let her have it. I started laying into her about how sick Parker had been, and that we were only following doctors' orders, when she stopped me mid-sentence. She had to ask me not only what RSV was, but to define it for her. It became clear to her at that point that she'd been lied to. RSV had never even been mentioned in the call. The caller never even mentioned that Parker was sick at all… so I decided to enlighten her. I gave her the full run down. All the doctors, clinics, and hospitals we'd been to, complete with names, medications he'd been prescribed, and what he'd been diagnosed with.

The look that washed over her face said it all. It was one you might get after being kicked in the stomach. You'd think I just told her that her dog died. You'd think she'd just crapped her pants.
She'd been duped, and she knew it. As far as she knew before coming to my house, I had been force feeding Parker for shits and giggles.
*"I don't think my baby is chubby enough. Let me just shove this formula down his throat! He'll fill out his clothes better! I love chubby babies!"*
Had those morons called CPS and told something even resembling the truth such as:

*"Yeah he's been sick. Nine doctors. We just don't agree! We think we know better and she's doing the wrong thing!"*
They never would have come to my house, and those girls knew that, and made the conscious decision to lie in order to make it happen. Flat out, no two ways about it, lied.

I'm sure it's not the first time the CPS worker had followed up on a false claim that had been made, but not even she could believe how far a perfect stranger had gone in this case. With how many doctors we'd seen, the call was absolutely baseless. *"Well, just be careful what you write on the internet."*
Words to live by, y'all.

After a full minute of head shaking, she then told us that she was going to report back to her manager that it had been a false claim, and *not* to bother us about the subject any farther. If she had *"anything to do with it"*, she said, we'd *"never be hearing from CPS again."*

With that, she was gone... but I was still fuming. So mad, so infuriated, that I must have had steam coming from my ears. Was I relieved that the plan to have Parker taken away had been foiled, and that nothing more would come from it? Absolutely. Words cannot describe how much, but the fact that there had *been* a plan in the first place made my stomach sick. You just don't get any lower than a person who will deliberately lie to try and have a baby snatched from their mother, because she just so happened to offend you. That's bottom dwelling scum-sucking status.

Once I'd composed myself, and Thomas and I had stopped exchanging looks of absolute disbelief- I wanted to jump online and tell anyone and everyone what had just taken place. To me, it was proof that Tweedle-Liar seriously *was* psychotic. But I knew I had to think carefully about my next step after the repercussions of the previous, so after mulling it over, I decided against broadcasting what had just taken place to the world. Did I really want everyone knowing Child Protective

Services had come to my house based on a report of child abuse? It didn't matter that it was a steaming load of horse shit, it was still humiliating.

By that time, I'd been told that there were "moles" on my Facebook; people pretending to be *'on my side'*, even though I'd stayed relatively quiet about the situation from the beginning, that were copying and pasting anything I said in reference to the situation back to their deluded leaders. Did I believe it? Absolutely not, but I took care of the threat by deleting *everyone* from the MomSpace message board that the threats had originated from, minus 3-4 girls who had shown support for me and put themselves on the line to defy the crazies on my behalf.

I couldn't risk any kind of leak, just in case. If those women got wind that CPS had actually come to my house, they'd celebrate victory. If I let them know how upset I was, they'd win. It didn't matter if the CPS worker smelled a lie from a mile away- the fact that they'd even *come* to my house most likely would have fueled the crazy even farther. They'd go on even more of a power trip, and I couldn't let that happen. This had *seriously* crossed the line, and it needed to end.

Aside from a few private conversations, I told no one what had happened that morning. There was no blog, no Facebook rants; I went on absolute radio silence.

It's one thing to fight with someone online who's only slightly crazy (while still pointless), but when you're dealing with a person who has crossed the line to sick, it's time to take a step back and reevaluate what you're doing.

In the act of being honest- I can't tell you that I said nothing at all. That's not exactly the truth- and not my style- but for once I attempted to be sneaky about it. There *may* have been a comment made in passing about nothing important or specific, with a few choice words directed at the girls responsible for all the drama that had suddenly taken up residence in my life. I

229

*may* have called them a name that I had only heard come out of the mouth of a cartoon character before.

Personally, I thought it was funny, and I needed a laugh… little did I know those crazies had been chomping at the bit; just *waiting* for the next thing I wrote that was about them, or that they could *claim* was about them.

I suppose at that point I was still vindictive enough to need to make a stab at them (even if just a silly one), and naïve enough to think it would go unnoticed if it were buried among other normal everyday things. Considering the severe lack of attention to detail they'd already exhibited, it wasn't totally stupid of me to think that they'd read the first few sentences of the blog and lose interest if it wasn't clearly about them… or get distracted by a piece of lint on their shirts. When you're desperate for something to bitch about though, I guess you'll sift through just about anything to find it!

From those silly little words buried deep within monotony, a new message board was spawned.
The members? Anyone who wasn't a *"Jenny Lover."* The purpose? To talk shit about me in a place where it couldn't be reported and they couldn't be punished. You can't make this shit up!
A message board just for talking about lil' ol' me? I'm FAMOUS!
When I learned about it, it was another one of those life moments that was *so* absurd, *so* ridiculous, *so* beyond the realm of ridiculous that I had to laugh and ask *"Is this a dream? How old are we again?"*

Creating a message board for the sole purpose of talking shit about one random internet girl and anyone who supports her reminds me far too much of those "Slam Books" that got passed around in middle school, just to make the insecure feel better about themselves; pathetic and childish.

Although I didn't tell anyone to keep the CPS visit a secret exactly, the few people I did tell knew I didn't want the newly formed *"I hate Jenny"* fan club finding out about it, but as these things tend to do- it slowly leaked to the interweb, and then to them.

My comparison to grade school antics is holding up rather nicely, don't you think?

Would you be surprised if I told you that every girl involved in the attacks on me, including the ringleaders, denied *any* involvement in making that fateful call?
One would assume they'd be giggling maniacally and rubbing their dirty little hands together in glee.
Nope.
Instead they claimed I was either lying... or one of my *real* friends must have called. Not them! Never them! There Jenny goes again, putting the blame on someone else! And because I had no absolute proof, I must then be wrong.

And then it hit me like a ton of bricks, *of course* they wouldn't fess up to it! Not only would they be admitting to filing a false claim with a government agency, but they would in turn become the bad guys of the whole debacle, and they couldn't have that! They had to keep everyone believing that *I* was the bad guy or they'd lose all power over their brainwashed minions.
Here I thought that anyone with half a brain would figure out that if a specific person threatened to make the call (when no one else had ever even had the notion), and then the call was made THAT night- it would be *way* too much of a coincidence for it to have been someone else. Magically, that slipped by the lot of them.

So now, not only was I an abusive parent, but a liar too. Why would anyone who didn't bother to ask me my side of the story from the beginning ever believe me before buying into all the useless drama proclaimed by the crazies originating it in the first place? I had become the perfect target.

To add insult to injury, once they'd heard about the visit CPS made to my house, they started attempting to take credit for every single move I made to further medical intervention for Parker. Appointments we'd been waiting on for over 2 months? That was, according to them, their doing. They had convinced themselves as a whole that everything I did was a direct result of things they had said to me, or because of their threats and actions.

That could not have been any farther from the truth, and I sat and seethed over it for a long time. Wanting to say something, wanting to speak out to tell them just how wrong and incredibly foolish they were forever thinking they could influence my decisions as a parent, but I bit my tongue.

Every time the Tweedles and their band of merry morons pulled something new- I thought I couldn't possibly get any angrier- but I *always* did. It was really starting to boil over inside of me. I was still dealing with a very sick baby, who with all the medical intervention we'd received, still wasn't eating, and whose breathing still wasn't back to normal. With all the appointments and testing and stress related to that- I *really* didn't need their bullshit interfering.

Every time I thought they couldn't do anything else, or that they had to be tired of kicking the same person around (because I definitely wasn't giving them the fight or satisfaction they were looking for)- it had been over a month since I'd showed any kind of rise to their bait- they proved me wrong. Other than a select few, I had still told hardly anyone about all that was going on behind closed doors. I pretended life was normal- not even my family knew.

Crazy knows no bounds and no limits; crazy doesn't realize when the dead horse has been sufficiently beaten.

To further prove how 'wrong' I was, and how the whole world was 'on their side', a rumor I'd heard before once again resurfaced. I had "moles"- very similar to the hideous ones you get burrowing through your yard- people who I was friends with on Facebook who were there for the sole purpose of reporting anything I might say relating to the situation back to The Tweedles. This time, though, they weren't claimed to be from the MomSpace message board since I'd already removed everyone the last go-round. This time they wanted me and everyone else to believe that my real life friends were the ones reaching out to them, supposedly outraged by my actions. Real life friends *and* girls I trusted from Holden's message board. *"You wouldn't believe which of her friends are contacting me!"*

The group that had been slowly growing of females who had banded together against me claimed to know everything I was saying about them at all times. They claimed to have access to my private messages, and all of my private posts. Was any of that true? Absolutely not! I did have a slight panic attack, complete with hyperventilating, sweating profusely, and a nauseated feeling at the thought, and had to make damn sure it wasn't true before being able to continue on with my day.

The ironic thing was- *I* was the one who had access to all of *their* private messages and to *their* private "I hate Jenny" message board. *I* was the one with the mole!

All along they insisted that they were finding out everything I had been saying, when really it was the other way around. They'd tried so hard to recruit people by lying so many times that not even *they* could keep the stories straight anymore. Tweedle-Liar and Tweedle-Bitch basically campaigned against me as if we were running for mommy president- only I wasn't even in the race. I sat back, and for the most part stayed quiet. I never reached out to anyone begging them to take my side like those girls had done. I just didn't feel the need to justify myself to anyone personally. I'd written the blog with my point of view, and I was done. I had no interest whatsoever in groveling for support. In my mind, anyone worth having in my life would come to me and *ask* me before assuming internet rumors to be the truth.

And that's just what a lot of ladies did. Instead of jumping on the drama bandwagon, like anyone who joined the newly formed message board of bitchery, some girls who suspected it was all crap came to me to show their support. There was no begging them to get involved, they sat back just as I was doing. Laid low and went completely unnoticed to the crazies. They stayed friends with them on Facebook, and pretended to be totally oblivious to what was going down- and soon they gained access to the exclusive club for Jenny-haters... and the haters had *no* idea.

You see- I knew they were pulling things out of their asses and making up lies just to get more followers- because I'm me and I think I'd know if I were any of the things they said I was. I knew they didn't have a mole on my Facebook, or on Holden's MomSpace message board. I knew they didn't have any of my friends coming to them- because I knew *everything* they were saying 'behind closed doors.' Every rumor I was hearing down the line was never backed up on their special little board- the naïve girls who had joined were getting fed the same crap as everyone else with no facts to back it up, but it didn't seem to matter to them.

I know what you must be thinking:
*This is absurd! Aren't you just as bad as them for getting so involved?*
But the comparison between them and me stops there. While the Tweedles and their devout worshippers would have used access to my private messages for evil in order to attack me and use everything I may have been saying against me, I wasn't interested in any of that.

I wanted to know if and when there would be another attack so I could fully prepare myself for it ahead of time, and I wanted to know what lies they were concocting and tossing around as fact to make even more people believe I was the terrible person they made me out to be. My interests were in protecting myself and my family from any further damage, and that was it.

I fully realize the ramifications of being able to read all the things being said about me by a number of strangers- it was no walk in the park to see all the nasty things being written, and to read the comments laughing about them, and others tearing me apart as a person. It most likely created more stress for me than if I *didn't* know what was going on, but stupidly I thought that if I knew what the lies were, I could then defend myself by proving it all wrong.

For further protection purposes, I also wanted screen shots of any admission of guilt and any threats made (one girl had already threatened to come to my house.) Another false CPS report was not going to go unpunished, and maybe a little perk of the insider's access was watching them squirm when things meant to be kept secret that they'd talked about on their special little board were suddenly public knowledge. Reading their freak outs when yet another one of them got unexpectedly banned from the MomSpace message board we'd all joined together so long ago was pretty damn satisfying, I must say.

While all of that may have been amusing, it wasn't all fun and games. There were some serious lies being put out there. After everything that had already happened, I didn't think anything they did from then on could surprise me anymore. Disgust me and make me lose hope for the human race? Yes. Surprise me? No. A visit from Child Protective Services on claims of abuse is some heavy shit, how could it get much more insane? Once again, I underestimated the level of crazy.

I have to give credit where credit is due, those girls were certainly… *determined.*

Posts talking shit and making fun of not only anything I'd done, said, or blogged, but about a good number of other Moms as well; every kind of insinuation you can imagine. Drug use, bad parenting, getting girls to join and then attempting to make their lives hell if they left; it was open season, and anyone who didn't join them or agree with them was prey. Those that said anything negative about "all the drama" had just slapped a blinking target on their backs. Joining that board was like joining the mob; when you're in, you're in- but the boss is this boss. If you're out- you're out; you're dead to them.

Mostly it was a lot of squawking and snarky comments, but there were also plans of attack against the MomSpace board. Plans for those who had been banned to get new IP addresses so they could create a new account (a big no-no) just to post, yet again, about the drama they'd been warned multiple times to stop talking about, only to find themselves once again banned.

It sounds like some huge paranoid schizophrenic conspiracy plot. When you stand back and look at the list of offenses thus far, it sounds made up, like the plot to some grown-up version of Mean Girls. It doesn't seem like it could possibly have been that devious or purposeful. This is a group of grown women we're talking about.
I wouldn't believe it either had I not gone through it myself. I never could have imagined people were this, to put it nicely, cruel, or that anyone could get SO hung up on pointless drama to take something so far... but it happened. No exaggerations necessary.

The newest 'tactic' of sorts appeared to be digging into my past, twisting what they found until they could turn everything I'd ever said into a complete fabrication on my part... 'Cause lying is bad, y'all!

According to the Tweedles, Holden never had reflux, my Mom never had Polycystic Kidney Disease, and I never had genetic testing done while pregnant to make sure that Parker didn't. How did they prove this was a lie? Well, because I never brought it up on the MomSpace boards again after the tests came back negative. Never mind the fact that I rarely posted on that board in the first place, or that I wrote numerous blogs about it; I didn't run back and immediately make a post about it, informing them of the results, so that MUST mean it was a lie!

The months Holden spent in agony due to reflux suddenly became a figment of my imagination because I *"stopped talking about it."* That *had* to be because I made it all up just for attention! Couldn't possibly be that we found a medication that worked and then, like 99% of all kids with reflux, he grew out of it.

These were all things that could have been discarded as the rantings of a delusional bitch with just a little common sense, but I think at that point, mob mentality had kicked in and finding out the truth for themselves meant nothing to any of the girls on the Tweedles' board. They *wanted* to be a part of the clique, wanted to have something to bitch about, and wanted to believe that I was all the things being said- because that would justify how horrible they were acting- so they did without question.

Although I never visited the *"I hate Jenny"* message board myself, and adamantly refused to return to the MomSpace board we'd all once been members of because the drama there never seemed to die down, I did see a hell of a lot of screenshots (pictures captured from a computer screen) from the friend who had gained entry to their private club of what was being said about me, and a lot more information passed to me by those privy to comments made via Facebook. Wouldn't you know it- they were all the same; one pesky term being repeated over and over again.

*Munchausen's by Proxy*

Yes, apparently I have it. Not only are the Tweedles smarter than a multitude of pediatricians, specialists, and children's hospital emergency room doctors- but now they're psychologists too!
Can they also control the weather and turn water into wine? Should I send them a spool of thread so they can spin it into gold?

It was all bordering God complex territory if you ask me.

*We decide how you take care of your child, and we know what is wrong with him because we know EVERYTHING! We will run your life and if you have a problem, we will TELL you what it is! Now bow down to us and our superior brain power!*

Yeah, I really somehow managed to fake a positive RSV test and paid off 9 doctors to all come to the *same* exact conclusions, AND got them all to tell me to force fluids!
OR- maybe I made it all up because I am mentally ill, and so desperately crave the attention that I'll get it by any means necessary!
Better yet: Holden and Parker don't even exist! I am a total and complete fake! I'm actually a 56 year old morbidly obese man with no children and twelve cats, sitting in front of a computer, stealing pictures of other people's kids, and passing them off as my own, because I have nothing better to do now that my ass skin has grafted to this chair!

Any of those things being true would have made them happier than pigs in shit, I'm sure.
Unfortunately for them, none of it was. And unfortunately for me, once again, they got to me. I was beyond pissed. More times than I can count, I drafted up a huge blog post letting them have it. Pages and pages worth of anger I'd held in for so long over the past weeks, while trying to be the bigger person about the situation. For once I didn't hold back, I didn't want to anymore.  I wanted them all to know exactly what I thought of them and just where they could stick their lies.

I never posted any of those blogs, I always decided against it. No matter how badly I wanted to, it would have been simple just to press the *'post'* button, but what good would it do? Nothing I'd said before ever helped, it just gave them new material to twist around, and I'm sure a curse word filled rant wouldn't do anything but make things worse. I couldn't even imagine how it could get worse than it already was- so I bit my tongue... again.

One with a rationally thinking mind would assume the story *has* to end there. Since I said nothing, and hadn't said anything in quite some time, Tweedle-Bitch, Tweedle-Liar, and all their devoted followers *had* to be bored enough to move on by now. They must have found some other unsuspecting Mother to torment relentlessly.

Remember- we left the land of rationality *long* ago, what kind of antagonists would they be if they didn't keep the drama going for absolutely no reason??

What purpose it served or good it did to continue this mess, I will never know, it just never got old to them. If the Tweedles were bored, it was easy enough to come up with something new to keep things interesting in order to keep other girls coming back for more. Without drama, they had absolutely nothing to offer.

For a while, I'd just been seeing screenshots of message board banter, and things passed down the line to me that had been said, all of which was annoying, but at that point, nothing new, when one day a message popped up from a friend of mine (one who had thought to be 'on their side', I'm assuming this is who they thought was their mole... sure wasn't!) that contained a strange statement.

*"Tweedle-Liar told me that you told her that you hope her baby has autism, and that she'd deserve it."*

I think I may have crapped my pants a little at that very moment. Of all the horrible things that you could say to someone, that is near the top of the list... And I hadn't said it!

How could I have? I hadn't spoken to Tweedle-Liar since...
well, *ever* that I could recall. I had blocked her from day one,
and made a point of not speaking to *anyone* involved at all
from that point on. No messages, no stupid Facebook comment
wars- I wanted no part in it... so how exactly did I make that
comment to her?

Upon being prodded for more information, the only answer my
friend received left a lot to be desired, and even more
confusion:
*"Oh, well I heard it from someone, but I can't say who."*
Seriously? People were gullible enough to buy that? Any idiot
on earth could come up with a better back story than that.
That is what she was using to get people on her side? Really?
I'd wondered for so long how Tweedle-Liar kept convincing
new people to join her stupid little board- but I couldn't believe
what I was reading.
Shit, I'd probably hate me too in that case... if I could actually
bring myself to believe a pathological liar with absolutely no
proof to substantiate her claims; I like to think I'd know better.
By nature I am a skeptical creature. If there aren't hard facts
and an enormous amount of evidence to back something up,
there's little to no chance I'll believe it. That's why we hadn't
been satisfied with the opinion of one, or even nearly a dozen
doctors, I needed solid proof. The flimsy story getting passed
around to back up the autism comment I had supposedly made?
That would *not* have cut it for me. It's just too bad other ladies
aren't nearly as questioning about something so serious as I
am.

Trust me, yet again, I wanted to snap. It would be a well-
deserved blog-lashing. I can toss around some hefty insults
when I'm angry enough, but saying that I hope a child has
autism is nothing I would ever even DREAM of saying, or
even thinking. Doesn't matter who the person is, or how much
I loathe them. I can be a bitch, a BIG one, I'm but not sick.

Try as I might to ignore to comment and move on, it just wouldn't go away. It's like that guy in the bar who just can't take no for an answer.

*Can I buy you a drink? Do you wanna dance? Are you sure I can't buy you a drink? Your husband can't satisfy you like I can!*

DUDE, just back off!

The more I heard that I had made this comment from a plethora of sources, and knowing that people were so easily buying into it, I had to laugh. What else could I do? It seemed that with each time the story was told, it changed a little bit depending on who Tweedle-Liar told it to. First she heard it from someone else, then it was through Facebook message... it was perpetually morphing.

And still, none of her minions picked up on the constant changing of story, even though they'd all been told something different just to hook them in. I found it somewhat sad that girls who seemed to be level headed and normal would believe her so easily. A couple of the girls who were the angriest about the supposed comment had even admitted to a mutual 'friend' that they had never even read my blog. Not even once. They listened to their crazy leader as if what she said were the direct voice of God, no questions asked.

Regardless of internet drama, life still had to go on as usual, as did my blog. I continued in my attempt to ignore it; I even attempted to find it funny. I took care of the boys, Parker just as sick as ever, and wrote blogs as though nothing out of the ordinary was going on in the background. Most of my friends to this day still do not know the full extent of what happened during those months. Keeping it quiet seemed like the most mature way to go about things, and I still honestly believed that if I said nothing, the Tweedles would *have* to just give up.

Time passed, and the autism comment still just wouldn't go away; even though months had gone by without me saying a word. And now it had changed from me saying it to some

241

random person and being passed along to Tweedle-Liar, to me actually *calling* her and leaving a voice mail telling her I hoped her kid had autism. It was totally fucking ridiculous, and I just couldn't bite my tongue any longer without drawing blood. If you're going to hate me, that's fine- but at least hate me based on truth and not some absurd make-believe fantasy created by a power hungry psychopath. I had to set the record straight for my own peace of mind, even though I was warned it wouldn't do any good, and from experience knew that to be true. When I hit my breaking point, not even logic and reason can seem to keep me from blogging. I couldn't contain my anger anymore. The affliction, exhaustion, appointments, incredible amount of lies- *four months'* worth of it- was all too much for one person.

It's like a sick addiction: You try to be the bigger person by staying away from it, but sometimes you just fall off of the wagon.

Like a compulsion to pick a scab, you know it's there- it's itching and bothering you- and while you *know* that if you just leave it the hell alone for long enough, it will heal- you just can't resist the urge to pick at it. And I am a habitual scab-picker.

## 4/14/10
# I had this all planned out

And then the screaming started and didn't end. Now my whole wonderful blog post I had outlined in my head is gone. Funny how a screaming child can completely blank your mind out.

Even if I could remember everything I wanted to type, I don't think i'd be in a good enough mood to type it. To be funny, you either have to be REALLY ticked, or really happy. I'm just done. Done is not a funny blog post. Done is an angry blog post; big difference.

Lately I've been holding back a little bit around here because of internet drama, and other than poking fun, I personally like to stay out of it. I've been harassed, lied about, and torn apart all for the amusement of others- and I haven't said a word. It just hasn't been worth my time to fully address the ridiculousness of the situation.

It's really easy to talk shit when you can hide behind a computer screen. Let he who is without sin cast the first stone.

People seem to think they're better than everyone else, know better, and are more knowledgeable on ALL subjects. I still won't address the situation in full, because it's still not worth it. I thought if I just let it be long enough, these people would get bored and move on to harassing someone else, but it didn't work that way.
I do have ONE thing to say while i'm on the subject though, one thing that bothers me enough to clear up.

There's this pesky little rumor about me supposedly making some comment about some girl I don't even know's child, and "*hoping*" the kid "*has autism*" and "*she'd deserve it.*"
I thought it was a joke at first, sort of like I thought the whole CPS thing was a joke. I might not like a parent, but the LAST thing i'd do is talk shit about their kid. Especially when it comes to autism, considering I have family members who are autistic, and friends who have autistic children, that is not my style. My style is more to wish herpes on someone- an adult; *never* a child. And i'd word it "the clap"- but I didn't. I've said nothing to anyone.

I asked where all these rumors came from, and heard that Tweedle-Bitch, who was the one claiming I said it about her child *"heard it from someone else, couldn't say who,"* and once she realized people were questioning that, considering I have

243

screenshots of all the lovely things she and others have said about me, changed her story. Now suddenly the comment was made via voicemail.

At that point I just had to chuckle to myself in a state of disbelief, it's that absurd. I'd like to hear this supposed voicemail, but I bet either it's 'deleted', or sounds nothing like me; funny how that works. Would you like to see my phone records? Or would that not be enough, because then someone would claim I made the call from a pay phone, as if those even exist anymore. The absurdity goes on and on.

I realize that saying all of this won't help anyone who is already "against" me to realize that they've believed a bunch of horseshit from the very beginning. Most people are far too stubborn or prideful to admit when they're wrong, or just want someone to tear apart to make themselves feel better- but I felt like it needed to be said.

No, the autism comment was **never made**. Never happened. Would never happen.

Do I care if you disagree with my choices as a parent, and the fact that I chose to follow 9 doctors' orders? No, not at all. I did what was right not only in my opinion, but in the opinions of all the doctors we have seen. If that's not what you would do in my situation, that's you- not me.

BUT- to only be roped into this ridiculous unnecessary drama by a big fat fabricated lie (and not just twisted truth like everything else that's been spewed all over the place lately)? That's just stupid and idiotic to me. I like proof before deciding. I like saying "Screenshot or it didn't happen!" Clearly others don't.

I'm sure this will give those who feed and thrive off of drama just one more thing to bitch about, and I don't really care. Me NOT saying anything didn't help, so why not speak my mind? Oh, and just an FYI: you can't tell if your child does or does not have autism at 6 months old. So the little karma comment implying that *my* kid would end up with autism doesn't exactly apply, expert. Not only because I didn't ever say it, but because it isn't diagnosable until 18 months of age. Sad to make those claims about your own child, clearly she must be worried about it herself to say that other people are wishing it on her kid when they aren't.

So believe what you want, even if there's proof to the contrary, even if you know deep down it isn't true. That's on you, not me. I have zero guilt about anything I've done; I hope you can say the same at the end of the day.

Back on subject- i'm not going to be scared to post about Parker anymore. I've done nothing wrong. I'm doing everything possible to get him help. Unfortunately, everything possible just isn't enough.

He's yet again decided that bottles just aren't for him, and every day for the past 4 days he's eaten less and less- when he was on the verge of being 100%. This includes solids. Fruit? Every single one but mango gets puked back up. Veggies? Although his stomach seems to tolerate them- he's been refusing those lately too, or puking them up.

The first thing we did was to call the doctor, who finally called back only to say she wouldn't see him for another week of refusing bottles. Way to go, Doc. If he keeps going at the rate he's going, he'll be back to eating absolutely nothing by that point, and lose all the weight he's gained (that is already being bitched about by the doctor), and we'll be back at square 1. I can't see how that's acceptable, so once again, we're going to try and make an appointment with the GI without a referral. I don't know what good it will do, but I want EVERY test ran… *again*. After almost 4 months of being "sick", something eventually has to come back positive. I don't know what that will be, but I know *something* isn't right.

Tonight Parker decided that he'd only eat a half an ounce before bed and that would be sufficient- and that's when I got

to my breaking point…with everything. There's only so much one person can take, there's only so much one BABY can take. Something's gotta give here, and without *more* medical intervention, it isn't going to be Parker.
Let's just hope it isn't more time and money wasted and no answers. I'm so sick of no answers.

I'm just frustrated, and i'm done. Nothing I seem to do is the right thing according to certain other people, and although Parker might be better for a week, he just ends up reverting back to "sick" all over again. Why? I don't know. I need to know, HE needs to know. He is almost 7 months old and has been sick for over half of that. It's just not right.
And if you don't like how I've handled it thus far, shove it. No one's forcing you to read my blog, and if you just want to tear it apart and make fun of me, and make assumptions and accusations- then you shouldn't be reading it in the first place. Get a life. Preferably your own and not mine.

That blog I thought for sure would follow suit with all the others I had written that so much as alluded to the drama unfolding in private, but it didn't. There was no huge uproar, no real backlash… but it didn't do anything to help the situation either.

By that point though, none of the *"I hate Jenny"* club even bothered reading my blog anymore. Everything their evil overlords told them was instantly accepted as the truth and nothing but the truth; The Tweedles must have been drunk off of the power! That whole bitch board had ventured so far into fantasy land that it was almost like they weren't even talking about me anymore. It turned into a character they created based on me, and had kept making up new comments, and new lies to keep the drama going, just to have *someone* or something to bitch about. That's a pretty sad existence.

The drama did finally die down, at last, almost 4 months after starting. That's not to say they let it go though. The *"I hate Jenny"* board is still up and running (last I heard), and while I'm sure that I'm still occasional fun fodder for the masses, the girls that are still members have moved on to making fun of and criticizing others. If it wasn't me, it was obviously going to be someone else. People like that always have to have someone to belittle.

Their antics got the majority of them banned from the MomSpace message board because they just could *not* stop talking about the situation like everyone else had months ago, and had been told to over and over again by the powers that be. At one point, they were all whacked out enough to claim that they were suing for *"violation of their constitutional rights"* over their bannings. No, I'm not kidding.
C-R-A-Z-Y, I don't think it will ever fully end. As long as there's something to disagree with, I'm sure those "women", if you can call them that, will be lurking in dark corners to find it. I have just gotten to the point where I don't care anymore. It took a long time to get there, but it feels damn good.

A funny thing to mention: Tweedle-Liar has since claimed that *other* people have made the infamous autism comment to her. Anyone she doesn't like- she'll say called her kid autistic. In reality, she's the one who seems to think so. It appears that she is *so* desperate to categorize her child as such, just for the attention it brings. Now who is the blatant case of Munchausen's by Proxy? Hypocrite much?

What made me the most upset, and the most sick to my stomach about the whole ordeal, was that the girls from the board-o-bitches claimed everything they did was in the *"best interest of Parker."* All for him and for his health, because they personally didn't think what I was doing was right- but anyone with half a brain could tell it had *nothing* to do with him from the very beginning. Their actions made that more than clear.

They used my baby as a weapon against me, as an excuse to attack me; that absolutely disgusts me.

Had I been the "abusive" parent Tweedle-Liar insisted I was, why threaten me with a call to CPS if I wrote *"one more blog"* about her?
Wouldn't you call immediately, regardless of what anyone said in defense if you thought a child was in real danger?
It was, in reality, nothing more than retaliation against me for not backing down. It was a sick, twisted form of payback. In their minds, attempting to have a stranger's baby taken from them based on ill-placed anger and lies over a stupid blog post and one Facebook comment was a fitting punishment.

 I should have let it go from the very beginning. I never should have written the blogs or responded to any comments, and instead just let them stew in their own pot of pathetic bitchiness, but when you fuck with my family, when you go so far as to try and have my baby taken away from me because you're mad about a damn BLOG I *supposedly* wrote about you? Then you deserve to be stood up to. There was no way I could sit and do nothing; the mama bear came out and it couldn't be stopped!
I got so angry so fast, so caught up in the heat of the moment, that I didn't see the booby-trap I was walking straight into. I let my emotions get the best of me when I should have taken a step back, re-evaluated the can of worms I would be opening by getting involved at all, and walked the fuck away.

So I did what I did- immature or not- it happened. I take part of the blame for egging the whole dumb situation. Had I not responded in the first place, things may have turned out much differently; but with all that said, I still believe they deserved a hell of a lot more than some colorfully worded blogs. To attack and harass a stranger on Facebook and message boards, call CPS on them with false accusations of child abuse, start a new message board just to talk shit about them, and then continue to terrorize them and make up despicable lies for *four* months; to do all of that, starting because of one Facebook comment and a blog… You tell me, does the punishment *really* fit the "crime"?

Had I known then what the consequences would be for throwing a little salt on the fire, poking the crazy with a stick, I absolutely would have done it all differently. I never would have replied to Tweedle-Bitch's first comment, never would have written any of the blogs… I probably never would have joined the MomSpace board at all.

To this day I still wonder the real reason this all happened and went as far and for as long as it did. Looking back, it doesn't seem like it really had anything to do with me at all. Those who love drama don't need reasons; just one excuse and they can make a fight out of just about anything. For Tweedle-Liar, the ringleader of the pack? I can only speculate, but to me, it was a desperate cry for attention, and the way she did that was by always playing the victim card.
*"She wrote the blog about me!"*
*"She's lying about me to her friends!"*
*"She called my kid autistic!"*
Maybe the chick just needed to get laid- badly; maybe she needed an extended stay in a white padded room; who knows! There's just no logical reason it should have ever gone so far and gotten so personal. There's unquestionably no excuse for it.

I'm most likely putting myself on the line by even writing this chapter. I wouldn't be surprised at all to receive more threats and another visit from CPS that later would be claimed that I *"made up"*, but I felt strongly enough about the subject matter of this story to put it all out there, no holds barred.

I think it's important to know that bullying doesn't *just* happen to school-age children. Adults, moms especially, are just as bad, and just as guilty of it. I know more women than I can count who have been bullied, stalked, and harassed online by other moms. None had it go as far as to have CPS called on them, thank goodness, but that's not to say it isn't happening out there.

Despite all of what happened, nothing anyone said *ever* influenced my decisions as a parent. I never believed anything the Tweedles or their board members said, and never took any of their advice, because it was all so preposterous to me. Contrary to their beliefs, their opinions meant nothing to me. Time they all could have, and should have been spending with their young children, was instead wasted on me, and for nothing.

During and after all the drama died down, my family was still going to more doctors to try and find a solid answer for what was going on with Parker. Even after his breathing problems subsided, he still never went back to eating normally. We went to a Pulmonologist for his breathing issues while those were still going on, and that didn't seem to help. We had already switched pediatricians, and it didn't make a difference. We had to wait two months just for a Cystic Fibrosis test that turned out to be only for insurance purposes, and not because they actually thought he had it (way to stress me out even more!), that of course turned out negative.

It wasn't until we gave up on the doctors we'd been seeing for months and bypassed the referral method, and booked an appointment with a GI doctor ourselves, that we got any kind of solid answers as to what was going on with Parker. After blood tests that showed an enlarged spleen that ended up being nothing, followed by an ultrasound that turned up nothing, to elevated liver enzymes that came back as, you guessed it, *nothing*, it finally got to the point where there was nowhere left to go but to just TRY a medication and see if it worked.

The only option at that point was to assume it was a condition called *"Delayed Gastric Emptying"* which by definition is:

*"A medical condition consisting of a paresis (partial paralysis) of the stomach, resulting in food remaining in the stomach for a longer period of time than normal. Normally, the stomach contracts to move food down into the small intestine for digestion."*

In layman's terms, that means that Parker could never digest what we were getting into him, causing him to never be hungry because his stomach couldn't properly empty. In turn he would puke up what had been in there, sitting for hours on end (which may have also had something to do with reflux). The medication he was given that was nothing more than an educated guess by his new GI doctor ended up working; he started eating more and puking a lot less.

All the bitching from the random internet girls, all the insistence that they were right and that they knew better than all the doctors we'd seen…
*It was a milk allergy! It was all reflux and we'll laugh when we are proven right! Just let him get hungry and he'll eat!* They were *all* wrong; dead wrong. Every single last one of them- though I'm sure they'll never admit to it.

Don't get me wrong, I didn't write this story out to discourage any Mom from blogging. Quite to the contrary- not only do I believe blogging to be beneficial to any mom's sanity- but I still recommend that everyone write one, public or private, it helps!

What I meant for this chapter to be is a cautionary tale. While I don't believe *at all* that what happened to me will happen to every Mom that decides to start her own blog about her day to day life with her child/ren (I'd like to think that it happens to *no one* else, I wouldn't wish those bitches on even my worst enemy), the point is- when it comes to writing a blog that's open to the worldwide web, it's extremely important to be careful.

Careful about what you say, how you say it, and who you may be saying it to.

I joined the MomSpace message board of Moms with babies born in the same month as Parker for support, just like every other mom who joined, and because I thought that being in contact with those who might be going through the same thing at the same time as me would be beneficial, and would comfort me if I were ever in need of guidance or help- and look at what I got in return.

# Part 3:
How to avoid being attacked by internet crazies

Writing an open and public blog means open to interpretation by the public; you just never know how someone else might read what you've written, and what kind of context they may take it in.

Most people that attack others on the internet are nothing more than bored morons, with no life and astonishingly low self-esteem on an e-power trip. It's incredibly easy to be mean, judgmental, and threatening when you're sitting at a desk behind a computer monitor and no one can see you or confront you. They never usually have any intention of following through on any of the threats they may make; it's all puffery. But in some cases, there *are* legit, balls to the wall, certifiably insane, padded room necessitating, batshit crazies- and it's important to keep that in mind. You never know who they are, what will set them off, or how far they could be willing to go to ruin a complete stranger's life.

I'm not some internet celebrity. My blog isn't even that popular when you look at the numbers to be totally honest. I'm just a mom who happens to write a brutally honest blog about my life, who got caught up something I couldn't control, and couldn't stop no matter what I did.

Moms are some of the meanest, pettiest people you will ever come across on the face of the earth. Not all mind you, but in my experiences on message boards and my blog, they beat high school drama by about 34 *thousand* miles.

253

Hard to believe, right? I really hate to burst that bubble. Moms are their own special breed of bully, especially on the internet where anyone can say anything they want without consequence or punishment. They aren't some prim and proper, hair neatly tucked away in a bun, jello-mold making, current Stepford version of Doris Day or Carol Brady. I don't know *any* moms like that. If someone who is now a mother was a bitch back in her high school heyday, chances are more than a little likely that becoming a mother did nothing to change that. I have good reason to believe kids just made the bitches *bitchier* and the crazies crazier.

In hindsight, I should have walked away from the situation I went through from the very beginning and never said a single word, because everything I went through was *so* not worth me attempting to stand up for myself to whacked out internet Moms who didn't give a shit about what the truth actually was. They just wanted someone, *anyone*, to attack. Facts didn't matter, and I wasted my time even trying to defend myself.

As the saying goes: Hindsight is 20/20.
Now I definitely know better, and can hopefully help to stop this kind of thing from happening just by telling my story, and advising you of what NOT to do when faced with a similar situation.

# 1. Don't take it so seriously

What you need to remember is that no matter what someone may say or how much it bothers you, ANYONE who will take time out of their day (that they should be spending, oh... I don't know... taking care of their kids?) to stalk, harass, lie about, and torture perfect strangers over the internet is a fucking PSYCHO, a total and complete loony toon. That type of person should be laughed at and probably medicated, not

cried over. Don't even take what they say with a grain of salt.
Don't take it at all! Crazy is as crazy does.

## 2. You will always be wrong

If step 1 doesn't feel satisfying enough for you to walk away
from the situation unfolding, and you feel the need to defend
yourself- DON'T! Step away from the computer! It doesn't
matter if you've seen 10 doctors, 100 doctors, or even if you
have a damn PhD yourself. That whacked out internet mom
who just so happened to be a nurse in a past life and has blown
14 kids out of her crotch, and now makes a living siphoning the
state's welfare funds to buy high priced swing sets will
*ALWAYS* know more than you. No matter what you say, no
matter how much solid proof you have, she will *always* be
right. Trying to prove her wrong will end up completely futile.
Trust me.

## 3. Ignore, remove, and block

Once you find your Facebook, MySpace, blog, *whatever,* is
exploding with hateful diatribe, block any and all those
responsible. Don't blog about it, don't comment on it, and
don't respond to it! That not only fans the flame by angering
the wackadoodles harassing you, but it gives them exactly what
they wanted in the first place- a rise out of you.
You're just handing them more they can use against you. By
responding at all, you're giving them the ammunition to load
their guns. It's high school all over again, and it's not worth the
time you'll spend typing out a response that won't get read for
factual content, but twisted around instead and then thrown in
your face. Just don't do it.  There's no reasoning with the
unreasonable. There is no place for reason in the mind of a
crazy.

# 4. Contact the authorities

It may sound absolutely ridiculous, and you might even feel silly or stupid, but if ignoring the bitches and subsequently blocking them doesn't work, if it's worse than that and they threaten your real life? Call the police!

No, seriously, do it. More laws against internet bullying are being passed all the time, because as time goes on, it becomes more and more frequent.

Perhaps the police won't be able to do anything to help you, but if you honestly feel that your life is threatened and that strangers on the internet have gone WAY too far- it's worth looking into.

File a harassment charge, get a restraining order; even if you know you'll never go through with the charges in a court of law, maybe it will be enough to stop whoever is doing the harassing from running their stupid mouths and making your life a living hell.

When kids start bullying each other there's always a parent or teacher in a position of authority over them to put a stop to it. They'll get threatened with suspension, grounding, or losing things they cherish. When it's an adult doing the bullying, who's going to stop them? You can't exactly run to your Mommy and tattle, who will then make an angry call to *their* Mommy, and then their bratty little ass gets swatted. It's just not that easy, there's not one specific person you can turn to that you know will get rid of your pesky problem. Those who choose to bully in adulthood get crazy with power, because it seems like there is *nothing* anyone can do to stop them. You can't ground a 30 year old woman, they're practically invincible.

The only way to go, the only *place* to go that has power over adults is the police.

Going to any means, even extreme ones, is absolutely worth if it avoids you having Child Protective Services come to your house because of lies told to them by strangers, or having some psychopathic delusional bitch showing up on your front step with a shank fashioned out of a crusty old toothbrush, ready to stab you in the throat *"Cuz you's not a good mom!"*

# 5. Retaliation

Heed my warning: DON'T DO IT! If the woman, group of women, or even a man have gone far enough for you to even consider involving the authorities- retaliating will most likely open up the gates of hell on your ass. No matter how low you attempt to sink in order to attack them on their own level, they can and will *always* sink lower. They can always get crazier- and if you attempt to push- they will push back even harder. The last place you want to be when the apocalypse begins is circling the bottom of the bitch drain.

I know how satisfying it can be to tear into anyone who may have been giving you a hard time, and they absolutely deserve it! But that warm and fuzzy feeling of vindication coursing through your veins will be short lived, and not even close to worth it once your harasser catches wind and starts the next round of madness.

I had many offers from friends to make retaliatory CPS calls against those who had called them on me… and while I'd have paid to see the looks on their faces once they got a knock on their doors- I cringe to imagine how much worse that would have made things. Plus it's illegal to file a false claim (when you know the claim you're making is false, ya hear that??). Trouble with the law? No thank you.

Take a step back and a few (or a lot of) deep breaths, and remember you are *not* as pathetic or insane as anyone who may be attacking you, so don't act like you are! It's easy to play the victim card, even if you have every right to do so, but that doesn't mean that it's worth it, or that you should. Don't sink to their level, no matter how hard they bait you to do so! Be the bigger person and just walk away. Believe me, you'll live to regret it if you don't.

# 16 Life after Bitches

Throughout the whole e-stalking debacle, I had both friends and family telling me that maybe I should just take a break. *Stop blogging! Step down as co-host of the MomSpace board! Just lay low for a while, let it blow over!*

If I wasn't writing anything online, the crazies wouldn't have any place to attack me. After all the drama, the emotional rollercoaster I'd been riding, and stress I'd been through from the time Parker got sick until the time it died down, over three months of straight bullshit and being kicked repeatedly, I can't say it wasn't an attractive idea. Each time it was brought up, I considered it. How wonderful silence would have been!

In the end, I decided against throwing in the towel. The blog? The board? Those were important things in my life, things I worked hard for and on, dedicated and had devoted myself to. They were things I loved and depended on for support and sanity, why the hell should I have to give them up because a group of strangers on the internet decided to collectively get their panties in a bunch and go completely batshit crazy on me?

If I walked away from my blog and my board- wasn't I giving them exactly what they wanted? Even if I refused to participate in the game they were playing the whole time it was going on, wouldn't giving up essentially be letting them win? Each time I considered taking a hiatus from my online commitments, I had to consider even harder the consequences doing that would have on my life.

Already knowing full-well what that group of girls was capable of, letting them beat me into submission would probably make them feel justified and even higher off of their ridiculous power trip.

*We've won! We beat her! Now let's move on and do even worse to someone else, just to feel like we've won one pathetic thing in our empty lives!*
The reign of terror would only continue, and I certainly wasn't going to let it be because I folded under the pressure.

Most people would have given up and walked away- and for *damn* good reason! Who would still want to blog or post anything on a message board or even Facebook after that?

Me! That's who. Just like my typical stubborn self, I wasn't backing down this time. The blog would stay up, and I'd keep posting on Holden's MomSpace board. It was mine, damnit, I'd been pushed enough. They'd tried to take my kid away and failed; no way in *hell* was I letting them take anything else.

Everything went back to business as usual- finally- It had to. Yes, I was still upset about the past 4 months of my life, and getting back to feeling even relatively 'normal' took some time.

Every time a car pulled up outside from that fateful day until months later, my stomach would drop. I will admit I was slightly paranoid, just waiting for the sky to fall again; wondering if and when the next round of shenanigans would begin- but was I going to let them see that fear and feed off of it like a bunch of flies chasing a cow with shit hanging from its ass? No way in hell.

Contrary to what the members of the *"I hate Jenny"* message board may think, they did nothing to change my life or how I parent... at least not how they had been aiming to. I'll never know the complete reason behind the attacks, but it all gave the impression that they wanted my child snatched, my emotions ruined, and mind in shambles; none of that happened. If anything, I am even more confident that everything I do for my kids is the absolute best for them. No longer are the times where I get stressed out when someone tries to tell me I'm

260

doing something wrong, or that I should be doing what *they* would do instead. No one can tell me that I'm a bad Mom, and more importantly- I just don't give a shit if they happen to think I am.

Even with the plethora of things about that awful experience that I'm still not really sure of, y'know, like... WHY? If there's one thing I am positive about-it's that it was *never* their intention to empower me, and that's exactly what it did.

It also taught me some of the finer points of blogging. Actually, it more like pounded them into my head.

Before, I didn't have much of a filter on what I wrote, or *who* I wrote it about. Anyone, everyone, just didn't matter, I'd blog about it all without a second thought. Now I have learned to *really* think before I blog, and once I'm done thinking- I think again.
*Sure, angry blogs might be fun to write, and funny to read, but is it really worth the fight this might start?*
The answer is usually no. I prefer now to stick with *total* strangers; ones who may be able to find my blog, but the chances of them actually sitting down and searching for it are slim to none. Stupid waitress, bratty kids at the park, random stranger who mistook Holden for a girl- those types. It's much safer that way, and I can *really* tear into them with no fear of retaliation. Win, win!

To blog about anything more serious than a picture perfect day where unicorns are prancing alongside you, and your kids are shitting rainbows, you're going to need to develop thick skin. There will always be someone out there who doesn't agree, doesn't like you, or is just having a bad day and looking for someone else's cheerios to piss in.

Regardless, writing about Parker's health was still important to me, not just to vent all the frustrations that had accumulated from months' worth of dealing with stupid doctors and stupid people, but to gain a clear head about the whole thing. His problems unfortunately did not end with the drama. Being sick for so long did a real number on his mind and his body. Finding a GI doctor to diagnose and treat him was only a temporary fix, the blog was the savior of my sanity yet again. Reflux, RSV, and delayed gastric emptying opened a can of worms that to this day we are still dealing with. At a year and a half old, he is still having trouble eating because of all of those things. When those girls told me to just let Parker *"get hungry and eventually he would eat,"* they could not have been more wrong (I'm sensing a trend here). He is now in Occupational Therapy for a food aversion because he never learned to eat on his own. What I was taught from our therapist is that eating for a baby is only instinct up until 3 months old, after that it is a skill that has to be learned. Seeing as how Parker got sick at 3 months old and couldn't eat for many different reasons, he never acquired that skill. A baby like him will literally starve themselves before they'll ever eat anything, so when I said the "force feeding" likely saved him- I was more right than I knew. The information you can learn by speaking to *real* professionals is astounding.

Do I blog to that effect? Not totally. There is no more full disclosure when it comes to all the details of Parker's eating and his therapy sessions. I've found that there's just no real need in my blogging to tell everyone *everything* about what's going on with him- because I know the chances of them understanding are highly unlikely. Unless you have a child who's been through it, there's no way to fully comprehend everything Parker goes through, and that we go through on a daily basis to help him, and I just won't open myself up to or tolerate that kind of criticism anymore. I learned that one the hard way.

When it comes down to it, there are a lot of things I look back on and regret about that situation. From responding to that first stupid comment, to letting it all get to me so much. The thing I truly regret the most though, is letting those females monopolize even *one* second of time that I could have spent being focused on Parker, and feeling terrorized and panicked instead. Absolutely NONE of it was worth it, and if I could go back and re-do the whole thing over again I would.

Has the drama completely ceased? No, and I don't think it ever will. For as long as I'm writing my blog, there will always be people who disagree with what I have to say, who don't agree that what I'm doing is right or what they would personally do- and therefore I will always be wrong in their eyes. I still get the occasional nasty comment; I still get messages telling me I am by far the *"worst and most negative parent on earth,"* that I am sick and that I must hate my kids to write the things I write, that it's *"so obvious"* that they *"ruined my life."* The difference between then and now is that not only do I know that none of that shit is true, and while yes- it does get under my skin- it will never be enough to ever make me believe that any of it is fact. Just a sad, bored, and delusional internet personality with nothing better to do than to project on to me the things they are dissatisfied with in their own lives.

I can admit that I am a slightly negative person; I make no strategic moves to hide that. Try having a sick kid for over a year and see how positive *you* can be on a daily basis! As a friend once told me:
*"It's just the territory for a mom of a kid with sensory issues!"*
 Do I wish I were less negative? Of course, it's something I strive for every day- but it is remarkably hard. One thing I won't do is hide how I feel, that has never changed from the beginning to now. I do, however, always make an honest attempt to turn my negativity into something funny.
I am fully aware that my humor is subjective and that not everyone will *"get it."* Sarcasm and parenting doesn't tend to mix well together for a lot of moms, but I don't think that gives people a hall pass to try and destroy me. As many faults as I have, I would never do that to someone else no matter how much I disagreed with how they raise their kids and the choices they make. It's just not my place, and I can't ever even dream

to know what is the "right way" to raise a kid for anyone other than myself. No one person parents the same way as someone else, people need to get off of their high horses and accept that fact. It's just too bad that most will never see it that way.

Now, I'm not going to sit here on my golden pedestal and lie to you by saying that I am better than everyone else and that I never judge anyone! How dare you, you should be ashamed! I'm better than that!
I'm not, *at all*. I do my fair share of being Judgy McJudgerson, complete with eye rolls, gasping, stifled giggles, and fist clenching. I just happen to judge in a way that won't hurt anyone- in silence. I am not a baby guru, I do not know all and see all; I'm still figuring out what to do with my own two brats. As long as you're not strapping your kid to the hood of your car and going for a joy ride on the edge of a canyon with sharp jagged rocks at the bottom, it's likely that I'll stay quiet and let you do your own thing. Someone else's kids are not my problem, and just because I don't agree with what they may or may not be doing doesn't make me right and them wrong.

Something I know now that I wish I knew a long time ago is that I do not need to defend or justify myself or my actions to anyone- especially not strangers on the internet. I felt like I did a lot of that in this book, but only because I've never really had the chance to explain "my side" before, and it felt important to me to do so for the story and for my own personal closure on the matter. I still catch myself immediately getting defensive these days, but with previous experience under my belt I now know it's not worth my time to even try.

What I choose to do with my kids is no one's business, and if anyone feels so inclined as to take issue with that, that's their problem and not mine. If people aren't willing to take the time to really get to know me and the things Parker has been through, then there is absolutely no reason for me to have to explain it to them. People like that don't deserve it.

What has been done cannot be undone though, so I had to learn from it, and never let it happen again.

I always say: If life hands you lemons, put them in your bra!

In my humble opinion, that philosophy has really worked for my family.

Life with kids is never what I would consider easy. A lot of the time it's not even fun. It's still challenging and frustrating no matter how long I've been a mom or how old my babies get, but mostly it's rewarding and I love *almost* every minute of it. I will never sugar coat parenthood and claim that kids are constantly the 'best things ever', I won't ever pretend that I don't have my moments where I want to throw myself out a window, because that isn't real- and that's not me. No matter what someone may say to me, I will always stick to my guns regardless of whether people fully 'get it' or not. The comments bother me, absolutely, who wants to read horrible things about themselves on the internet? But that will never change me; I won't shit glitter just to be accepted by those who don't and won't ever understand where I'm coming from.

I've accepted the fact that some people will never even attempt to listen to the facts, and will instead believe whatever the hell they want to; to make themselves feel better about their own choices, to have a laugh at someone else's expense, or just to be a dumb bitch, and I've moved on with my life.

Thomas and I have been married for 4 years, kicking those 'young marriage' statistics in the ass! Three out of five days I can admit that I think he's a total douche, and he probably thinks I'm a bitch... but it works for us. We support each other through anything and everything life throws in our direction, and that's really what matters in the end.
Holden is now 3 ½, weirder than ever, and has been back to being fully potty trained for about a year now. No more shitting on my floor and hiding it in strategic places around the house

for me to find later after following a trail of stink. What a nice surprise those rogue turds were! Don't get me wrong, there's still the occasional *'crap in my pants and cry about it'* scenario, but he's grown up a lot. It's very bittersweet, yet awesome, watching as my baby becomes a little boy with his own likes and dislikes, and quirky sense of humor. I have entire blog entries dedicated to the strange things he says.

Not far behind him is Parker. A year and a half has come and gone and I have no idea where it went. Time passes far too quickly with your youngest child. You always think you'll have the time to cherish their infancy, but in the blink of an eye it's gone and you realize you didn't sit down and take it all in nearly enough. He may still be having trouble in the food department but that in no way defines who he is. Parker is silly, light-hearted, funny, and incredibly loving. Looking back on all the blogs where I was having conniptions about his gender, and wasn't sure I'd ever be happy with the unexpected pregnancy and forthcoming child, all seem beyond stupid and overdramatic to me now.

I can't imagine Parker or Holden turning out as girls, can't imagine my life being full of so much laughter if they both didn't come out with a penis between their legs.
Mostly, I can't imagine a house full of creepy ass fixed-eye staring, demonically smiling dolls- and I don't want to! Dolls give me nightmares. I'm much happier with a house full of matchbox cars that I slip and almost break my neck on just about every day.

We absolutely still have rough days… and a lot of them at that- but I have the blog to help me push through those, and to be able to wake up the next morning not feeling like I want to sell my boys to the gypsies. Kids are mysterious, frustrating little creatures. Every day is a new adventure and a new blog. To me, that alone makes blogging worth it, but it's not the only reason I kept it going for so long.

Although in the beginning I started the blog not just to have a place to vent my frustrations on becoming a new and relatively clueless mommy, but mostly for monetary purposes. It turned into so much more than that as time passed. Sure, the money is a nice little motivator when I feel too tired to type after a day of projectile poop and incessant screeching, but now it's really just the icing on the cake.

The more I blogged, the more I remembered just how much I *love* writing. Even before I was ever singing my own songs I was writing them. Writing had always been a huge passion of mine growing up, I think I just forgot about it as I got older and more interested in the performing arts. Being able to rediscover that and to be able to mix it with something I'm even more passionate about- my kids- has really changed my life and given me purpose and a sense of self I never felt before.

From trying to make a little extra pocket change to writing a book, all because of a little blog! A blog that has put me through hell none-the-less.

Just like I never saw kids in my future, even months before I got pregnant with Holden, I never thought I'd write a book based on being a mommy blogger back at the blog's conception either. My how things change. From the time I started the blog to now, I don't think I ever could have imagined everything that would happen, or where I'd be now because of it. It seems my life never goes quite how I plan- but somehow in the end it always turns out pretty good.

I felt alone when I started the blog. One kid, no friends, and feeling pretty damn miserable not knowing what to do with myself and having no one to talk to, to having 2 little boys and being surrounded by good people who support me- most of whom have kids too, and a decent number of them are just weeks away from popping out spawn #2. There's something in the water I swear, and this time I am making damn sure to steer clear of it!

267

Once a week at least I get asked when Thomas and I will be trying for baby #3. Everyone thinks that based on how I felt in the past, that I want a little girl *so* badly that I'd be willing to go through another horrendous pregnancy just to get one. I am not that person anymore! Not only does the thought of having three ankle biters running around absolutely petrify me and instantly give me more gray hairs, but I can't see what good it would do the world to have a big pregnant me trudging around, hating the world again… other than the hilariously hormone induced blogs it would produce.

So no, there are no babies planned for my future- even though I think about all the new material I'd have for years to come… I just don't think it's worth the pelvic pain, achy tits, and a vagina so swollen and discolored that it looks like I ordered off of the "LARGE" side of the Arby's menu. These are things I could live without *ever* experiencing again.

All too well though, I know that accidents can and do happen, so I'll avoid making the mistake of saying "never."
Just not right now and hopefully not any time soon! My body could seriously use a break from expanding with a miniature human and then tearing my crotch nearly in half for the 3$^{rd}$ time. I'm just not sure it can come back from that kind of devastation; I think Thomas might appreciate the break as well.

Even if I were psychotic enough to get myself sperminated again, I'm absolutely positive it would end up being another boy, and I'm not bullshitting you when I tell you that I'm ok with that. I even have a name picked out.
Everything Parker went through went a long way in teaching me that happy and healthy are way more important than penis or vagina.

If it does happen- IF- it's safe to say that the blog will be one of the first places I go to share the news.

268

# Poop and the Paranormal:
My two favorite things!

Blogging does not *always* bring backlash and drama. I fear I've made it seem that way over the course of this book. Out of all the time I've been writing the blog, I can honestly say that the good far outweighs the bad. Sure, I've been yelled at, criticized and harassed, not to mention the run in with CPS, but I believe that has more to do with extremely bad luck than being a casualty of the blogging world as a whole.

The last thing I want to do is make the process of blogging so scary and dangerous sounding that no one ever wants to try their hand at it. Why do anything if it doesn't make you happy; if it's not fun? That in a nutshell is what blogging *should* be. You should write what makes you happy and say screw everyone else, but also have a cautious approach to it. It's hard to balance the two, but it can work out, and when it does- it's fantastic. I don't consider myself that controversial, but to some that is *all* that I am, so really I'm just setting myself up. You don't have to do the same if you really believe in what you're saying, and have a good time doing it (and if you can let the occasional nasty comment roll off of your back).

When I was toying around with the idea of writing a book, not really sure if I wanted to take the plunge and commit myself to such a long and painstaking project, I had a lot of different concepts in mind. The specific idea of basing a book around my experiences as a mommy blogger was almost a last resort on the list of possible book subjects I had. I thought about writing my life story, but decided it would probably be too long and too boring. Then I considered a paranormal based book, since my life has been full of strange and unexplainable occurrences.

When I asked friends and blog readers for their opinions on what they might want to read about in a book by me, to get a better feel for what would make an interesting read, the answer was always drama, poop, and my personal experiences with haunting and the things that go bump in the night.

So I thought I would round out the end of this book with a handful of blogs on my all-time favorite things to write about; things that never brought me any controversy or drama. Proof that blogging can be fun and bitch free! Two things that get me physically excited to write about, that I actually chuckle to myself while writing: Poop with a tiny dash of the Paranormal. What did you expect?

Those things don't really go hand in hand, but when you deal with as much poo as I do on a daily basis, you become fascinated by the strangest things.

After careful consideration, and a massively failed attempt at fitting everything into one book, I decided to take the ambitious approach and write two instead. One for the drama and poop, and one for all the haunting experiences in my life. While it killed me to cut out an entire section of this book, I did leave in my all-time favorite blog, which just so happens to fit into the paranormal category. It will give you just a taste of what's to come in my next book (whenever I might finish it).

Maybe to some Moms "poop talk" is a taboo subject, but with so many different types, I don't see how it can be ignored. The colors! The consistencies! The way it defies all logic and gravity! How can one *not* have questions that must be answered?

While absolutely disgusting- I have always been what I consider a "pooper." I suppose you could say I poop more than the average human (and way more than any normal female will ever admit to.) Poop does not make me uncomfortable like it seems to with most women; quite to the contrary, I find nothing more hilarious than a good old fashioned poop story.

Even my days on tour as a musician- poop was a large part of life. I can remember being told by fellow tour mates that they'd *"never pooped as much in their entire lives as when I was around."* My poo was contagious! That's just a shining example of how much I go; and when you go that much, there's no use in being shy about it. I have no shame! Poop never gets old; it never gets less funny- and with kids? It never, ever ends.

If you can't laugh about the subject of poop- becoming a parent will be a repulsive and dreadful experience all around.
I'm like a kid in a candy store when I have a poop story to blog about, it just doesn't get better than that! I become giddy with anticipation, just waiting for the comments full of *"EW!"*'s and *"OMG!"*'s to come flooding in. To me, there is nothing more hilarious or satisfying than horrifying people while simultaneously making them laugh hysterically.
If I wanted to, and if I thought anyone would actually read it, I could full an entire book with only stories about poop. That is *just* the level of hilarious I find things that seep out of people's asses. Regrettably, I don't think anyone else is quite as enthusiastic.

Still, since this is my book, and my goal when starting this project was to give the best and the worst of my blogging experience, I always knew there would have to be at *least* one chapter dedicated solely to the subject of bowel movements. Especially since about 45% of my blog is shit (and I don't mean poor writing, but literally 45% of my blog is dedicated to doodoo) - and this book *is* my blog, it just has to be included.

271

So here they are, for better or for worse: my favorite, most hilarious, gaggingly awful poop blogs of all time.

10/17/08
# Why I hate onesies

I understand why onesies are so popular- they make it so your kid doesn't have to wear pants- and who wants to wear pants all the time anyways?
It's perfectly acceptable for warm weather, but once cold weather hits and you're layering all kinds of things over onesies (shirts, pants), they start to turn into kryptonite.

Why you may ask?

Think of it this way...

You're trying to get your kid changed quickly because they pissed through their clothes (as babies often do), and are becoming increasingly agitated by being stuck in urine soaked garments, but because they're wearing a onesie... it takes an hour to get them changed.
You have to remove pants, unsnap onesie, pull onesie off, put new diaper on, put new onesie on, snap up new onesie, put pants back on.
To shorten the process for you, I will sum it up as just this: *pain in the ass.*

If baby was just wearing a t-shirt, the most damage they'd do (hopefully, depending on how much your kid pisses) is peeing through their pants. So you'd just remove pants, change diaper, put new pants on- and DONE!

Just wait for the gravity-defying baby poop blowout, we've all been there.

For some reason or another, your kid lets loose the A-bomb of poop-- **diarrhea** (or for Holden, just incredibly loose, dark green, magma-like crap.) You don't realize it's happened until you go to pick your (now) fussy baby up only to realize your hand has suddenly become incredibly warm. You pull it away to find out why; it's covered in soggy death-poop. Turn baby around and it's ALL the way up their back, down their legs... *everywhere*. This is where you try to hold back the dry-heave, but fail miserably.

Pulling a onesie soaked in diarrhea over your baby's head is probably the least fun thing you could ever dream of doing. Getting them to hold still (or if they're young enough, sit up without breaking their little baby neck) so that the liquid-crap doesn't get in their hair, mouth, and all over you, is NOT an easy maneuver to accomplish.
It took two people to get that thing off of Holden without giving him a lovely poo-helmet, and a onesie STICKS to babies... like when you wear a t-shirt in the pool and get that super-suction effect- it's exactly like that.

I have not had a disturbing experience like that happen since I put the BAN on onesies in my house. Any time he's had a blowout since then it's-luckily at most- seeped down his leg, which is still disgusting but not as devastating as wearing a poop-filled sack, AKA, a onesie.
The onesie just seems to spread the doo around within itself because they are a *tad* snug fitting (or maybe because my baby was pretty fat).

It's not just the poop that bothers me though; it's all those damn snaps.
When Holden was younger, I got it into my head that the full-bodied rompers were *OH EM GEE, CUTEST THINGS EVER!!!!!* and he had probably 10 of them.
You can call me a glutton for punishment, because that's exactly what those were: punishment. The massive amount of snaps made diaper changing a MUCH longer and far more

annoying process than normal. Damn those snaps! I was constantly snapping them up wrong, putting his crotch snap where his ankle snap should be, or getting them all the way snapped up only to realize I was *JUST* one off. Trust me, after the 50th time it becomes the bane of your existence.

And just to further the obnoxiousness, Holden had massively chunky legs; so instead of looking like regular pants, the rompers ended up looking like spandex leggings.

Great, my kid is David Bowie in Labyrinth, which can only be pulled off by Bowie himself.

I have found that t-shirts are a breath of fresh air. I'm all for working smarter and not harder, and pulling on a t-shirt instead of going through the pains of pulling and snapping and unsnapping is no longer for me.

That and putting a 1 year old boy in a bodysuit just seems *wrong* to me. I don't want him hosting *'Sweating to the Oldies'* when he grows up.

7/28/10
# Poor Holden, when will he learn?

With all these commercials talking about regulating your digestive system, we as adults have learned that not pooping every day is a BAD thing for our systems. Backing yourself up can cause a lot of issues in your tummy and your general sense of well-being.

Toddlers do not know this, especially not stubborn toddlers such as Holden. He has become so confident in his pooping skills that he doesn't think he needs to go every day (when he used to go 2-3 times a day), backing himself up to the point where he ends up crapping his pants because he's been prairie-dogging it for hours and just can't hold it anymore.

After getting in trouble more than a few times, he has learned not to *completely* crap his pants- but still for some odd reason refuses to poop every day like I know he needs to. Every other day he takes a MASSIVE crap... larger than what comes out of an adult, and surprise surprise, has to strain to do so. I keep reminding him: you NEED to go poop, Holden, It's good for you! Pooping is important!

The kid just won't listen...but after today I think he may have finally learned his lesson.

After not pooping at ALL yesterday, today once Thomas got home, we both informed him how important it was to empty himself out every day so he didn't poop his pants and lose his toys again.

Right after dinner I saw him get a very panicked/pained look on his face. I knew right then he needed to go, or possibly had *already* gone. I snatched him up and ran him to the bathroom, somehow managing to get my belt loop caught on the stupid bathroom door for a good 30 seconds.

Finally got Holden seated on the potty and he rested his head on my arm and pushed with all his might. Little kids act like taking a shit is equivalent to giving birth.

I heard a plop, and then Holden started to scream:
*"MY BUTTHOLE!! MY BUTTHOLE!"* all while giving himself the reach around and grabbing himself in pain. Screaming turned into crying and screaming, and both Thomas and I looked in the toilet thinking he'd dropped something large enough to tear himself almost in half and thereby causing this searing pain he was experiencing...but what we saw was a smaller than usual turd. A mini-turd, tiny-turd, baby-turd.

I imagine it must have been one of those rock hard, possibly sharp (you know you've had one of those in the past! Don't lie!) poops you can sometimes get with too much fiber intake that hurt his poor little poop chute.

As a mom I inspected the situation, as any mom would do. I bent him over, spread those cheeks, and made sure his hole wasn't bleeding. It looked ok to me, though I don't know much about how buttholes are supposed to look, but the poor thing was still writhing in pain and crying... so I did the only thing left I could think to do.

I took out the Dermaplast from when I gave birth to Parker (a numbing spray that relieves nether-region pain), bent Holden over- and sprayed his crack down like a dog that's been rolling in the mud all day.

What, you may ask, was his reaction?
*"Thank you!"*

I felt the same way when my snatch was throbbing from almost tearing myself in half while popping Parker out in record time.

A few minutes later I asked Holden how his butthole felt. His response may leave me laughing for days:

*"AWESOME!"*

ROFL. Literally.

Maybe now Holden will learn that pooping every day instead of every OTHER day is important to the health and well-being of his fragile little anus. Hemorrhoids at such a young age would be a NIGHTMARE; for all of us!

## 12/14/10
# The Poop to end all Poops

If you've been following the blog for a while, you'd know that I am a big fan of the good old fashioned poop blog. When you're a mom, I fully believe that you just have to accept poop-talk as common place, and if you don't have a sense of humor about it, you might as well throw in the towel. Baby poop is a strange fickle creature, and even the most experienced mom will have questions as to consistency, color, and frequency. It never seems normal, so when another mom asks me about poop- I never find the line of questioning weird or abnormal. Poop talk is a way of life once you're wiping it off of a hiney multiple times per day, and when it comes to poop I have been through the ringer. I've dealt with projectile poop, runny poop, hard poop, diarrhea, constipation, poop in all colors of the rainbow, poop full of mucus, and being pooped on *and* at. After all of that, poop should not faze me anymore... but I think today may have changed my point of view. After today, I think poop may give me recurring nightmares for a very long time.

It's no secret that Parker has had poop issues for some time now. I don't know why it started or what triggered it, but once the constipated came on- he just hasn't been the same.

Screaming when he poops? Check. Not pooping for a full day and then not being ABLE to poop? Check, check. Big hard turds? Check.

Today was by far the worst and most repulsive and terrible experience yet, and not just for me- but for Parker as well. If he wasn't scared of pooping before because of how much it seemed to hurt him- after today I fear he will NEVER want to poop again, and I can't imagine the problems that could cause.

The constipation, while awful to watch Parker scream in pain, has sadly become commonplace. I had a feeling he may benefit from a trip to the doctor to see what the hell could be done to help him- but now I think it's a necessity.

Multiple times throughout the day he screamed for five minutes straight, straining and trying with all of his might to poop, only when I went to check his diaper, there was nothing there. Not even a skid mark. In the past when this has happened, he'll at least relieve himself later in the day and feel fine, but that didn't happen today.

After he woke up from his long nap, he almost instantly started screaming and straining, but this time he not only didn't poop, but he didn't give up trying to either. He literally screamed and pushed for an hour straight.

During that hour I tried just about EVERYTHING to help him. I tried feeding him water, he didn't want it, tried pushing his legs back to help him push out the crap that seemed lodged in his anus- he fought me with the strength of 5 men. I even tried pressing on his abdomen but that only made him scream louder. I feared he would break every blood vessel in his face from straining so freaking hard for so long.

Snack time came and went. I knew Parker wasn't going to eat since by that point he was screaming so hard that he was dry heaving, so I snacked over his head while I held him and tried to calm him, and let Holden snack next to us. It finally got to the point where I knew the poo wouldn't be coming out on its own so I gave him a dose of baby laxatives.

Another 30 minutes go by, and while he finally drank some water, he was still screaming and straining without relent. I decided more desperate measures needed to be taken. I took him into his room, and plopped him on the changing table with the full intent of giving him a suppository- which is a seriously frightening thought to me. I can handle poop ON me, but I can't handle shoving things up my kid's butt as high as I can possibly get it while he fights me tooth and nail. Fingers and buttholes do not mix in my world.

When I pulled his diaper off and lifted his legs to insert the suppository I was greeted by a butthole stretched larger than ANY butthole I have ever seen (and ever care to see again), with a gigantic poop trying to squeeze its way out. I think I screamed and gasped at the same time, I couldn't believe what I was seeing…the horror!!! But I knew it had to come out. I didn't even know how long it had been that way, and felt terrible I hadn't taken him into his room to inspect the situation, and help him out sooner.

Holding back the dry heaving, I pressed on the skin right above his butthole to help stimulate the urge to push, and push he did. Instantly, two poop balls the size of fists came out. I screamed, he screamed; I cried, he cried, and then another one tried to come out; another one that was stuck and not going to come out on its own. I had to press that spot again to try and help him, and very quickly that one passed as well, but what I saw after his stomach was empty was even more disturbing than watching it come out.

His poor little hole was turned basically inside out. It was gaping and bleeding. My initial thought was *"OH MY GOD HE NEEDS TO GO TO THE ER, HE BROKE HIS ASSHOLE,"* but once I saw that he was completely calm, I decided it was better to ask a few friends first.

While what he had just gone through was awful, it's also sadly pretty common. Children can get constipated for SO many reasons, or no reason at all. I can't let it happen again though, not to that extreme! My biggest fear is that he will remember this experience the next time he has to go #2, and just *not* go. He'll end up holding it for so long that there will be NO way to push out the size of crap that will have been building in his colon. Can you imagine a shit ball bigger than a fist? He'd have to have the poop surgically removed!

After this experience, and I can't believe i'm going to type this, i'm not sure I can find poop funny anymore. It definitely lost some of its sparkle and a lot of its humor today.

The only upside is that he felt MUCH better once those huge turds had passed, so much so that he took 8 steps, and then 10 steps!
That's my little pooper… I mean trooper!!

12/19/10
# Do you smell that?

In the past, I have written a handful of blogs about the seemingly impossible to answer strange questions of parenthood. There is one that I have ALWAYS wondered about more than the rest, and I can't be sure if it's been blogged about here before- but I think it's worth another mention.

My puzzling parenting mystery is this: Why don't small children have a gag reflex when it comes to bad smells?

In my experience as a parent, and my EXTREME aversion to bad smells (insta-gag), I have learned the fine art of breathing through my mouth. Most times, this works perfectly. Diaper changes with liquidy, disgusting, putrid baby poop aren't nearly as horrid when you don't have to smell them; but while I can breathe through my mouth and block out the smell- I know Parker and Holden are both breathing in those poop fumes, and they have always seemed completely and utterly unfazed by it. Hell, when Parker was a little younger and had THE worst (and loudest) explosive poops known to man, Holden would walk up to him, bend down, and take in a huge whiff of poop, only to laugh afterward while yelling *"EWWWWW!"*
If I did that? There would be an even MORE disgusting mess to clean up because you better believe i'd have puked all over Parker.

Is gagging when met with horrible smells and sights a learned trait? I know some people just have stronger stomachs and minds when it comes things of that nature, maybe children just have the strongest stomachs known to man.

I guess I just can't reconcile it in my head how they don't find bad smells... *bad.*

280

The reason I've been pondering this question yet again is because of a very recent, and incredibly awful experience we had over the weekend.

We were out getting something to eat when Holden, for the millionth time, announced mid-meal that he had to go pee. Because Parker refuses to let Thomas walk away from him when we're in a public place- taking Holden to the bathroom was my job.

As soon as we opened the door to the bathroom, I was hit with what was honestly THE worst smell I have ever smelled in my entire life. It smelled like someone's insides were rotting and they walked into the women's bathroom and sprayed the entire contents of their intestines all over the walls. It smelled like every dirty diaper I have ever changed, put into a vacuum sealed room and left to ferment for a year. To steal a line from one of my favorite movies- *" It smelled like a turd covered in burnt hair."*

I was absolutely HORRIFIED. The wet gags were instantaneous and uncontrollable; meanwhile, Holden is just strolling around the bathroom like the air is as fresh as a daisy, none the wiser.

It definitely did NOT help the situation when we entered the only stall available (and there were only 3 total), and Holden points at the toilet and announces *"Look! DOODOO!"*- it was streaked all over the inside of the toilet like a 5-car pileup. Honest to God, I've never had to fight back puking so hard.

I implemented my trusty technique of just breathing through my mouth in order to power through this potty trip and get out as quickly as possible. This worked only long enough for me to pull Holden's pants and underwear down and then the smell became SO strong that I could taste it; actually *taste* the smell of diarrhea on my tongue. At that moment, I didn't think I could last any longer. I almost snatched Holden up and yanked him out of that bathroom, pants and underwear around his ankles, just to get away from the smell.

Realizing that was a bad idea, I decided against it; but not wanting Holden to sit on that disgusting toilet, I held him midair and forced him to pee that way. He wasn't happy about it and kept whining that he *"didn't know how!"* while i'm yelling back at him *"PLEASE HURRY OR I'M GOING TO PUKE! THE SMELL IS TOO BAD!!!"*
I cannot IMAGINE what the people in the stalls next to us were thinking. I don't know how THEY were handling it without upchucking their newly consumed meals. Then again, they didn't have the vision of diarrhea streaks all over the toilet they had to use.

And still, through all of the madness- Holden never mentioned a single thing about any bad smell. I don't even know if he had any idea why I was freaking out so bad.
BAFFLED! Literally the worst stench that I have EVER smelled and he didn't even bat an eyelash.
Baffled, and insanely jealous at his masterful non-smelling ways. I need him to teach me that skill! I bow to my sensei!


## 2/3/11
# Breaking a promise

I know I promised no more poop blogs- and I can tell you that I had *REALLY* hoped not to write any more for a while; to take a long, needed, and much deserved break from poop- because I am SICK of it!!

Per usual, things didn't quite go that way. For the past week I have been basically SWIMMING in poop, and it shows no signs of letting up any time soon. Oh how I long for the days when Parker was constipated, at least then I wasn't changing upwards of 20 diapers a day.

Holden is all better from his run of the stomach flu, that's the only positive thing that's happened this week. When a kid doesn't wear diapers and has the runs, that stuff can go ANYWHERE and usually does. With a diaper, at least the shits can be caught, somewhat at least.

Never in my life have I seen a child crap as much as Parker has in the past few days. And the kid isn't eating ANYTHING, total food refusal. It's like he has alchemy of the anus and is conjuring up diarrhea out of the air quite literally for shits and giggles. He is the wizard of poop, the king of crap, the master of mud-butt.

Today tops any disgusting poop story I have ever told- so if you feel like diarrhea talk might turn your stomach tonight- i'd suggest not reading any farther. If you find it funny to laugh at my misfortune, than this blog is just for you.
I wish I had something else to write about, but seeing as how every 5 minutes I had to change a disturbingly warm swampy diaper, it's really ALL I did and have been able to think about.

It started with the usual- liquid poop out the wazoo. Not fun, but sadly not unusual 'round here lately.

And then it hit. The poop of the century. I had no idea just how bad until I took a peek into Parker's diaper to assess the damage, and saw it just sitting there, lying in wait... two inches deep. Ugh, i'm getting queasy just typing it.
It was so bad that I knew if I laid him down to change him, it would spread and pour over the edge of the changing table. So I had to pull the diaper off of him standing up. Once I got him cleaned up, 4 wipes later, I realized I couldn't just bundle it up like a regular diaper and toss it in the can- it was just too full... and while Luvs doesn't lie when it says it contains blowouts, it did NOT absorb the sheer quantity of liquid bowel drainage sitting in this diaper.

I had to do the worst thing I've ever had to do as a parent; worse than stimulating an anus to coax poo out of it. I had to take the overflowing diaper over to the toilet, tip it on its side, and dump it out. It felt like it was pouring into the toilet forever, there was just that much shit. Never have I dry heaved and gagged stomach acid into my mouth so many times in under one minute. Keeping my eyes closed and breathing out of my mouth was NOT helping my plight, the sound of it alone was enough to make the strongest stomach turn upside down.

You might think it couldn't get any worse from there. That HAS to be the worst thing that could happen. Wrong.

After Parker adamantly refused lunch, he took a very restless nap. I could hear his stomach turning as he slept, and he STILL stank from the monster craps he'd already taken.

Once he woke up, I took him to the bathroom as I always do so he could relieve himself. I should have expected him to need to explode after the previous events of the day, but all he did was let out a wet toot. He insisted on getting up right afterward, so I let him. He stood holding on to the sink while I reached to get his diaper to put back on him, and then started to scream for no apparent reason. He can be cranky when he wakes up so I didn't think much of it, when I heard it-
*BRRRRRRPPPPPPPPPPP,*
I found my legs, the floor, and the bathroom carpet SOAKED in liquid baby shit. I screamed probably louder than I've ever screamed in my life. VOMIT! It was everywhere. As if I hadn't already gagged enough, now I was bringing up hot stinging stomach bile. Paper towel does *not* absorb watery diarrhea, it just spreads it around. Cleaning it up was nearly impossible, and on my top five of most disgusting tasks ever.
I tore my pants off, tried to clean up the floor, and threw the pants and the rug straight into the wash.

After that I think I was just numb to the poop, nothing that came out of Parker from that point on could compare to being spackled with diarrhea. He may have crapped something like 15 times after that, WITHOUT EATING ANYTHING, and it did not faze me.

I've become immune to it y'all, that's how bad it's gotten. How can such a little person expel so much crap without eating any food?? It makes no logical sense!

Oh, did I mention that during nap time Holden decided to crap himself, then grab it in his hand, and CARRY it to the bathroom instead of holding it in his butt, and releasing it into the toilet? 'Cause that totally happened, icing on the cake.

I'm thinking my next move should be to invest in a baby butt plug. Then I can choose when he shits and WHERE the shit will go. Sounds like a million dollar idea to me.


2/18/11
# Making fun of Mommy

Ever since that whole incident in the restaurant where I was smacked in the face with the WORST smelling poop I've ever had the misfortune to smell, my ability to hold back a gag has practically vanished. In situations where I used to be able to just hold my breath or breathe through my mouth and get through the situation without any kind of complications, I started experiencing more difficulty.
And then the stomach flu tore my house apart. After over a week of vomiting and diarrhea and those diapers so full of liquid shit that you could swim in them- the ability to suppress gags again completely vanished.
Gone. No more!

I literally have NO control over it. If Holden poops in the potty, which never used to bother me in the slightest, even when he was calling it *"banana doodoo"* or telling me *"that doodoo smells like chicken!"*, now causes the insta-gag reaction from me.

Parker's craps are even worse because he empties his bowels into a little potty that I then have to empty into the big one... and sometimes chunks get left behind. GAG GAG GAG! I am lucky I haven't actually crossed the threshold into full-on vomiting yet.

It's gotten SO bad, in fact, that I even find myself gagging at my own crap; trust me, it ain't that bad.

I can't look at the poop, I can't think about the poop, if the poop is there, and I know it's there- you can bet I'll be gagging.

Since Holden's battle with the stomach flu he's developed a strange fascination with puking. I guess at first his stomach was still a little upset and he would INSIST he had to puke (which he pronounces "POOK") *"I have to pook mommy, my tummy hurts!"* but once the tummy ache went away, it turned into more of a joke for him to run around making gagging sounds.

Only a few times at first, but once he noticed *I* was gagging all the time because of the sheer volume of crap coming out of himself and Parker, it became the most hilarious thing in the world to him to make fun of me.

He takes a crap? Instantly he's play-gagging at it *"EEHH EHHH EEHHHHHH! That's DISGUSTING! I'M GONNA POOK! EEHHH EHHH EHHH!"* (Sound out those EH's as your best vomiting impression.)
Even If I DON'T gag, he gags. Every time Parker takes a dump Holden comes running into the bathroom:
*"I'M GONNA POOK! EEHHH EHHHH EHHH! IT SMELLS LIKE CHICKEN AGAIN! EHHH EHHH EHHH!"*

Now he's even moved on to farting

*"EW DADDY FARTED!!! EHH EHH. I'M GONNA POOK EVERYWHERE! IT SMELLS SO BAD!"*

The kid takes a hell of a lot of pleasure in my misfortune. There I am, trying SO hard not to actually vomit because for some stupid ass reason, I can no longer handle fecal matter being in my general vicinity, and he's running around the house fake-gagging and laughing like a maniac.
It must be nice to have no sense of smell!

Seriously though, isn't it a little young for him to be making fun of people? It's a tad high on the sadistic level for a 3 year old, is it not? I know kids his age are really frickin' evil, but I didn't think they quite had the mental capacity yet to actually make fun of someone on purpose. It wouldn't surprise me at all if Holden is the only one. I lie in wait for the day his sense of smell kicks in... 'cause then i'm going to drop a huge load in the toilet and lock him in the bathroom with it.

It's the little things in life that can make you happy, y'all. The little things.

5/29/10
# Reddits

Before you read this blog, I just have to say that no matter WHAT you read here tonight, I do still believe there is something strange, possibly even paranormal, going on in this house. The events that have transpired over the past few weeks, leading to the resolution tonight do NOT discount the eerie feelings and other strange phenomena I have experienced here!

With that being said: Recently things have been weirder than normal as far as Holden's "experiences" go. We went from

287

random things happening, to him becoming very specific about something going on in his room.

Instead of just saying he was scared of *"the doors"* or *"the wall"* like he has been for a while now, he started saying there was something in his closet. But not just something, *someone*; and it had a name.

For weeks he would say there was something in his closet, and he'd say a name neither Thomas nor I could understand, but it definitely wasn't an English word (or not one I've ever heard before anyways.) He'd tell us he was scared of it. He'd tell us it wanted him to *"get out of the closet."*

Every single time this came up, he'd walk to the same exact place in front of his closet, look under the door, point, and say its name.

I've been in Holden's closet MANY times. There's nothing in there but a ball popper I had to hide because it drove me absolutely INSANE, an inflatable treasure chest, and a baby activity table; nothing that sounded anything near what he was saying:

*"Reddits"*

I wasn't sure if that's what he was saying, but it was the closest thing that registered in my mind that seemed to match what was coming out of his mouth- and Thomas heard the same thing. So the thing in his closet became Reddits.

Holden talked about Reddits CONSTANTLY. Informing us repeatedly that it was in his closet, followed by going and pointing, and would say that he was scared of it. He was scared when we'd open the closet doors to show him that there was no Reddits there.

It started to disturb us. Was he seeing something in his closet we couldn't see? What could he possibly have to be so scared about? Holden doesn't have a very active imagination; he's not one to make things up.

It got to the point where not even *I* wanted to go in his closet. After all the weird things that have happened around here, it just seemed to fit that he was seeing some sort of ghost. He never let it go, so it HAD to be there.

Finally today I decided to get to the bottom of this strange situation.

During dinner I began asking him random questions about Reddits to figure out what the hell it was that he was seeing. I asked him certain questions in five different ways *just* to see if he'd give me the same answer.
Is Reddits your friend?
*"Nope!"*
What is Reddits?
*"It's in my closet"*
What color is Reddits?
*"Green"*
When he said green, I thought he was maybe seeing the poster we have on the wall in the living room of a green monster like thing, and maybe it was freaking him out and he was having dreams about it. So I pointed at the poster and asked him if THAT was Reddits.
*"No, that's the monster! Hi monster!"*
Canceled that one out.
Then I thought...maybe it's my mom again, it wouldn't be the first time I thought she was around, so I went and got a picture of her and showed it to him:
*"Who is this?"*
*"That's Grandma!"*
*"Is that Reddits?"*
*"No, that's not Reddits!"*

Ok, not that either.
Maybe Reddits is an animal? I asked him what sound Reddits makes. He said that Reddits oinks like a pig,

*"oink oink!"*- As if that didn't confuse me more. He also told me that Reddits is a girl.

Any way I asked him, no matter how I worded the questions or tried to trip him up, he *always* gave those answers.

The only thing left to do was to confront it. After dinner I told him to go into his room and show me Reddits. I wanted to see her in all her green oinking glory.

Once again, he went to the same spot on the carpet right in front of his closet, leaned down, pointed under the door and said *"right there."*

Thomas and I opened the door... and I was genuinely nervous about it. I didn't want some creepy green ghost chick jumping out at me and oinking.

I found nothing there but the activity table, just as I suspected. I showed him, and try to assure him.

*"Look Holden, there's nothing there!"*

He started breathing heavily, physically recoiled, and then tore ass out of his room. To him, Reddits was there.

I open the other door (the closet has 2 sliding doors), which is easier to open and get into- and call Holden back into the room. He did NOT want to at all, he started to have a full on panic attack about it, so I snatched him up and *forced* him to look into his closet. This was going to end, now! I named everything I could see. None of them were Reddits.

I put him down and said forcefully, *"Holden, SHOW ME REDDITS"*

He leaned into the closet and pointed into the corner of the other side and said *"RIGHT THERE!"*

I managed to get myself around all the junk and *way* into his closet so I could scour it for anything I might have missed upon first inspection.

And then I see it. Instantly I knew.

I reach down into the dark corner and grab it, and come back out yelling *"AAAAHHHHHHHH!"* holding it up like a hunter with a big kill.

This, of course, made Parker go absolutely supersonic, with his mouth wide open and face deep red because he was totally scared to death at the reaction I had.

In my hand I held it. A small, green, plastic piece of lettuce from Holden's play kitchen.

## LETTUCE!!!!!!!!!!!!!!!!!!

Upon seeing what I held in my hand, Holden's eyes lit up like a Christmas tree.

*"REDDITS!"* he yelled, grabbed it from me, and ran off as fast as he could.

For *WEEKS* he's been asking for a damn piece of LETTUCE stuck in his closet. He could see it from under the door and that's what he kept pointing at.

He wanted that thing SO frickin' badly he even took it in the bath with him.

*LETTUCE.*

Why he acted so damn scared of it? Why he said it oinks like a pig, or that it's a girl? Or that it wanted him to get out? All of that is still a mystery; likely just Holden's weirdness at play.

I can't believe "Reddits" is actually "Lettuce." I feel like a total moron! I'm can't help but to laugh and facepalm myself about it.

Lettuce. WTF. That's all I can say.

291

Holden needs to learn to pronounce his Ls so I don't freak myself out for weeks again by thinking there's a damn ghost in his closet.

# Like Jerry Springer, I have final thoughts too

When I look back on everything I've gone through in the past few years, not just as a parent but a blogger as well- even though there have been SO many pitfalls, downsides, and mortifying nightmarish experiences- I have to laugh at it all. What else can you do?

People, as a whole, have it all wrong! I was told I'd have to completely change as a person once I became a mother. Give everything up that I loved and put my kids above all else. No more this and no more that, no more sarcasm or cursing or complaining, it all had to end- and my life would now revolve around my children, and that would be the end of the story.

I'll admit that it's partially true... but it's not quite as it seems. Yes, my priorities *absolutely* changed. They had to. I couldn't be a party girl anymore. I couldn't just go out at the drop of a dime, whenever I felt like it, without a care in the world because there was no one that would suffer due to my spontaneous and irresponsible actions.

Here's the thing about it: I didn't mind. I *chose* to have Holden. I chose to change my life, and anything that I changed was because I wanted to, not because I felt like I had to sacrifice my life. There was absolutely no regret about anything I 'gave up' in order to properly care for my child.

Once a week at least I'm asked when I'll go back to playing music. Don't I miss it? Don't I want to continue pursuing my dream? The answer is no, and I don't say that begrudgingly.

293

It's just not my dream anymore. I do think about it from time to time. What if I didn't have kids? Where would I be now? But I don't think about it in a resentful manner. If I wanted to still play music like I was before having kids I absolutely could. Here's the thing: I don't want to. I played music 'professionally' for seven years. Could it have worked out for me in the way I wanted? Sure, had I kept at it, it's very possible. But after I had Holden, it wasn't what I wanted anymore. My passion became Holden, and after that, Parker. And I have zero regrets about it whatsoever. It was my choice, 100%, and contrary to what seems to be popular belief- I'm happy about it!

Things may be hard, I haven't and won't ever make excuses about that. Dealing with sick kids, shitty diapers, and getting randomly pissed on is never an easy thing to learn to live with- and all with a smile on your face- but there's no way I'd change it for anything. Even with all of the frustration, all of the dry heaving and disgusting smells- I love my life, period. Even if it's not where I thought I would be 5 years ago- that just doesn't matter to me anymore. I'm not that girl anymore, and I'm proud of that.

For most of my life I've gone through what sometimes seems like constant pitfalls and loss, with a few moments where I felt truly happy, but really I was only ever *almost* happy.

Everything I had dreamed of always seemed so far out of reach no matter how hard I worked or how badly I thought I wanted it. I could never get a tight grip on any of it. I was flailing, lost.

Now? I feel... well... completely insane- but in a good way. I'm finally *honestly* happy. Satisfied and clear on who I am and what I want. I'm not in a constant life limbo, struggling to figure out who 'me' really is, and what the 'me' really wants. I know who I am, I know what I want- I'm finally exactly where I've always wanted to be, I just didn't know it before.

The toddler tantrums will never be fantastic, and the explosive leaking diarrhea diapers are definitely not the highlights of all of my days, and I can't tell you that there aren't times that I still feel like selling the kids to the gypsies and then flinging myself off of the nearest bridge.

Gallons of chunky curdled projectile baby vomit and seven hour long screaming marathons in the wee hours of the morning may even make castration or other forms of sterilization sound appealing.

Of course those things suck! Of course there are bad days! Parenting is a tough ass business, not for the faint of heart or weak of stomach. It's up and it's down, it's awful and it's amazing- and for as long as I am one I will always be honest about that, I will never make excuses for my feelings, and I will never sugar-coat it no matter what anyone else may think.

In every house where a child lives, that stupid cutesy poster with the slightly disturbed looking cat on it and the tag line that reads *"You don't have to be crazy to work here... But it sure helps!"* should be prominently displayed. That, in a nutshell, is the mindset of a parent.

This is my life. I love it, and even with those *beyond* bad days I wouldn't change any of it for a damn thing. No, not even a record deal.

Anyone who tells you that you have to give up your entire life for your kids isn't doing it right. Life changes, priorities change, people change; that's just how it goes. You don't have to lose what makes you *you* the second you squeeze a kid out of your vagina. A child should add to the person you already are, not take anything away.

From beginning to end, everything I experienced during this crazy parenting and blogging journey (and I do mean everything), the most important thing for me, and for my kids really, is that I stayed absolutely true to myself. I don't want to be some fake ass pod-mommy, pasting on a fake smile and bullshitting my way through life. I want my kids to know who I *really* am, and to be proud of that person.

I didn't lose myself the day I became a mother- I *found* myself.

# Holdenisms

*"Turkey Tetrazzini!"*

*"Caca poo poo pee pee platter!"*

*"I'm gonna kick you in the face!"*

*"I'm gonna SUCK YOUR TOES!"*

*"I just don't want to, cradle cap!"*

*"That one's the smallest turdy poop I've ever seen!"*

*"My pecker is prickly!"*

*"Mommy, I think my pecker is ticklish!"*

*"I like when peepee comes out of my pecker!"*

*"I want to play with cars and trucks and... EAT PARMESAN!"*

*"MOMMY! ARE YOU LISTENING? I FARTED!"*

*"What the POOP? I don't give a FART"*

*"If you don't take that pea off my fork i'm going to smack your face with that balloon on the TV!"*

*"You little baby butthole!"*

*"I don't want to go to Cinderella's castle 'cause she's not cute!"*

*"We're gonna leave her here. She's gonna be a street-walker!"*

297

www.holdinholden.blogspot.com

www.facebook.com/holdinholden

Twitter: @HoldinHolden

holdinholden@yahoo.com

Made in the USA
Charleston, SC
06 July 2013